DECOLONIZING FEMINIST ECONOMICS

Decolonization and Social Worlds

Series Editors: **Alana Lentin**, Western Sydney University, **Ali Meghji**, University of Cambridge, **Syed Farid Alatas**, National University of Singapore and **Jairo I. Fúnez-Flores**, Texas Tech University

---

This series provides a radical new platform for high quality monographs which respond to the call for a decolonial revolution in sociology and the social sciences. Taking us beyond the boundaries of Eurocentrism, the series aims to expand the scope and imagination of the field.

Also available in the series:

- *Critical Racial and Decolonial Literacies*, edited by Debbie Bargallie and Nilmini Fernando
- *White Supremacy and Racism in Progressive America*, by Miguel Montalva Barba
- *Coloniality and Meritocracy in Unequal EU Migrations*, by Simone Varriale

Find out more at:

bristoluniversitypress.co.uk/decolonization-and-social-worlds

DECOLONIZING FEMINIST ECONOMICS

Possibilities for Just Futures

Gisela Carrasco-Miró

BRISTOL
UNIVERSITY
PRESS

First published in Great Britain in 2025 by

Bristol University Press
University of Bristol
1–9 Old Park Hill
Bristol
BS2 8BB
UK
t: +44 (0)117 374 6645
e: bup-info@bristol.ac.uk

Details of international sales and distribution partners are available at bristoluniversitypress.co.uk

British Library Cataloguing in Publication Data
A catalogue record for this book is available from the British Library

ISBN 978-1-5292-3648-4 hardcover
ISBN 978-1-5292-3649-1 ePub
ISBN 978-1-5292-3650-7 ePdf

Cover design: blu inc
Front cover image: unsplash/Mario Álvarez
Bristol University Press uses environmentally responsible print partners.
Printed and bound in Great Britain by CPI Group (UK) Ltd, Croydon, CR0 4YY

FSC
www.fsc.org
MIX
Paper | Supporting responsible forestry
FSC® C013604

To my parents, Montse and Salvador

and Alèxia and Sal

Contents

Series Editors' Preface

Syed Farid Alatas, Jairo Funez-Flores, Alana Lentin and Ali Meghji

The *Decolonization and Social Worlds* series began at Bristol University Press as a response to the ongoing coloniality of knowledge. The series is co-edited by Syed Farid Alatas, Jairo Funez-Flores, Alana Lentin, and Ali Meghji, along with an international advisory board featuring some of the leading figures in the field.

A central aim of the series is to excavate how coloniality works – both historically, and in its contemporary expressions. It is undeniable that the social sciences emerged in the high era of colonial imperialism. Classical social scientists – from Durkheim to Weber, and Giddings to Geddes – were prominent exponents of the politics *and epistemologies* of European empires. From Weber's Orientalist reduction of the 'Hindu', 'Muslim', and 'Confucian' worlds, to Durkheim's assertion of indigenous people as being pre-modern, Geddes' colonial town-planning in India and Palestine, and Giddings endorsement of 'democratic imperialism', social scientists have had significant relationships to colonial imperialism. We are now at a stage in social science where we know quite while about the histories of these relationships between social science and empire – both from the perspective of how social scientists worked in the service of empires (such as Britain's training cadets in sociology to better administer colonial populations), and from the perspective of how social scientists reproduced the epistemologies deployed by empires to legitimize colonialism (such as the idea of the colonized as being in need of development and progress). While the *Decolonization and Social Worlds* seeks to continue these discussions about social science and colonial imperialism, we also seek to further push the boundaries of social science knowledge by considering alternative histories, theories, movements, and social relations from the borders of the colonial world system.

Within the series, we therefore seek to address multiple areas of social scientific inquiry. To name just some of these areas, we are interested in unearthing the work of forgotten (or denied) scholars, in decolonial and anticolonial social movements and struggles, in new ways of thinking about the historical and contemporary relationships between the metropoles and colonies (or core, semi-peripheries, and peripheries of the world system), in social scientific histories of colonial imperialism, in the evolution of empires, in indigeneity and indigenous critiques of coloniality, and in the historical and contemporary incarnations of the coloniality of being, knowledge, and power.

Now decades after the wave of decolonization of the mid-20th century, we still see clear colonial divisions in the contemporary world order: in terms of ongoing settler colonial projects; in political economy, wealth, and poverty; in war and militarism; in international political order and organizations; and in knowledge production. There is always a vital need for conceptually and empirically informed decolonial scholarship to address all of these complexities, and we hope that the series goes someway towards contributing to this already rich, vibrant area of social scientific inquiry.

In its essence, this series looks for a world of many worlds.

Preface: Decolonizing Feminist Economics as Dispute

Decolonizing feminist economics is not a utopia; it is a battle.[1] This book proposes a decolonizing feminist economics that yearns for truth and possible worlds to build shared futures. It begins with uncomfortable questions and the idea that economics must address common problems. In this way, it charts maps and prepares the ground for possible solutions. It does not lack answers; rather, it rehearses them without closing them off.

For decades, Anglo-Saxon feminist economics has been the most visible and materially influential form of feminist economics worldwide. While this dominance is waning – thanks to the rise of anti-capitalist, ecological, anti-racist, anti-imperialist, anti-patriarchal, and decolonial feminist energies outside the Anglo-Saxon sphere – its legacy remains significant. This book critiques its Eurocentric practices and ideas, aiming to disrupt its hegemonic framing and to open space for alternative, transformative and decolonizing approaches to feminist economics.

When we speak from within feminist economics, our critiques are often directed outward (against capitalism, sexism) and rarely inward. It's as if there is a kind of belonging and protection – a 'home' – among the few, though increasing, dedicated to feminist economics. It seems we allow ourselves space (so difficult to secure) to do 'our own work' without breaking ourselves. Yet this feeling of 'home' does not help; quite the opposite.

Feminist economics must be relentlessly honest, starting by questioning itself. Feminism has shown us that a radical movement that speaks to itself frankly accomplishes a much more meaningful task than merely telling truth to power. In this sense, feminist economics cannot be a fantasy of converging interests, of plans without unforeseen and undesirable consequences, nor a comfortable space among 'us'. Conceiving it as a place of belonging prioritizes unity and ignores those who may disrupt its harmony. Feminism should be based on 'unexpected alliances', not on a place of complete belonging.

The book does not aim to be a home nor a utopian economic programme; it seeks, when necessary, to inhabit discomfort and uncertainty. Yet I hope it offers, for some, a space of resonance. It does not aspire to convince or persuade, although I wouldn't mind if it did. Rather, it engages in dialogue with voices that have long helped to imagine other ways of inhabiting the world, understanding it, naming it, imagining it collectively, and organizing against that which we wish to transform.

A truly transformative feminist economics arises from an uncomfortable and uncertain feminism. This entails exposing oneself and committing. There is nothing more distressing than listening to an academic present her 'topics' with the addendum: 'I am interested in …' rural women, for example. How can someone be interested in rural women? They either concern her or they do not; they either affect her or they do not. To be affected is necessarily to break something within oneself and reassemble it through new alliances.

In a world of suffering and struggle, Indigenous peoples are key to understanding an economic reality that constructs its power upon their erasure and denial. Conjuring this erasure is, therefore, essential to combat power. It is not about making Indigenous peoples *the* topic or adding their perspective to economics, but rather addressing economics in a way that contains their position and their outcry. This demands a radical alteration of how we see and understand economics, inevitably leading us to confront the economic and power structures that perpetuate so much suffering.

Examining economic facts today requires a large dose of imagination: a determined commitment to connect what we know with what we still do not know and to open ourselves to unfamiliar experiences and perspectives. We have stopped imagining, and thus, stopped thinking about more just possible futures because we have internalized the belief that we already know what will happen and, above all, how it will end. Yet perhaps one of the primary roles of decolonizing feminist economics today is to remind us that we know far less than we think. Only then can we be in a position to learn, listen and question.

Although not everything is possible, neither is everything finished.

Barcelona,
2 November 2024

Introduction: Economics Against the Apocalypse

> There is no mystery to what an 'economy' is. … [A]n economy is just a group of people interacting with one another as they go about their lives.
>
> Greg Mankiw (2021 [1998]: 4)

> Capitalism Kills.
>
> Graffiti on top of the parking ramp that Winston Boggie Smith was killed at on 3 June 2021, Minneapolis, United States

The future

'We are heading towards a profound economic crisis' is one of the sentences that resonates frequently in recent years, showing no signs of abating. Captured by apocalyptic narratives predicting the end of the world and the irreversible destruction of our living conditions, the very concept of the future has been overshadowed by a present fraught with despair, disillusionment or, worse yet, indifference. But could it be that this very attitude of resignation is what might be driving humanity towards the brink of its own sustainability?

If we have run out of a sense of future, Marina Garcés (2017) contends, it is because what may happen has become completely disconnected from what we can do. This disconnect has led to the deactivation of critical thinking and a delegation of intelligence, leading us to a comfortable and cowardly credulity. In this context, Garcés (2017: 56; translation mine) argues that '[t]he credulity of our time delivers us to a double-faced dogma: either the apocalypse or solutionism. Either the irreversibility of destruction, even extinction, or the unquestionability of technical solutions that are never in our hands to find'.

The question that fuels apocalyptic narratives and fosters the cancellation of the future now points to the challenging viability of an economic system based on limitless growth and an extractive and productivist logic that is both unsustainable and unjust. The apocalyptic condition of the present, coupled with constant crisis and emergency, have placed the need to save lives (of some) at the heart of the economic contest rather than the Earth and its limits. Confronted with this need, as Garcés elucidates, the dominance of capitalism offers a depoliticizing and threatening solutionism: adapt or face extinction. This translates into an economy of dispossession that attacks life, allowing the capitalist system to perpetuate itself under patriarchy, colonialism and ecological degradation.

The survival crisis generated by its own system is masked by apocalyptic narratives that justify economic measures of self-regulation or so-called 'development'. These narratives create a naturalized assimilation between our life systems and capitalism in particular, portraying a world without us – either because humanity has become extinct or because the saviours are no longer human, but rather post-human. Ultimately, these narratives never aim to end capitalism but rather the human species: saving the world from destruction becomes synonymous with saving, at all costs, the structures of capitalism.

When we think of capitalism, we tend to assume that markets and trade are synonymous with it. However, markets have existed for thousands of years across various times and places, while capitalism is relatively recent – only about 500 years old (Graeber, 2014). Capitalism is a political, cultural and economic system dominated by – and centred around – the imperative of investors to turn a profit (Marx, 1976; Harvey, 2014; Kallis, 2018). It is, therefore, a system defined *by interest* that draws ever-expanding quantities of nature and human labour into circuits of accumulation (Graeber, 2014; Hickel, 2020). While capitalist economies vary in certain aspects, they share fundamental institutional attributes such as paid labour and private ownership of the means of production, widespread market exchange, bank credit and bank-credit money, private enterprise production of commodities (Ingham, 2013; Kallis, 2018) and converting the means of sustaining collective life into private forms of capital production.

Like any other social formation, capitalism reproduces its order through its expenditures, but it has five distinctive features. The first is its history, deeply rooted in the extraction of social and economic value from women and marginalized and racialized groups, particularly Black and Indigenous people (Federici, 2004, 2012). Although both colonialism and patriarchy predate capitalism, they are profoundly reconfigured by it. The second feature is its organization around the imperative of constant expansion, or 'growth', which entails the endless reproduction of capital. This growth occurs not for any particular purpose but *for its own sake* (Kallis, 2018; Hickel, 2020).

The third feature is private consumption: expenditure that sustains the capitalist class and perpetuates a racist hierarchy. Giorgos Kallis (2018) argues that for capitalism to continue uninterrupted, initially unproductive expenditures have to be gradually (and at an increasing scale) privatized and commercialized, resulting in an endless cycle of expansion. In an economic system where everything is a commodity, inequality proliferates rapidly. In this regard, Dylan Sullivan and Jason Hickel (2023) assess the history of capitalism by examining empirical data on real wages, human height and mortality rates from the 16th century onwards. They found that the rise and global imposition of capitalism were associated with significant declines in social indicators. Wages often fell below subsistence levels, and mass mortality crises occurred in several regions. In the global South,[1] they state, recovery only began in the 20th century, coinciding with the rise of progressive and radical anti-colonial movements that reclaimed control over national resources and production (also see Kumar, 2005). Under capitalism, life presents greater challenges for those with modest means. In this unequal system, money buys class. While one's origin can influence the ability to acquire money, it does not fully determine one's fate. This potential for mobility (competition) fuels capitalism's dynamism.

The fourth characteristic is that capitalism is rooted in a conflict between capital and life, wherein the lives of others and the Earth are exploited, transforming the means of sustaining collective life into private modes of capital production (Pérez Orozco, 2014). This occurs because the capitalist economy is driven by what is most profitable for capital. Growth is a principle of capitalism, not of the consumer. The difference between people's needs and the needs of capital is quite evident. For example, there is an overproduction of items like fossil fuels and fast fashion, while essential needs, such as affordable housing, are chronically underproduced because they are less profitable or not profitable at all. The paradox of capitalism lies in the fact that, despite massive production and resource consumption, basic needs remain unmet, and life itself is under threat. Ultimately, either capital is sustained, or life is.

The fifth characteristic of capitalism (in fact, this is the one that sustains the other four) is its unlimited promise of prosperity (Garcés, 2023). This promise of (non-)future is based on growth, efficiency and freedom. These values are empty and relative; they can only be perceived when contrasted with systems, cultures and people who are *less* effective, *less* free and produce *less* wealth. This unlimited and continued promise of accumulation is contingent upon our adherence through labour and consumption. Only by participating in these ways can we partake in the promise of growth, enrichment, success, development and prosperity. In this manner, the promise of capitalism permeates everything and functions as an interpretive structure of reality and of ourselves.

Yet, how can capitalism maintain the promise of an unlimited future in a limited world? The failure to fulfil the capitalist promise of prosperity has caused widespread discontent, which translates into melancholy and resentment. In this sense, this future's apocalyptic ideology carries a dual message: it prompts older generations in high-income countries to confront their privilege and the apprehension of its potential loss, while simultaneously plunging young people in these societies and many populations in low-income countries into despair and depression.

It is possible that the world as we have known it is coming to an end. However, we cannot assume that the end of one world is the end of *the* world, as if humanity has not already dismantled numerous worlds before. It is a disconcerting manner of forgetting the fact that the world presently in upheaval has emerged through the wreckage of others and much death, as is occurring once more.

With echoes and demonstrations around the world, Palestine has become the paradigm of a future to be reclaimed. Slogans like *Palestine is anywhere* or *Palestine is everywhere* must be understood as rejections of colonial expansion, a condemnation of ongoing and repeated acts of genocide, and affirmations of liberation and sovereignty. These calls also evoke a sense of vindication and shared sentiment among past and present dissidents and international liberation movements connected across the globe: from Palestine to Guinea-Bissau, from Rojava to Chiapas, from the Brazilian Amazon to Western Sahara. Through their resistance and demands, these territories call for a new world – one that envisions possible futures that are just and diverse.

There are alternatives

Mark Fisher (2009: 2; emphasis in original) coins the concept of capitalist realism to name the dominant ideology by which it is determined: 'not only is capitalism the only viable political and economic system, but also that it is now impossible even to *imagine* a coherent alternative to it'. Fisher argues that capitalism engenders its own cultural logic rooted in economic and productivist rationale, fostering a position of cynical superiority. This economic paradigm dismantles the conditions that would animate any alternative way of conceiving reality, that is, another economy. Consequently, he explains, the capacity to formulate alternative economic paradigms is thwarted, creating an invisible barrier that constrains both thought and action. As Fisher (2009: 4) articulates, '[c]apitalism is what is left when beliefs have collapsed at the level of ritual or symbolic elaboration, and all that is left is the consumer-spectator'.

Capitalism portrays itself as the only conceivable world: 'This is what it is', we are constantly told. Yet, this sense of inevitability neutralizes critique, leaving us feeling powerless and indifferent. It is a world where everything seems possible, yet no alternatives exist (Garcés, 2002). In this sense, capitalism constructs a narrative that presents itself as natural and inevitable, concealing its deep cultural and ideological foundations. Fisher (2009: 3) argues that capitalist realism imposes a pervasive sense of resignation, suggesting that we are trapped in a state where 'the end has already come', leaving us with an apocalyptic future characterized by mere repetition and variation.

Following Fisher's ideas, in the realm of consumer capitalism, genuine interruptions or innovations are rare; cultural creations quickly become products to be bought and sold. Consequently, we resign ourselves to the belief that creating a just and sustainable way of life beyond the current economic system is impossible. Margaret Thatcher's famous declaration, 'There Is No Alternative', still holds significant influence today, reinforcing this resignation and limiting our resistance to symbolic gestures like consuming anti-/post-capitalist cultural products such as dystopian Netflix series or 'alternative' music.

However, there is a key to breaking the chains of our present impotence: critique. By returning to a classic definition of critique as a discourse that yields practical, liberating effects on our perceptions, actions and potential, we can uphold its relevance and address the challenges it presents today. This relevance depends on our ability to infuse critique with new meaning, situate it within the current conditions of our world and manifest it in our concrete experiences. In nearly all its connotations and traditions, critique involves revealing something that eludes our sight: a concealed truth, the conditions of possibility, a contradiction, an irrationality, the intolerable, the boundaries of our existence, and so forth. Therefore, critique is an outcome of vision, an interruption, that is not passive contemplation but is intended to wield a transformative power: transformation of the self, of history, of the material conditions of life, and so on.

If we aspire for critical discourse to instigate the liberating effects as outlined thus far, our aim must be to incite the collective dimension of our existence – a 'we' – to awaken or elevate it. In this regard, economic critique remains, in some respect, a pragmatic discourse aimed at revealing what lies beyond our immediate perception and facts. However, this vision no longer aligns with the modern enlightened consciousness nor can it be merely professed or declared. It demands action. It necessitates embodiment. But how?

We may claim that words and theories constitute actions and content ourselves with the role of critical thinkers listening to ourselves. Yet, this is insufficient. Indeed, many of us have encountered how the academic realm of critical studies such as heterodox[2] economics or postcolonial and decolonial studies often perpetuates a sort of intellectual isolation, one among many other isolations, thereby reinforcing a sense of helplessness and apathy. It is evident that it is not in our hands to decide or programme the process of decolonization. But it is urgent that we question and transform the conditions for the creation of critical economic thought today and this needs decolonizing.

In the absence of critical engagement, economic thought risks becoming futile. Despite accessing its insights, we remain uncertain of how or from where to relate with it. The question, however, is not about *how long* this economy that leads to impoverishment, injustices and indignation will persist. Instead, this book proposes a shift in focus: *why must the economy be this way and not another? What kind of economies do we want?* This marks the essential starting point for a critical, feminist, decolonizing, imaginative and committed approach of the economy in the era of programmed apocalypse.

Economics and the economy

Economics, whether orthodox or heterodox, has lost its transformative capacity, its ability to generate action. Having failed to engage with the complexities of our times, economics has retreated into a discipline that is remote, entrenched in mathematical formulas and driven by *solutionism* – that is, anticipating solutions to problems before thoroughly analysing them, motivated by an ideology of efficiency and technological immediacy. The focus has shifted from self-improvement to the pursuit of ever-increasing privileges in a stagnant era that has abandoned the quest for a better, more just futures for all.

Economics is often perceived as a closed system, wrapped in abstract language that shelters it from confronting a present shaped by power relations and composed of diverse people, thoughts and imaginaries. This detachment, even when acknowledged or denied, paradoxically elevates economics to a position of academic privilege. Economics is esteemed for simplifying the complexity of our societies, offering manageable numbers under the guise of objectivity, treating 'facts' and 'solutions' as rigorous. Yet, mathematical modelling conceals underlying power dynamics, interests and values. Gender, heteronormativity and race, for example, are deeply ingrained in this practice.[3]

Most economists aspire for their discipline to appear 'scientific', more akin to physics, 'the gradual realization of universal, unimpeachable mathematical truths', with the result that they have dispensed with its previous political and social connotations (Graeber, 2019: np; see also Mazzucato, 2017). Nevertheless, physics studies inanimate objects, whereas economics deals with people and the Earth. It extends beyond mere interpersonal interactions among individuals navigating their daily lives without major issues, as Mankiw (2021 [1998]) suggests in the epigraph to this chapter. Our direct experience and observation about the life around us, along with an extensive body of research, reveal the often-violent consequences of economic decisions on individuals, communities and the Earth. 'Capitalism kills' echoes globally, underscoring the human and environmental toll.

Feminist economics, alongside other heterodox branches, questions the methodologies that grant economics its status as a science but still inherits the prestige and object of study of economics (Harding, 1995; Peter, 2003;

Barker, 2005). From my experience in the field of feminist economics, however, this commitment goes beyond self-interest (career advancement, publishing, obtaining tenure, and so on) to a genuine desire for knowledge that materially benefits women, especially those impoverished.

In this book, I understand economics not as a form of physics or as an independent system governed by its own immutable laws. Instead, as explained in Chapter 1, I view economics and the economy as a social, cultural and political construct: an invention by specific people in particular societies. This construct is constantly evolving and can be contested. Nevertheless, regardless of what the term 'economy' means, it is inherently material. That is, an economy is the means by which a human population provides itself with its material needs upholding their *values*.

However, '[the economy] was an object that no economist or planner prior to the 1930s spoke of or knew to exist. ... In the sense of the term we now take for granted ... the idea of the economy emerged ... in the 1930s and 1940s' (Mitchell, 2011: 124 and 125). Every human society has had some form of an economy, even if they lacked a specific term for it. An Indigenous collector of medicinal plants and seeds in the Petén in Guatemala, for example, might not perceive her activities as contributing to an economy. The concept of an economy, along with particular ideas about how it should be organized, is part of what Cornelius Castoriadis (1997) refers to as the 'social imaginary' (Kallis, 2018) – constellations of power that frame the economy (as well as politics, culture and society) on multiple levels in diverse historical and social or cultural contexts.

A market economy, for instance, is intricately woven into its institutions, which, in turn, shape individuals to act as the rational maximizers envisioned by market economics. This leads to a self-reinforcing loop where market economics is validated by the very environment it has created. Although this might imply a closed system resistant to new economic ideas, change is an inevitable part of the process. Our current understanding of the economy differs greatly from that of previous decades or centuries. This evolution happens because reality constantly challenges and tests existing frameworks, promoting a dynamic interaction between values, imaginaries, ideas and lived experiences.

Creating new imaginaries (as this book aims to do, particularly new imaginaries for economic transformation) is a vital step in unleashing the social potential to change the world. Thus, we can say that the economy is an instituted process driven by imagination. In this regard, one of the key questions this book explores, especially in Chapter 7, is whether imagination can be harnessed as a tool for economic transformation, fostering confidence and resistance amid growing crises.

Ultimately, the economy involves humans interacting with material environments to provide for their needs and *values*. Although it may seem forgotten, economics – as the study of how societies organize themselves to provide their material conditions to meet their needs while upholding their values – has, at its radical origins, an ethical purpose: to ensure the well-being of as many people as possible with a positive impact on the Earth and social relations. In this sense, the ethical economic question guiding this book is: how can we live well, together (Chapter 7)?

Living well poses the very meaning of human dignity and freedom as universally reciprocal and co-elaborated, thinking from a 'we' based on a common, not a unique, world. Our ability to openly question our dignity and, consequently, our well-being and freedom is not preordained but essential to our humanity, as articulated by Ailton Krenak (2023). Thus, dignity is not an economic attribute or another; instead, it is the very possibility of considering the status of human experience from the perspective of improving its condition. In this sense, the book emphasizes the necessity for an economic critique from its very foundation: the way in which economics gives us back the ability to elaborate the meaning and value of the human experience from the affirmation of its freedom and dignity. In this context, the book explores economic knowledge not only in relation to power but also with an emphasis on emancipation, aiming to construct, together, a more habitable and just world.

Decolonizing for action

The dispossession of Indigenous peoples is the central and original injustice in our economies. Rebalancing this relationship is fundamental to achieving a just economy and envisioning better futures for all. This principle lies at the heart of decolonizing feminist economics, the proposal of this book. This is not to take an essentialist, romanticized or 'nativist decolonization' (Moosavi, 2020: 16) approach based on a multicultural economics – that is, including a variety of economic perspectives without touching the core of economics. Instead, decolonizing aims to recognize and valorize Indigenous struggles, agendas and knowledge – so far silenced and ignored in economic thinking – to transform economics. By doing so, it can reveal new facets of power structures and offer diverse economic experiences that may unveil new paths to social emancipation and liberation.

The process of decoloniz*ing*, as a gerund, encapsulates the power of incompleteness and seeks to imagine and redefine power, change and economic knowledge through multiple practices, epistemologies, ontologies and axiologies. Decolonizing for action involves actively disrupting the colonial past and its ingrained assumptions, aiming to radically break away from the colonial legacy and its oppressive axes, namely capitalism, patriarchy and ecological degradation, towards liberation and freedom.

In this book, I use the generalized political collectivity 'Indigenous' or 'First Nations' to refer to communities resisting colonial domination and advocating for sovereignty and self-determination. While not all decolonization projects specifically address Indigenous issues, particularly those of diasporic and migrant identities, this book explores how decolonizing methodologies advance Indigenous struggles and futures, potentially fostering coalitions among various communities affected by colonialism.

Assertions of Indigenous identity are often dismissed as essentialist, implying an unchanging 'essence'. However, while the category of 'Indigenous' lacks a universal meaning, it broadly encompasses common experiences of colonialism and imperialism across various communities, language groups and nations. For Indigenous peoples, Indigeneity is rooted in a distinct relationship to land and the knowledge systems they maintain, which significantly impacts sovereignty (Ngũgĩ, 1986; Smith, 1999), including economic sovereignty. Marie Battiste writes:

> Indigenous knowledge is also inherently tied to land, not to land in general but to particular landscapes, land-forms, and biomes where ceremonies are properly held, stories properly recited, medicines properly gathered, and transfers of knowledge properly authenticated. Ensuring the complete and accurate transmission of knowledge and authority from generation to generation depends not only on maintaining ceremonies, which … law treats as art rather than science, but also on maintaining the integrity of the land itself. (Battiste, 2002: 13)

In this sense, one's relationship to one's land is critical in decolonizing struggles, though it does not necessarily manifest as a physical marker. Diverse histories and realities of distinct Indigenous groups must be seriously considered, ensuring that, for example, the particular realities of diasporic Africans are included in this concept instead of being denied or subsumed (Adefarakan, 2011). This approach moves away from exclusive or hegemonic essentialist notions of 'Indigenous peoples' narrowly predicated on obligatory residence on ancestral land, towards a more complex and inclusive understanding reflecting the varied experiences of Indigenous peoples under colonialism and imperialism.

Therefore, 'Indigenous' involves a recognition of difference, where serious attention is given to the multiple and diverse experiences that Indigenous peoples have. Just as it is necessary to acknowledge that Indigenous identity is not singular, it is also necessary to recognize that Indigenous people's relationships to the land or territory are not singular. In addressing 'Indigenous' as a category of political subjectivity, one necessarily must wrestle with particular and contextualized histories of domination, oppression and liberation.

In economics, land is traditionally considered a factor of production, much like labour, and is viewed as an element in the creation of goods and services. As discussed in Chapter 4, it is often perceived as an empty, abstract space to be controlled for production efficiency and market access to maximize profits. However, Indigenous philosophies and worldviews regard land as a living entity and the source of Indigenous knowledge and economic sovereignty. Indigenous economic sovereignty challenges capital accumulation by enabling Indigenous peoples to regain control (delinking) over their own productive capacities and organize them according to local needs and desires. In this context, a new form of sustainable, non-destructive growth is still needed in many areas of the global South to meet people's needs.

When Indigenous peoples produce and consume for themselves without external pressure, these resources are no longer available cheaply to fuel consumption and accumulation in the global North. This disrupts the imperial arrangement on which Western capitalism has always relied: cheap labour, cheap resources, control over productive capacities and accessible markets. In this regard, Samir Amin (1990 [1989]) coined the term *delinking* to describe the process of moving away from this dependency relationship, where economies in the global South are subordinated to the interests of the global North and forced to comply with the demands of capital. Therefore, Indigenous peoples and struggles cannot be ignored or relegated to mere case studies, citations or tokens in the decolonization of economics; they must be central. This does not mean that the discussion must focus solely on Indigenous peoples (as if they were *the* subject), but rather that decolonizing economics must be framed in Indigenous futures and economic sovereignty if it truly wants to be decolonizing.

This necessarily involves a new understanding of economics and a question addressed to the heart of it: can economics stop being imperialist? Over 40 years ago, Claude Ake (1979: i–iv) argued that Western social sciences represent 'the most subtle and pernicious forms of imperialism – imperialism in the guise of scientific knowledge'. Ake contended that Western social sciences, whether consciously or inadvertently, impose capitalist values, institutions and development models on the global South. They aim, he stated, to reshape the global South in the image of the West, propagating ideologies and practices that serve imperialist ends.

Although this critique was not new – figures like Samir Amin (1976) and Paul Baran (1957) among others had already pointed it out – Ake pushed for a critical rethinking and reconstitution of our field's intellectual genealogies. He sought to move beyond the limiting narratives of disciplinary origins and originality inherited from the modernist West. Ake advocated for the development of an alternative system of knowledge production, one that appreciates the diverse histories that produce varied knowledge bases around the world. For Ake, and for much of the postcolonial and decolonial debate that has followed, this understanding is crucial for transcending the restrictive contexts of knowledge production in the modern world.

However, Indigenous knowledges and practices have not been recognized as valid contributions towards constructing better societies and economies. They are often dismissed as superstitions, opinions, subjectivities or common sense, and thus are not considered 'rigorous' enough to be included in economic discourse and practice (see Chapter 1). Consequently, Indigenous knowledges and 'worldsense' (Oyěwùmí, 1997: 3) must occupy the 'economic' space to re-signify it.[4] This is not to say that Indigenous knowledges and people are inherently anti-capitalistic or 'better' *per se*, but to show alternative ways of economic thinking that highlight the antagonisms governing our worlds.

This entails a deliberate effort to eliminate colonial and patriarchal biases and assumptions that have historically influenced Indigenous ways of life and economies. The decolonizing examination aims to generate feminist economic knowledge that goes beyond Western-centric modernism, ensuring well-being and economic justice for all while engaging with non-capitalist forms of knowledge and economies. Yet, to be truly transformative, decolonizing requires action.

What unfolds when we take action? We begin to transform, sustain, nurture and care for the just and diverse worlds we aspire to inhabit. Feminisms have shown us that action is not just about visible outcomes, victories or defeats, but also about *the continuous process of doing and undoing*. This ongoing, generative activity is inherently transformative.

Decolonizing feminist economics

Decolonizing feminisms thought and feminist economics share the commitment to imagine and build non-oppressive systems for just futures. Both criticize dominant power structures and challenge the ways in which knowledge is produced and disseminated. They seek to overcome exploitative paradigms that perpetuate injustice and inequality, including extractive industries, resource exploitation and global trade. However, decolonizing feminisms argue distinctly that decolonization and dismantling the patriarchal system are interconnected and reinforce each other. Therefore, it is not possible to analyse the origin and configuration of patriarchy without examining the origin and operation of colonialism and the process of original accumulation. Indeed, as analysed throughout the book, feminist economics makes little sense if it does not also involve decolonization and degrowth to avoid reproducing dominant strategies of capitalist modernity, extractivism

(Chapter 4) and climate colonialism (Chapter 5 and Chapter 6), and to open spaces for decolonizing critique, imagination and resistance (Chapter 7).

While feminist economists critique mainstream economics, their commitment to scientific research, albeit unintentionally, often reinforces Western-centric modernism (Wood, 1997; Charusheela, 2003; Zein-Elabdin, 2003, 2016; Carrasco-Miró, 2020a) and the paradoxes associated with the discipline's scientific ambitions (Barker, 2006). This gives rise to four key challenges, which I identify and explore ways to address in Chapter 2 of this book. First, feminist economics' focus on identity politics often centres women, which can overlook deeper analyses of structural economic inequalities that extend beyond gender divisions. Second, feminist economics' cultural bias tends to privilege the historical context of European modernity, thereby erasing certain cultures and economies by excluding colonialism and coloniality[5] from analysis. Third, feminist economics may inadvertently perpetuate capitalism and Western-centrism through concepts like equal opportunities, empowerment and human rights, which can function as equality fictions. Finally, the failure to envision economies beyond growth and Western-centric modernism limits the potential for critical and transformative economic thinking.

Addressing these concerns, I propose a decolonizing approach to feminist economics to confront heteropatriarchy, colonialism, capitalism and ecological degradation. Decolonizing feminist economics is not, however, a critique of economic models but a questioning of what kind of economies we want, what futures we can imagine. It further envisions a world free of these oppressive structures and aims to ensure material life, liberation and dignified subsistence without diminishing life. Decolonizing feminist economics is about possible Indigenous futures. In Part III, I develop a framework of eight interconnected principles for what decolonizing feminist economics may entail: *embodying* feminist economics; *centring* Indigenous sovereignty and freedom; *interrogating* Orientalism, Eurocentrism and developmentalism; *advocating* for plural economic knowledges; *questioning* the meaning of value; *resisting* capitalist growth economies; *advancing* economic justice – reparations, land return and wealth redistribution; *embracing* a common world as a political commitment.

Decolonizing feminist economics aims to recover, revalue and strengthen Indigenous knowledges, practices, struggles and lands,[6] while introducing disruptions into dominant economic thinking from its borders. This includes acknowledging economic distinctions and affirming the epistemic rights of cultures that have been either racially or economically undervalued. These cultures represent diverse economic modes of social and material organization, each characterized by fundamentally distinct forms of subjectification, creating different worlds that are intricately interconnected. Decolonizing feminist economics involves not only recognizing these differences but also undoing existing power structures that perpetuate inequality. This includes challenging and dismantling *simultaneously* heteropatriarchy, colonialism, capitalism and ecological degradation structures. It necessitates, therefore, both addressing unbalanced power dynamics that contribute to these oppressive systems and envisioning a world free of heteropatriarchal, capitalist and colonial structures where the sustainability of life is truly at the centre.

Decolonizing feminist economics is also grounded in African and Black feminist theoretical frameworks such as intersectionality (see Chapter 3). Intersectionality takes into account the way that different social and political identities can create different experiences of gendered oppression and focuses on opposing various forms of oppression, including patriarchy, white supremacy, classism and heterosexism. It has largely arisen from the unique positions Black women occupy – facing racism and white supremacy from white feminists, and confronting the often-internalized sexism and patriarchy of African/Black men, all within the broader contexts of capitalism and Eurocentric societies (Combahee River Collective, 1977; hooks, 1981; Davis, 1983; Crenshaw, 1989; Collins, 1990; Amadiume, 1997; Mama, 1997). As discussed in Chapter 3, intersectionality is a powerful and necessary conceptual feminist tool for decolonizing because it critically interrogates unjust power structures and inequities while also acknowledges that these spaces of injustice and disempowerment are contested in pursuit of solidarity, transformation and just futures.

Possible just futures

In real-time, we are witnessing an accelerated hardening of the material conditions of life. The intrinsic crisis of capitalism becomes increasingly evident, both in its social impact and in the scientifically proven limits of the Earth and its resources. Amidst this reality, the fascination with the apocalypse, framing the end of the world as irreversible, has deeply permeated economic thinking. Those who navigate this apocalypse and its various forms of salvation will secure economic but also political, technological and cultural power. However, it is precisely these apocalyptic economic fantasies that have led us to this point. How can we continue to think, live and engage with a world whose future remains uncertain? How do we challenge the burgeoning apocalyptic dogma that is becoming the economic framework of meaning without succumbing economic thinking to the hypocrisy of selling futures?

In embracing a feminist economics decolonizing approach, this book proposes both critical economic thinking and economic imagination as essential to emancipate ourselves from the apocalyptic dogma and do so with the confidence that the possibility of doing and thinking is among us to live well, together, in just futures. Despite how difficult it may be at this moment to imagine a future that is genuinely better, more economically just, than our present, we have to keep trying. However, for futurism to transcend unrestrained fantasy, there must be a credible path to get there from here.

To achieve this, we may need to develop new ways of thinking and rethinking ourselves, as well as imagining – not just thinking – economies in relation to a future that is grounded in the present. That is a future time not relegated to the beyond but forged in our everyday lives. Predicting or cancelling the future seems today less analytically rigorous than actively participating to shape it. While we do not know how the evolution of the economy will be, one certainty is that resignation, tinged with realism, guarantees an outcome least transformative of all. Awaiting the revolutionary or decolonial breaking point, always postponed, is practically equivalent to inaction.

In this context, the political concept of the 'possible' becomes key. The possible is not about pointing to the unreal or indulging in fantasies but about being measured by the realities it seeks to address. In this sense, the possible is what allows us to think, justify and navigate the uncertain, mutable and enduring. In the cracks of our fractured world, freedom manifests as the ability to choose between different possibilities, while the future represents the power to realize them (Garcés, 2002). Engaging with the possible is, therefore, not merely an abstract exercise but a concrete effort to shape and bring about more just futures.

Disobeying the apocalypse

During his brief life, Étienne de La Boétie (1530–1563) posed a fundamental question on freedom. His essential concern was to unravel why people submit to tyrants when, by uniting, they could quickly achieve their liberation. The question to elucidate is the reasons for the voluntary obedience of the many to the powerful: If a tyrant is one person (or a dogma of thought), and their/its subjects are many, why do they consent to their own slavery? This is the path that served de La Boétie to observe how servitude prevailed at the expense of freedom:

> For the present I should like merely to understand how it happens that so many men [*sic*], so many villages, so many cities, so many nations, sometimes suffer under a single tyrant who has no other power than the power they give him; who is able to harm them only to the extent to which they have the willingness to bear with him; who could do them absolutely no injury unless they preferred to put up with him rather than contradict him. (de La Boétie, 2008 [1578]: 3)

De La Boétie encouraged the automatic defeat of tyranny if people refuse to tolerate their own enslavement. For him, tyranny is a self-destructive system, and although the people have not consciously chosen to be under the oppression of the tyrant, they have the moral responsibility to break the bond of submission established with the despot. He argues that individuals often associate and remain under the tyrant's yoke for the supposed security it provides, which translates into exploitation. However, even though their freedom is restricted, the subject naturally has the desire for freedom, even if not empirically aware. How to live together without dominating each other: this is the essential question with which La Boétie challenges us and continues to unsettle us, even today. Though belonging to a distant historical time, La Boétie's work still maintains its initial strength for anyone capable of saying no, of disobeying. In the case of this book, disobeying the programmed apocalypse under a tyrant economic system that attacks life.

In this sense, *Decolonizing Feminist Economics: Possibilities for Just Futures* insists on two questions that it does not intend to resolve but aims to keep thinking together: How to fight against economies that attack life? What knowledge and economic practices are necessary today to develop and share a sustainable planet and dignified lives for all? Feminist post-extractivism, ecofeminisms, and post-growth/degrowth[7] are contemporary political-economic concepts and movements multidimensional in nature, sharing different critical features and proposing just futures I explore throughout this book. They provide a critical economic analysis of the current capitalism, not only in terms of economic and cultural crises but also in more global terms, understood as a civilizational crisis.

These proposals suggest anti-patriarchal economic practices beyond growth, explore paths to freedom and liberation, and discuss the ecological limits of the Earth. They constitute the starting point for practising and envisioning new economic horizons of change and civilizational alternatives, grounded in an environmental rationality that diverges from the *Homo economicus*,[8] extractivism and the economistic mindset that commodifies life in its various aspects. Throughout the book, I further propose how decolonizing feminist economic can enhance and strengthen these movements and suggest various paths for future research and collective action to continue disobeying the apocalypse.

PART I

1

Towards a Decolonizing, Feminist and Trustful Economics

Introduction: Contributing to current debates

Decolonizing economics

Despite the growing political and scholarly urgency in understanding how other cultures encounter 'the West', economic and politico-economic approaches, including heterodox economic approaches, have been slow to engage with the profound ideas and challenges presented by postcolonial and decolonial thought (Kayatekin, 2009; Pollard et al, 2011; Kvangraven and Kesar, 2023). This hesitancy can be attributed, in part, to the perceived autonomy, prestige and hierarchical nature of a more 'scientific' disciplinary knowledge within the field of economics. This dominance persists despite the increasing prevalence of discussions on postcolonial, anti-colonial and decolonial thought in other academic domains like critical and cultural studies, queer studies, critical race theory, gender and feminist studies.

The result is an academic landscape that compartmentalizes knowledge, perpetuating the disciplinary authority of economics – a legacy of the 19th-century reorganization of knowledge coinciding with Europe's imperial expansion (Klein, 1990). The entrenched disciplinary specialization and hierarchization from this period continue to influence the contemporary economy of knowledge in our universities, reinforcing the division of labour that caters to distinct academic markets and bolsters the dominance of economics. However, this kingdom of economics has not gone unchallenged. In recent years, there has been a surge of critical voices advocating for the *decolonizing of economics*.

A decolonizing revision compels disciplines to relinquish their current autonomy and authority. Adopting a transdisciplinary, anti-disciplinary or counter-disciplinary approach – rather than traditional interdisciplinarity, which preserves the philosophical core and methodological tools of separate disciplines – helps to expose the shared pre-analytical premises of economics, thereby diminishing the perceived autonomy of these disciplines. These methods do not merely add social or political perspectives to mainstream economics; rather, they interrogate '*how we think about economic systems*' by drawing on a variety of theoretical and disciplinary insights, centring on 'history, power, structures, and social relations' (Kvangraven, 2022: 519; emphasis added; see also Charusheela and Zein-Elabdin, 2003). In this sense, I employ anti-/trans-/counter-disciplinary methods in this book as essential tools to seek solutions outside – and against – the current framework of the economic thinking and resist colonial 'techniques of specialist knowledge as they work with strategies of power' (Spivak, 1996: 215).

Decolonizing economics distinguish itself from existing initiatives promoting diversity and pluralism in economics. In general, decolonizing economics focuses on 'a) tackling the historically produced Eurocentrism in the field of economics and its claim to neutrality and universality, b) more openness in terms of theoretical and methodological approaches, and c) tackling structural exclusion in the economics discipline in order to remove barriers to equal representation in terms of identity' (D-Econ, nd: np). These critiques are pivotal in fostering a paradigm shift within economics. Decolonizing economics not only insists on including economists from the global South but also emphasizes centring their voices, challenging the prevailing hegemony in economic discourse. Moreover, the focus on decolonizing teaching in economics underscores the importance of reshaping how economic knowledge is imparted, ensuring a more inclusive and diverse pedagogy (Kvangraven and Kesar, 2023).

But what happens with the economies – the object of study in economics? What do decolonized economies look like? Can an economy be decolonized? Under what conditions? Is it possible to think economies beyond economics? How might economics address common problems instead of specific outcomes or topics, including 'being decolonized'? Importantly, there is a significant challenge that radically affects decolonizing economics: the scarce or non-existent articulation with anti-patriarchal or feminist studies, theories and practices. This contrasts with anti-colonial struggles that tended to be very aware of the deep connections between capitalism, colonialism and patriarchy (Vergès, 2021). Decolonizing economics, therefore, must be likewise anti-colonial and anti-patriarchal.

Decolonizing feminisms

Decolonizing economics share with decolonizing feminisms a commitment to envisioning and building alternative systems that pave the way for just futures. They both critique dominant power structures and challenge the ways knowledge is produced and disseminated. They interrogate the Eurocentric foundations of knowledge, recognizing the tendency to marginalize the experiences and perspectives of colonized peoples, with a specific emphasis, as articulated by decolonizing feminisms, on Indigenous people, women and non-binary individuals. Their joint mission is to transcend colonial and economically exploitative paradigms, including extractive industries, resource exploitation and global trade.

Distinctively, decolonizing feminisms assert that the processes of decolonization and the dismantling of patriarchal systems are interconnected and mutually reinforcing (Espinosa et al, 2014). The anarchist feminist Bolivian collective, Mujeres Creando, and Maria Galindo (2013a; 2013b; 2021) encapsulate this interconnected struggle, asserting that decolonization is not possible without depatriarchalization. They argue persuasively that 'the patriarchy was intrinsic to the creation of the colonial world. … [I]f colonial relations (and neo-colonial relations) are built on patriarchy: decolonization cannot occur without depatriarchalization' (Galindo, 2013a: 6; translation mine).

In that sense, depatriarchalization in a decolonizing way is presented as a theoretical conceptual alternative to the logic of inclusion, to identity logic, as well as to the solipsism that are the three tendencies in which mainstream feminism has become entangled. Depatriarchalization emerges here as 'another distinct theoretical approach capable of posing different challenges, starting from a different analysis, and, through a creative and renewed reading of the universe of women, establishing new transformative and subversive horizons' (Galindo, 2013a: 140; translation mine). Decolonizing feminisms, therefore, underscores that the focus of decolonization should extend beyond political and economic liberation and the non-Indigenous and Indigenous to encompass the deep-seated entrenchment of patriarchal systems within social, political and economic realms that perpetuates inequalities within societies and communities.

The analysis of the Indigenous and gender condition within decolonizing feminisms is not merely a recognition of multiple forms of oppression faced by Indigenous women; it is an acknowledgement that gender and Indigenous conditions stem from the same technology of hierarchization. This technology consistently assigns women and Indigenous peoples the role of the defeated, stripping them of their voice and the possibility to affirm their place in the world (Gargallo, 2007). Thus, any examination of the origin and configuration of patriarchy necessitates an understanding of the origin and functioning of colonialism and the process of original accumulation (Federici, 2004). In that sense, decolonizing economics holds limited significance if it does not encompass depatriarchalization.

While there is not a unifying/totalizing 'decolonial feminisms' located in a particular place or option (this will contradict the core idea of it), feminisms and anti-patriarchal struggles engaging with decolonization – this includes anti-colonial feminism, decolonial feminisms, third world feminism, communitarian feminisms among other decolonizing feminist movements and struggles around the world – have in common a plurality of ideas and approaches concerned with multiple and interconnected power structures such as heteropatriarchy, capitalism, whiteness, colonialism and ecological degradation – and the resistance to them. They provide analytic tools, albeit in different ways, and political agendas to 'decentre the West' and confront and resist the challenges that these oppressive systems present to the lives of women, communities and the Earth.

Decolonizing feminisms explore the theoretical and practical frameworks for thinking through significant concepts in feminist theory, activism and beyond such as questioning the representation of the feminist subject within feminist theories and understanding the intersection of very diverse elements of economics, corporeality, politics, religion, spirituality, liberation and difference. From diverse socio-political locations and multiple and transdisciplinary perspectives, feminisms/anti-patriarchal struggles engaging with decolonization propose new, decolonizing ways of thinking about feminist knowledges, methodologies and practices in light of capitalism and extractivism. However, decolonizing feminisms cannot be an effective intervention unless it also addresses economies and economics.

Feminist economics

In the middle of these debates, feminist economics has remained practically absent. Decolonizing feminist approaches and decolonizing economics have rarely engaged with feminist economics. Although there are occasional mentions of feminist economics in the decolonizing economics literature such as in the work of Ingrid Kvangraven and Surbhi Kesar (2023) or the Association for Heterodox Economics, these references are celebrated but often lack substantive development or meaningful connections to the broader decolonizing project. As a result, the contributions of decolonizing economics to feminist economics, and vice versa, have remained largely gestural. Conversely, while decolonizing feminisms offer a profound critique of cultural hegemony and colonialism, this critical lens does not consistently extend to the theorization of the economy within much of the scholarship. Despite invoking economic forces in their analyses, decolonizing feminisms often draw on theories that diverge from current scholarship in mainstream economics. Similarly, recent collective works within feminist economics, such as *The Routledge Handbook of Feminist Economics* (Berik and Kongar, 2021), and notorious conferences in the field like the Annual International Association for Feminist Economics conferences, reveal a conspicuous absence of engagement with anti-colonial, decolonial or postcolonial thought.

Addressing this gap requires investigating epistemological and material alternatives, such as exploring incomplete records, identifying missing links, acknowledging voids, and examining rifts within feminist economic thinking and practice. This book contends that these productive ruptures have not been adequately explored and seeks to contribute to the emerging approach of decolonizing feminist economics. In doing so, the book responds to the call made by postcolonial feminist economists Eiman Osman Zein-Elabdin and S. Charuseheela (2004) to emphasize the significance of non-Western approaches, including Indigenous forms understandings of the economy, feminism and the non-Western moral imperatives derived from non-capitalist modern knowledges, societies and groups. In order to do that, the initial focus will be on understanding the culture *of* economics.

The culture *of* economics

Economic activities do not occur in a cultural vacuum; they are inherently influenced and shaped by the social and cultural meanings that comprise various everyday practices, ideas and worldviews (Polanyi, 1957; Pollard et al, 2011). Consequently, economies are always cultural artefacts, reflecting and embodying the values and norms of a particular society or community. However, within economics, culture has often been dismissed as a negative or neutral factor, and its role in economic behaviour and decision-making continues to be underestimated. Current economic approaches to culture often range from treating it as a constraint on 'rational' individual behaviour, subservient to 'material' considerations, to an isolable realm of meaning (such as tastes and preferences) or a force propelling economic growth (the cultivation of entrepreneurialism). Alternatively, some approaches embrace culture but with an implicit hierarchy where modern Europe assumes a higher ontological order, relegating other cultures to a subaltern status in the discipline. However, culture is rarely valued for its own sake – the culture *of* economics.

Eiman Osman Zein-Elabdin (2004: 28) argues that this 'disembodiment from culture' in economics has led to a process of double erasure. On one hand, certain cultures and economies are erased by theorizing them as inferior (less developed or developing). On the other hand, there is an erasure of the work of cultural hegemony, privileging the historical context of European modernity in different world regions. This partially explains the slow engagement of economic approaches with critical theories concerning postcoloniality (Zein-Elabdin and Charusheela, 2004; Pollard et al, 2011; Zein-Elabdin, 2016) and decolonization, allowing economics to remain largely entrenched in its Western-centric modernist cultural framework.

Western-centric modernism, as defined in this book, is characterized by a distinctly Western, particularly European, social vision that elevates specific practices and institutions to the status of universals. These include an industrial capitalist economy, a liberal-democratic nation-state, extensive bureaucratization, differentiation of social functions, and the redefinition of interactions among individuals, between individuals and the state, and between individuals and society. It also encompasses the colonization of the non-European world and the expansion of capitalist social relations.

There is a gap, however, between the civilizing modernist project of domination and the critical option of emancipation, which needs to be explored anew. Modernism also includes a variety of conceptual innovations centred on universal ideals such as emancipation, freedom and democracy. These ideals serve as the foundation for both capitalist modernity and the resistance against it (Srnicek and Williams, 2015). For instance, they have inspired abolitionist movements around the world, supported numerous women's rights struggles in Africa, Latin America, the Caribbean and Asia, and continue to drive contemporary campaigns for land rights, Indigenous rights, wages, security, basic health, dignity, self-determination and autonomy.

Despite this, the association between capitalism and modernization remains entrenched, overshadowing progressive visions for the future. It is crucial to recognize that multiple modernities are possible and to embrace new perspectives on the future. In this context, I agree with Nick Srnicek and Alex Williams (2015) that modernity should be contested rather than rejected. Similarly, as Samir Amin (2009 [1989]: 17) suggests, we should aspire to a universal project that transcends European particularism – a 'modernity critical of modernity'.

In that sense, to invoke modernity ultimately raises questions about the future: What should the future look like? Whose future is it? However, reclaiming a sense of the future, following Amin, cannot simply adopt a modernism that positions the West/Europe as the normative ideal, where societies and their futures are ranked based on their proximity to this Western/European ideal. Samir Amin (2009 [1989]) terms this culturalist distortion Eurocentrism, where European culture is viewed as inherently superior.

> Eurocentrism is not, properly speaking, a social theory, which integrates various elements into a global and coherent vision of society and history. It is rather a prejudice that distorts social theories. It draws from its storehouse of components, retaining one or rejecting another according to the ideological needs of the moment. (Amin, 2009 [1989]: 166)

In economics, Eurocentrism appears in two interrelated forms: the assumption of the superiority of Western modernity (implying the capitalist system is the only possible future) and the disregard for culture itself. This belief in supra-cultural laws governing economic behaviour and dynamics takes the cultural framework for granted, making economic tendencies and material aspects of life seem detached from culture. This is evident in concepts like innate individual rationality and supremacy of the market as a medium of resource distribution and management in neoclassical theory[1] and a priori historical necessity in Marxism and other heterodox economics, including feminist economics (Zein-Elabdin and Charusheela, 2004). As a result, the role of culture becomes obscured while Western-centric modernist principles influence the foundational premises of economics.

Challenging the ontological separation between economics and culture is essential for effectively addressing economic problems. The modern division between culture and economics hinders our understanding of the world and does not reflect the ways in which we actually live. If we understand culture as the process through which we give meaning, shape, and navigate the relationship between human beings and the surrounding environment, it becomes clear that culture is not a product we can choose to enjoy or not based on individual preferences. Instead, it is an intrinsic and essential part of our lives. In that sense, culture should be seen as a process through which economic meaning and rationality are articulated and experienced. Therefore, the 'culture–economy link' (Zein-Elabdin, 2011a: 53) must be considered as an organic, interconnected whole, rather than as mechanistic or hierarchical. To fully explore a non-dualist analysis of the culture–economy relationship, we need to engage with the full breadth of contemporary economic thought, both heterodox and orthodox, while avoiding the exclusive attribution of epistemic authority on the 'material' to the field of economics. In this regard, a concept regarding economic hybridity may better describe economies found at the intersection of multiple cultural currents.

Gloria Anzaldúa (1999 [1987]) offers valuable insights here through concepts like *mestiza*, *nepantla* and *El Cenote* as pathways to creating new and transformative knowledge. Anzaldúa (1999 [1987]: 98) articulates 'La conciencia de la mestiza', a consciousness that transcends dualisms (mind/body, male/female, white/non-white) by uprooting these dualistic thinking structures from both individual and collective consciousness. In examining these dualities, *nepantla*, the 'in-between' space, is revealed and takes form in *El Cenote*, which she describes as a 'mental network of subterranean rivers of information that converge and well up to the surface' (Anzaldúa, 1999 [1987]: 244), empowering us to reclaim our *mestiza* intellect. Anzaldúa asserts that this transcendence is possible by making the *mestiza* existence visible in our daily lives and through the 'images of our work' (Anzaldúa, 1999 [1987]: 102).

In the context of economics, a *mestiza* methodology introduces hybridity by resisting the strict categorization of economics within idealist or materialist frameworks. Instead, it envisions *nepantla* in economics – a non-dualist concept challenging the modernist division between 'the economic' (as the mind) and 'the cultural' (as the body). A *mestiza* methodology in decolonizing feminist economics thus aims to dismantle dualistic thinking by advocating for an 'in-between' space (*nepantla*) in contemporary economies. Here, culture is not merely acknowledged but *embraced*, as in *El Cenote*, as a critical component of economics and our understanding of economies as networks of cross-cultural intersections of knowledge. This approach rejects the notion of economics existing independently 'out there' or in isolation, akin to the Coatlicue state – a state of mind that, according to Anzaldúa (1999 [1987]), resists new knowledge and deep transformation.

Thus, a *mestiza* methodology in economics begins with the observation that the economy is deeply embedded within our societal fabric and intersected by multiple cultural currents. It calls for situating and contextualizing economic research in ways that reflect these diverse and hybrid economic realities. A *mestiza* methodology seeks to build a decolonizing feminist economic framework that acknowledges this hybridity and collective sense-making. Integrating the 'culture–economic link' into economic research thus requires *mestiza* methods that embrace data collection, interpretation, and presentation practices that recover previously silenced forms of economic knowledge.

Epistemicide of economies

Acts of silencing, when executed as epistemicides, signify the demise of knowledge within subordinate cultures (Anzaldúa, 1999 [1987]; Santos, 2014). As argued by Frantz Fanon (1963) and Amílcar Cabral (1966), the eradication of such knowledge is not a mere epistemological artefact; it embodies the systematic disqualification of social groups, particularly Indigenous people and the destruction of practices rooted in these knowledges. These authors, along with other anti-colonial thinkers, argue that foreign domination – whether imperialistic or otherwise – aims for one of two outcomes: either the complete eradication of the population in the colonized nation to eliminate any potential for cultural resistance, or the successful imposition of foreign control that leaves the indigenous culture unharmed (see, for example, Cabral, 1966). This second scenario requires the economic and political subjugation of the people to align with their cultural identity. By ignoring the historical trajectories of colonized nations, imperialism and colonialism deny the evolution of their cultures. This results in cultural oppression and efforts to undermine or extinguish the core elements of Indigenous cultures.

Within the field of economics, these silencing acts have been particularly pervasive, imposing a singular view centred on limitless growth, capitalism and Western-centric modernism (Zein-Elabdin and Charusheela, 2004; Santos, 2014; Escobar, 2016; Spivak, 2016; Carrasco-Miro, 2018a). The Eurocentric nature of economics has stifled, devalued and erased a plethora of economic knowledges, hindering the equal participation of non-Western and non-capitalist economies (often labelled as 'less developed', 'developing' or 'global South') in the global construction of social meaning and economic well-being. Examples of epistemicide in economics include the eradication of Indigenous spirituality (essential in their economies), the abandonment of traditional productive or food practices (particularly the ones done by women), the extinction of native languages, and the displacement of Indigenous economic systems, governance structures and natural resource management methods.

In today's landscape, global capitalism and its motto of economic growth appear as the seemingly inevitable civilizational paradigm – the only envisioned agenda for the future. However, the exclusions, oppressions and discriminations stemming from this system extend beyond economic, social, ecological and political dimensions; they also permeate cultural and epistemological realms (Escobar, 1995; Kapoor, 2008; Santos, 2014). These consequences encompass the implications of presuming that the Western modernity paradigm of knowledge, rooted in capitalism, rationality, liberalism, secularism, heteropatriarchy, whiteness and the nation-state, represents a superior and universally applicable perspective. Simultaneously, within this modernist paradigm, knowledge, peoples, economies and cultures that deviate from the Western modern 'ideal' are treated as non-existent, irrelevant, underdeveloped and incomprehensible (Said, 1978; Ngũgĩ, 1986; Amin, 2009 [1989]; Espinosa et al, 2014).

Postcolonial and decolonial scholars refer to this ethnocentric universalism as the colonization of knowledge (Fanon, 1963; Césaire, 1972 [1950]; Anzaldúa, 1987; Rivera Cusicanqui, 1987; Smith, 1999; Quijano, 2000; Simpson, 2001; Tuck and Yang, 2012). These authors emphasize the geopolitics of knowledge as an ethical possibility for challenging epistemicide and envisioning a new humanity capable of escaping colonialism. Thus, decolonizing economic knowledge becomes a complex project that involves not only cultivating a sense of disconnection from the West but also disrupting the status quo to make visible the diversity of knowledges and reconstruct humanity.

Epistemicide of economies carries several implications. Firstly, it curtails the diversity of economic thinking and economic imaginaries, impeding the exploration of innovative and context-specific approaches to economics. By side-lining alternative knowledge systems, societies miss valuable insights and practices that could contribute to more sustainable and just economic systems. Secondly, epistemicide perpetuates power imbalances, reinforcing the dominance of certain groups or regions in the global economy. The marginalization of local and Indigenous economic knowledge, for example, can exacerbate social inequalities and undermine the agency and autonomy of marginalized communities. It also hinders the dignity and ability of these communities to shape their own economic futures based on their unique social, cultural, economic and ecological contexts. Acknowledging and involving different economic knowledge systems in economic analysis requires recognizing and valuing knowledge, which may sometimes be embedded in non capitalistic, non Western cultural economic values, knowledge and strategies of existence.

Recent years have seen efforts to challenge this Eurocentric bias in economics and promote more plural and diverse perspectives. Scholars and activists have advocated for the decolonization of economic knowledge and the recognition of different economic systems and practices. This includes integrating Indigenous economic knowledge, understanding the importance of social relations and community-based economies, sustainability, non-market forms of exchange, and embracing pluralism in economic thinking. These various economic knowledge systems embody new forms of power that surpass conventional boundaries of resistance and voice. Their emancipatory nature does not solely stem from being Indigenous, post-capitalist or non-Western; rather, it arises from surpassing the typical economic hegemonic schemes of innovation and power.

Shiv Visvanathan notes:

> The idea of cognitive justice … sensitizes us not only to forms of knowledge but [also] to the diverse communities of problem solving. What one offers then is a democratic imagination with a non-market, non-competitive view of the world, where conversation, reciprocity, translation create knowledge not as an expert, almost zero-sum view of the world but as a collaboration of memories, legacies, heritages, a manifold heuristic of problem solving, where a citizen takes both power and knowledge into his [or her or their] own hands. (Visvanathan, 2009: para 37)

By incorporating the dynamics of economic knowledge into a democratic imagination, the principles of knowledge are reframed, leading to a new reflexive conception of democracy centred around concrete economic communities of practice. This allows for the emergence of epistemological possibilities that give credibility to the forms of economic knowledge that underlie those practices. This is inseparable from the epistemological diversity that distinguishes and organizes the world in ways that differ from capitalistic and Western-centric modern thinking.

The close connection between these values and aspirations suggests that 'there is no global social justice without global cognitive justice' (Santos, 2014: 63). This underscores the necessity for economic thinking to be part of the broader struggle for cognitive justice, recognizing that overcoming the epistemicide of economies is inseparable from addressing global economic injustices. Only by acknowledging and valuing diverse economic knowledge systems can we hope to dismantle the entrenched power structures that perpetuate economic inequality and cultural hegemony. In this endeavour, the quest for cognitive justice becomes not just an intellectual pursuit but a transformative force capable of reshaping the very foundations of economic understanding and practice.

From a logic of maximization to the common good

At the very foundation of economics lies the question of what is the purpose of economic activity. While mainstream economics, following neoclassical economics, still explicitly name human needs and their fulfilment as an important goal to achieve, the purpose of economics is not clearly defined in current economic literature. The most shared definition, which is descriptively about efficient management of scarce resources, does not include an explicit aim, as efficiency always needs a purpose which it serves. In mainstream neoclassical economics the concept of needs is implicitly assumed or described as 'what people want to have' (Mankiw, 2021 [1998]: 2) in a supposedly natural scarce world, and considers decisions of individuals as being made completely independently of other people's needs.

However, economics is not a value-neutral discipline. For instance, the operationalization of rationality as endless profit maximization implies *values* of materialism and selfishness. Individual economic choices and policies impact on others and the Earth so inevitably they involve moral and ethical judgements. Individual consumption choices, such as purchasing products and using resources, for example, can contribute to resource depletion and environmental degradation. Excessive use of fossil fuels for energy or excessive consumption of water can contribute to climate change and water scarcity, affecting not only the individual but also other communities and ecosystems. Economic policies that promote fair wages, maternity leave and social safety nets can reduce income inequality and improve overall societal welfare.

On the other hand, policies that prioritize profit maximization at the expense of workers' rights or social benefits can exacerbate inequality and lead to social unrest. Economic choices and policies in one country can have global consequences due to the interconnectedness of economies. For example, trade policies, tariffs or subsidies can affect international trade flows and impact industries and employment in other countries. Similarly, environmental policies or lack thereof can contribute to transboundary pollution and affect global ecosystems and climate patterns. Economics is a value-generating discipline.

In this regard, the student movements around the world have been demanding a change in economics education and a different way of teaching economics, one that considers its ethics (values), for over two decades.[2] The International Student Initiative for Pluralism in Economics, for instance, wrote an open letter in 2014:

> We, over 65 associations of economics students from over 30 different countries, believe it is time to reconsider the way economics is taught. We are dissatisfied with the dramatic narrowing of the curriculum that has taken place over the last couple of decades. This lack of intellectual diversity does not only restrain education and research. It limits our ability to contend with the multidimensional challenges of the 21st century – from financial stability, to food security and climate change. The real world should be brought back into the classroom, as well as debate and a pluralism of theories and methods ... it is essential that core curricula include courses that provide context and foster reflexive thinking about economics and its methods per se, including philosophy of economics and the theory of knowledge. Economics education should include interdisciplinary approaches and allow students to engage with other social sciences and the humanities. Economics is a social science; complex economic phenomena can seldom be understood if presented in a vacuum, removed from their sociological, political, and historical contexts. To properly discuss economic policy, students should understand the broader social impacts and moral implications of economic decisions.[3]

Similarly, in 2011, Harvard students taking the economics course (Economics 10) taught by influential economist Greg Mankiw, Beren Professor of Economics at Harvard University, wrote an open letter directly to him:

> Dear Professor Mankiw,
>
> ... Harvard graduates play major roles in the financial institutions and in shaping public policy around the world. If Harvard fails to equip its students with a broad and critical understanding of economics, their actions are likely to harm the global financial system. The last five years of economic turmoil have been proof enough of this. We are walking out today to join a Boston-wide march protesting the corporatization of higher education as part of the global Occupy movement. Since the biased nature of Economics 10 contributes to and symbolizes the increasing economic inequality in America, we are walking out of your class today both to protest your inadequate discussion of basic economic theory and to lend our support to a movement that is changing American discourse on economic injustice.[4]

Furthermore, there have been numerous calls for the decolonization of universities and the decommodification of education worldwide. These discussions often include conversations about white supremacy and the enduring legacy of colonialism. One notable example is the Rhodes Must Fall movement which began in 2015 in South Africa and later spread to the

United Kingdom, and resonated globally. Rhodes, known for his role as a British imperialist and his racist views, became the emblematic target for #RhodesMustFall, a radical student movement centred on the decolonization of education. This movement addressed issues such as institutional racism, the need for curriculum reform and access to education (Luescher, 2016). The Rhodes Must Fall movement sought to decolonize education by employing tactics of disruption inspired by decolonial, Black consciousness and feminist intersectional theories (Ahmed, 2017), framing their struggle as a resistance to the dehumanization of Black people, which they argue 'is a violence exacted only against black people by a system that privileges whiteness' (UCT Rhodes Must Fall Mission Statement, 2015: 1).

The strong emphasis on the change in the academic economics curriculum becomes relevant for the economics discipline's own evolution, considering that the shift in the students in economics will have an impact on future academic debates. The advocacy for economics ethics and pluralism goes hand in hand with the recovery of debating real material issues, the social impacts, power dynamics and moral implications in our societies, and improving public debate.

Economics should engage with questions of what is just, sustainable and fair, rather than solely focusing on maximizing individual preferences, personal fulfilment or market efficiency as if they had no impact beyond a number. This involves acknowledging that economies generate and are influenced by changing social and cultural norms, values and structures, and society being more than the mere sum of its individual members. This means a more robust ethical, moral and political engagement with questions of value and the common good in economic theory and decision-making. This means deliberating rather than calculating which economies we want and discovering which notions of a good life in a particular context are the best that can be achieved given the circumstances. Economics, therefore, must transition from a logic of maximization to one of the common good.

Economics is known as the cynic science – assuming that prices are all anyone needs to know (Sandel, 2013; Mazzucato, 2017). As early as 1977, Nobel laureate economist Amartya Sen (1977: 336; emphasis in original) criticized 'the *purely* economic man' as 'close to being a social moron'. Today, when we think about economics, we refer to interests, the market or efficiency, or directly as a necessary evil, not as a feature that contributes to the good life of people and the Earth. However, and precisely for that reason, the change in economics must be based on the ethical question of how we want to live together. By shifting the misguided emphasis on growth-driven markets towards a focus on the common good, economics can transcend its cynical reputation and embrace a more trustworthy approach that encourages decolonizing, feminist and anti-patriarchal approaches, active participation, critical thinking, deliberation, imagination and, therefore, a true commitment to shaping societies that are more just and sustainable.

Questions for decolonizing a feminist economics graduate course

Here are seven questions we might consider when thinking about decolonizing a feminist economics or gender and economics graduate course:[5]

1. What and how do we want to learn in this feminist economics/gender and economics graduate course?
2. What conceptual, historical, poetic, and aesthetic knowledge and tools are shared to foster critical thinking?
3. Is the Eurocentrism, Orientalism and developmentalism, inherent in hegemonic economic and gender discourses, being critically interrogated?
4. Are previously silenced and marginalized economies, economic practices and social groups – those systematically subjected to injustice, oppression and destruction by capitalism, colonialism, heteropatriarchy and ecological degradation – being validated and recognized?
5. Are issues of land (both local and global), economic sovereignty and Indigenous futures being included and meaningfully discussed from a decolonizing feminist/anti-patriarchal perspective?
6. How is this feminist economics/gender and economics graduate course contributing to the creation of alternative frameworks and better futures for all, including the Earth? (Which concepts, strategies and imaginaries are being explored?)
7. Is there space to collectively imagine the kinds of economies we want?

2

The Problematics of Feminist Economics

Introduction: Feminist economics

Feminist economics emerged as a response to the recognition that mainstream economics often overlooks or undervalues the contributions and experiences of women in economic activities and develops research to overcome these failings (Benería, 1981; Berik and Kongar, 2021). It has conceptualized economics as a social institution, criticized the presumed gender-neutrality of economic outcomes, and challenged economics as hegemonic discourse.

Feminist economics situates its starting point in Western academic literature with works such as 'The underestimation of women's economic activities' (Benería, 1981), *If Women Counted* (Waring, 1988) or *Beyond Economic Man* (Ferber and Nelson, 1993; Berik and Kongar, 2021). The establishment of the International Association for Feminist Economics (IAFFE) in the United States in 1992 and the *Feminist Economics* journal further institutionalized the field, encompassing mainstream and nonmainstream feminist economists and feminist scholars from diverse disciplines and across the globe. Since then, feminist economics has developed its own concepts, analytical frameworks and methodologies, and gained representation and recognition in many international organizations and governments worldwide. All of this has been hard-fought and not easily attained.

There is a variety of approaches and levels of analysis in feminist economics that outline different views on the feminist political subject and the different possibilities of emancipation. These approaches include Marxian political economy, institutionalist economics, ecological economics and neoclassical economics. Despite feminist economics' plural character, there are common objectives, and general tendencies reflected in the mission statement of the IAFFE: 'Our common cause is to further gender-aware and inclusive economic inquiry and policy analysis with the goal of enhancing the well-being of children, women, and men in local, national, and transnational communities' (see also Berik and Kongar, 2021).[1]

With gender as central category, feminist economics includes both studies of gender disparities in the economy and critical work directed at biases in economics to create a more inclusive, just and equitable economic framework. Topics it addresses include the economics of households, labour markets, care, development, the macroeconomy, national budgets, and the history, philosophy, methodology and teaching of economics.

In recent years, feminist economics and feminist economists have experienced increased popularity and recognition in economic analysis and policy making. As feminism has gained traction in societies, institutions increasingly demand economic frameworks that address gender disparities and acknowledge the contributions and experiences of women in economic activities. Feminist economists have played a vital role in advancing this agenda by conducting research, developing policies and providing valuable insights to help policy makers and organizations develop more equitable policies that promote gender equality and social justice.

However, feminist economics still grapples with criticisms posed by postcolonial, anti-colonial, third world feminisms, African/Black feminism, *feminismos del Sur*, communitarian feminism and decolonial feminisms on its developmentalism and teleological assumptions about history and society that persist within the field (Mohanty, 1991; Spivak, 1999; Zein-Elabdin, 2003; Charusheela, 2009; Rivera Cusicanqui, 2018). Despite stellar efforts by postcolonial feminist economists,[2] I agree with Barker (2000), Wood (2003), Bergeron (2004), Zein-Elabdin and Charusheela (2004) and Zein-Elabdin (2016) that, so far, much of feminist economics analyses remain intransigently Western-centric modernist (Carrasco-Miró, 2020a, 2021, 2025a).

This chapter responds to the call for a deeper examination of feminist economics by exploring the theoretical limitations of its current status and suggesting ways to overcome them. It argues that feminist economics loses its relevance if, in addition to depatriarchalizing, it does not undertake a serious revision of its core subjects of inquiry, particularly its approaches to non-Western women, non-Western cultures and economies, colonialism and the process of decommodification. Following the insights discussed in the previous chapter, I intend here to unfold and analyse feminist economics' key cultural underpinnings. This entails recognizing the implicit or explicit cultural imprints of the growth paradigm, extractivist and productivist logic, and modernization theory. But more importantly, this chapter exposes feminist economics' discursive strategy: its ideological suppositions and rhetorical constructions, its gaps, bias, disavowals and discontinuities, its production and naturalization of hierarchies, and its institutional tendency towards reproducing or extending power.

To do that, as follows I discuss what I think are today four main problematics in feminist economics: the problem of the subject, the problem of cultural bias, the problem of equal opportunities and gender equality, and the problem of imagination and feminist contradictions. By doing so, I also propose pathways forward using a decolonizing framework to overcome these limitations.

The problematics of feminist economics

The problem of the subject in feminist economics

Although many feminist economists are careful to reject any hint of gender essentialism, the tendency, stemming from the inherent task of a feminist research programme, has been to particularize women as the subject in feminist economics. One example of this is the recent publication of the book *A Herstory of Economics* by Edith Kuiper (2022), a well-known feminist economist and former president of the IAFFE. Kuiper (2022) explains in her introduction that the book takes into consideration intersectionality and acknowledges difference in experiences among women in positions of privilege and disadvantage. But the focus of the book, Kuiper states, is

> on women's writing on economic issues, and not, for instance, on economists' writing on women's issues, because it is here – on the basis of their gender – that women economic writers and economists have been exploited. … The book focuses on the work of people who, *as women* [Kuiper clarifies she focuses on cis-women and not trans on p 10], developed a perspective on the economy that was and is very different from that developed by men *as men*. (Kuiper, 2022: 10; emphasis in original)

Focusing on women as the subject of economics does not necessarily invalidate feminist analysis, but, regardless of intentionality, the collective arguments imply that gender is the central bias in feminist economics. Theorizing gender as the generalized 'Other' in feminist economics is, nevertheless, problematic (Zein-Elabdin, 2003).

In Judith Butler's work *Gender Trouble* (2006 [1990]), there are two fundamental questions that concern the author and that are exposed at the beginning of the text as a presentation of the problems that feminism is facing. In the first place, 'the question of the "subject" is crucial' (Butler, 2006 [1990]: 2). In line with the Nietzschean lineage tradition represented by authors such as Michel Foucault, Jacques Derrida and Gilles Deleuze, Butler adheres to the proclamation of the death of the subject. In second place, but directly implicated by the crisis of the Western-centric modern idea of the subject and the essentialist metaphysics of identity on which it is based, is the question of women's identity, according to this author. In fact,

Butler (2006 [1990]: 1] begins their text by denouncing an error, namely that 'feminist theory has assumed that there is some existing identity, understood through the category of women, who not only initiates feminist interests and goals within discourse, but constitutes the subject for whom representation is pursued'. Butler wants, in effect, to challenge the assumption that the term 'women' indicates a common identity and, therefore, also questions 'women' as the subject of feminism.

In addition, this erroneous assumption, that of the existence of a certain common identity, is linked to another great error of feminism that Butler wants to escape. They asserts: '[t]he political assumption that there must be a universal basis for feminism, one which must be found in an identity assumed to exist cross-culturally, often accompanies the notion that the oppression of women has some singular form discernible in the universal or hegemonic structure of patriarchy or masculine domination' (Butler, 2006 [1990]: 6).

The essentialist notion of 'women' is in solidarity with the universalist idea of 'patriarchy' and both belong to that way of doing feminism that 'has come under criticism for its efforts to colonize and appropriate non-Western cultures to support highly Western notions of oppression, but because they tend as well to construct a "Third World" or even an "Orient" in which gender oppression is subtly explained as symptomatic of an essential, non-Western barbarism' (Butler, 2006 [1990]: 6).

In this vein, a feminist economics that embraces the metaphysics of identity rests on three deeply contestable hypotheses. The first is the idea that 'women' (from the global North or the global South) are one and the same: one empowered, the other not; one sexually liberated, the other not, and so on (see Mohanty, 1991). If the limits of the female subject are perfectly delimitable, it is because there is an identity, an essence, because we are, ultimately, the same. The second idea is that the boundaries surrounding the victims of patriarchy coincide exactly with the boundaries of 'women'. The third is that the subjects of economic struggles are the victims. All these assumptions are essential to affirm that feminist economics is primarily a struggle for women. Yet, any feminist economics that aspires to be critical and transformative must question each one of them.

The last of the affirmations, that of feminist economics being made by the victims, that is to say, that it is the condition of victim that constitutes the path of access to the subject position of feminist economics, rests on the strange and metaphysical belief that, since women are the most dominated and constrained by patriarchy, they are, at the same time, the privileged subjects to understand with clairvoyance, and without interference from power, patriarchy or capitalism itself. I believe that any emancipatory project must include the victims in developing theory as well as in political struggles, they cannot not be there, but not sacralize them. In that sense, agents of feminist economics are those who criticize the heteropatriarchal, capitalist, colonialist, ecocidal system, who defend an alternative society, an economy otherwise, to the extractivist and productivist mentality, and therefore its actions, who have the vision to build it, not just those who share pain and grievance.

But, in addition, we must deeply question the fact that only women are victims of patriarchy and the economic system. As Eiman Osman Zein-Elabdin (2003: 321) has argued, '[g]iven the overlap between gender and other historical instruments of domination, for instance colonialism, the particularity of women's economic subordination can be carried only up to a point, and gender itself cannot be fully sutured as an analytical category'. Economic subordination and oppression is shared not only among women but also encompasses a significant number of men, trans and non-binary individuals who have been historically constructed as irrational, deviant, disempowered or 'less developed', and to whom the market/non-market divide, which many see as the root of the gender bias in economics, also applies.

The key in the basic neoclassical model, which feminist economics criticizes, is the theoretical construction of the economic agent and the 'non-economic' rather than her/their/his gender (Zein-Elabdin, 2003). The gender bias in economics, therefore, is derivative from the theoretical bias towards market exchange, growth and capitalism as it evolved in modern Europe. At a discursive level, the bias towards material accumulation results in the devaluation or exclusion of values and practices of slowness, moderation, conviviality, sharing, gift-giving, loyalty, whether they are exhibited by 'women or men or children', and the ideological groups associated with such practices as irrational, disempowered, less developed or directly pre-modern. A feminist economics that rests on a metaphysics of identity needs to ignore that there are many other victims of the gender and economic system beyond women and this is highly problematic in its fight for economic justice.

It would be inaccurate to claim that feminist economists have overlooked the link between the devaluation of women and that of other groups. My argument here is that, even when mindful of these connections, feminist economic analyses have tended to approach other devaluated groups as an abstract theme within the gender–race–ethnicity–class nexus and have not yet pushed their analyses of domination to engage these complexities in a more constructive way (Zein-Elabdin, 2003; Carrasco-Miró, 2020a; Banks, 2021). In this regard, Nina Banks (2021) has examined the extent to which feminist economists have incorporated an intersectional framework in their research published between 2009 and 2019 in *Feminist Economics*. While not all feminist economists publish in *Feminist Economics*, the journal is the leading outlet for disseminating feminist economic research and ideas. Banks (2021: 121) concludes that her findings

> [i]ndicate[s] that feminist economists have generally not embraced [intersectionality] as an analytical framework. … Of particular concern

> is the very small number of articles that examine race as it interacts with other dimensions of identity and oppression. Notably absent are articles by African American economists. Moreover, articles that are US-centered tend to focus on the general category of 'women' without disaggregating data by race and other categories.

My point is not that racism, colonialism or ecological degradation is more important than gender, but, rather, that all are inextricably bound up with one another as overlapping vehicles of oppression. Problematically, the tendency in feminist economics to focus on gender, particularly on 'women', further leads to the elision of other cultures.

For example, consider Oyèrónkẹ́ Oyěwùmí's (1997, 2002) work on the Indigenous Yoruba context. Oyěwùmí focuses on the epistemological underpinnings of the Western notion of sex and gender, explaining that gender, and particularly the category 'women', does not operate in Yorubaland in the same way it does in Western discourses.

> The traditional Yoruba family can be described as a non-gendered family. It is non-gendered because kinship roles and categories are not gender-differentiated. Significantly then, power centers within the family are diffused and are not gender-specific. Because the fundamental organizing principle within the family is seniority based on relative age, and not gender, kinship categories encode seniority not gender. (Oyěwùmí, 2002: 5)

Regardless of the rich debate about Oyěwùmí's research and gender in the Yoruba context (see, for example, Bakare-Yusuf [2003] and Adefarakan [2011] for a critical reply to Oyěwùmí's work), what is significant is that it underscores the fact that the discussion is not solely about gender. Rather, gender is also bound up with spirituality and issues of embodiment, power, culture, imperialism, colonialism and the (un)critical acceptance of Western discourse as normative.

One could certainly establish the primacy of gender within very specific contexts, but subjects of economic policies and analyses vary, and their boundaries often shift. Depending on the context in question, other systems of hierarchy and the goals pursued, economic policies may focus on one social group, another, or several simultaneously.

The last of the theses at stake, actually the one on which the others rest, has to do with not questioning the identity of women. I think the only coherent response here is the assumption that we do not know very well what women are, that it is a problematic subject, that we are working with a fiction and that we do not believe in the sameness of that subject (Butler, 2006 [1990]; Preciado, 2021). The fragmentation present in different struggles for possible just futures has nothing to do with the diversity of subjects, disciplines or the plurality of the social space, but with the metaphysics of identity. In this sense, if the problem is not the diversity of politico-economic struggles and proposals against heteropatriarchy, capitalism, colonialism and ecological degradation, but the mythologized identity or the centrality of gender, the solution is to defend difference.

Butler (1997) argues in this direction when discusses that difference is not simply the external differences between movements and coalitions, understood as that which differentiates them from one another, but, rather, the self-difference of movement itself, a constitutive rupture that makes movements and alliances possible on non-identitarian grounds, that installs a certain mobilizing conflict as the basis of politicization. Fractionalization, understood as the process whereby one identity excludes another in order to fortify its own unity and coherence, makes the mistake of locating the problem of difference as that which emerges between one identity and another; but difference is the condition of possibility of identity or, rather, its constitutive limit: what makes its articulation possible is at the same time what makes any final or closed articulation impossible.

Women are not identical to themselves, children are not a delimited essence, men are not determined. Thus, identity is a political construct – necessary for strategic purposes but potentially harmful when it becomes overly simplified or essentialized. The difficulty of feminist economics is thus contained in the slipperiness of difference in all its illusive forms and entails scrutiny of each context. This requires transcending an implicitly essentialist notion of gender, such that it holds no presumption that gender underlies economic processes except in culturally specific ways.

Feminist economics, therefore, must be capable of analysing and combating the structural economic inequalities that run through societies and not only the inequality that separates men from women (boys from girls); it must be able to reveal the detrimental effects of capitalism not only on women; the damage of patriarchy not only towards women; understand colonialism. The political power of feminism depends, in the end, on us putting a little doubt on the identity of women because only by relativizing the categories that separate us as the different subjects can we build an economic just project that calls us all together.

The great challenge that feminist economics faces today is to escape, as it escapes from the traps, from possible identity withdrawals that threaten to deactivate it. Rebelling against solipsism and fragmentation, against the forms of neoliberal subjectivity and against the politics of 'what about my issues', means putting a little more doubt on who we are and abandoning the search for the true subjects. The more dedicated a critical study is to policing the borders of its subject, the less capacity to transform the world it has. We need to regain the certainty that the differences that separate us from others are not insurmountable abysses, that we can build economies based not on who we are, but on the world we want.

The trap from which we have to escape is that of identity, and deactivating it involves making an economy not based on shared grievances, but based on common desires (which kind of economies do we want?). For these economies, feminist economics can be a promise for everyone. If there is something revolutionary about queer theory, so problematically structurally absent and yet necessary in feminist economics,[3] it is its anti-identitarianism and its miscegenation, the gathering of diverse subjects around a political struggle that summons them not for what they are but for what they want to build together. Feminist economics will only succeed in being radically transformative if it takes over the battles for the 99 per cent of people (depatriarchalizing, decolonizing, anti-capitalist, radically ecological), that is, if it is not only for and about women.

The problem of cultural bias in feminist economics

The issue of cultural bias within feminist economics is intrinsically intertwined with the broader paradigm of developmentalism. This connection is anchored in the very foundations of developmentalist thought, which erects a framework for understanding global economic dynamics through the lens of Western modernism and progress as economic growth (that is, development), often at the expense of non-modernist, non-Western knowledges and worldviews.[4] At its core, Western developmentalism operates under the premise of an ontological and epistemological hierarchy, positioning Western modernism as the zenith of societal advancement. This hierarchical paradigm, in turn, engenders an inherent cultural bias that casts non-Western, non-modern societies and people as 'developing' or 'disempowered' in comparison to the purportedly superior Western 'developed' counterparts.

This ontological and epistemological hierarchy translates into a power dynamic wherein Western institutions wield authority in shaping and defining concepts such as progress, development, gender equality and women's empowerment. This power dynamic is further perpetuated by institutions of influence, including academia and developmental agendas such as the Agenda 2030 and its Sustainable Development Goals (SDGs). In this framework, Western modernist ideologues assume, for example, that women's problems in non-Western contexts lie elsewhere – for example, in non-modern/'traditional' cultures and non-Western men – and never in the actual economic structures or politics of institutionalization itself (Charusheela, 2003; Carrasco-Miró, 2016).

Most feminist economists have contested the oversimplified assertion that economic growth automatically translates to women's empowerment, questioning contemporary neoliberal empowerment policies. Despite this critical stance, a closer examination of economic discourses reveals that Western-centric modernist claims persist within feminist economics. Embedded in these claims are automatic assumptions about the liberated woman self, such as the belief that paid labour inherently empowers women.

In feminist economics, paid labour is usually portrayed as a source of autonomy, choice and self-esteem, liberating individuals from the confines of home, culture or tradition. However, there is little doubt in these narratives that contemporary paid labour, even in the global North, is associated not with empowerment and freedom but with precarity, exploitation, domination, dispossession and structural disempowerment.

Beneath the assumption that paid labour is a universal source of empowerment lies a shared Western-centric modernist ideology defining a particular notion of the human being rooted in individual autonomy and freedom of choice (Charusheela, 2003). Empowerment is conceptualized here as an individualistic, secular, legitimate, rational and natural domain – the sole ground from which one can achieve emancipation. In light of this, it becomes evident that the Western-centric modernist cultural underpinnings that steer interventions geared towards comprehending women's economic empowerment might not seamlessly align with the lived realities of the women whom feminist economics purports to 'empower'. In my earlier work (2020a), for instance, I draw on economic patterns within contemporary Mesoamerica and discuss Indigenous notions of reciprocity, the sustainability of life, territory-body and land-territory, and how their presence challenge current development discourses of women's economic empowerment. I argue that the fact that women's economic empowerment in several Indigenous epistemologies is not based on the individual's autonomy to make choices suggests a need for a broader feminist economics.

Alongside paid work, feminist economists have devoted considerable attention to the conceptualization of unpaid work, which is often considered being at 'the heart of gender inequalities' (Women's Budget Group, 2020) and is a key issue in feminist theory and policy. Feminist economists have long advocated for its recognition in national accounting and economic models (Waring, 1988; de Henau and Himmelweit, 2021). In their approach, they suggest that women's subordination primarily stems from their exclusion from employment and the market, viewing their entry into the workforce as key to emancipation. While it is true that paid work has provided women with financial independence and social recognition, the expectation of everyone earning a wage is not necessarily celebratory.

Efforts to reduce unpaid reproductive work to facilitate paid labour merely exchange one form of unfreedom for another, typically shifting this work to a poorly paid workforce – a redistribution rather than a reduction of labour (Hester and Srnicek, 2023). In contrast, post-work futures offer valuable insights here. Helen Hester and Nick Srnicek (2023: 28; emphasis added) argue that reducing unpaid work is not solely about enabling more paid work or alleviating drudgery; it is crucial because '*it expands the availability of free time*' – a prerequisite for genuine freedom. Free time allows us to determine how to navigate our finite lives, pursue chosen paths, and expand the realm of freedom by maximizing autonomously chosen activities and what to do with our time.

However, is it possible to regain control of our time? In his latest book, *The Politics of Time: Gaining Control in the Age of Uncertainty*, Guy Standing (2023) argues that time has always been political. Throughout history, the powerful have defined and controlled how we use our time, and, as he explains, this remains true today. Mental illness is on the rise; while some people experience more freedom over their time, many others find their time increasingly stolen from them – especially the vulnerable and those in the *precariat* (people living without predictability or security, a condition that impacts both material and psychological well-being). However, Standing, as well as Hester and Srnick, suggests that we can reclaim control over our time. Reclaiming our time, in this sense, means not only reducing work hours but also adopting a new philosophy of work (and, consequently, of time) – one that is post-capitalistic, where care is central rather than avoided. For example, a guaranteed basic income would provide universal access to national wealth, ensuring basic sustenance for all and freeing up time. Another example is the communization of care, which reimagines practices of care outside isolated, disjointed, and dysfunctional living spaces, with a renewed emphasis on community resources, collective housing, and socialized care practices. These could offer real opportunities for restructuring social reproduction. Additionally, a shorter work week and shared jobs without a reduction in monthly salaries could help combat unemployment and create more time for leisure and community. These are not utopian ideals but solid proposals already being successfully implemented in various places, such as Mexico (see, for example, Basic Income Earth Network, nd). If feminist economics is about prioritizing the sustainability of life, then life itself – not work – should be at its centre.

Delving into the current theoretical discourses surrounding unpaid work or the care economy within the global North also reveals a prevalent emphasis within feminist economics on making women's unpaid work count as an economic (market) activity in a growth-based economic model. This inclination is encapsulated in the words of Nancy Folbre, a renowned feminist economist and director of the programme on gender and care work at the Political Economy Research Institute, University of Massachusetts, in a recent interview in the *How to Save a Country* podcast hosted by Felicia Wong and Michael Tomasky (2023). Folbre explains that '[t]he care economy is about the production and the development and also the maintenance of human capabilities. This doesn't factor into GDP [Gross Domestic Product]'. In response to the interviewers' concerns regarding GDP, Folbre (Wong and Tomasky, 2023: np) claims that 'I don't think anybody really argues for just completely extirpating GDP. We need it for historical continuity, but we should not be so obsessed with it. We should have a dashboard of indicators of which GDP is one'.

This conversation encapsulates a common trajectory within feminist economic debates concerning unpaid work – an endeavour to incorporate unpaid work within GDP measurements or other growth measurements, aiming to rectify its historical oversight. Nonetheless, these discourses are based on a principle of reparation more linked to palliative care than caring for an actual transformative change. How can we transform the understanding of unpaid care work so that it not only serves to protect and repair a damaged economic system but also fosters meaningful change?

Discussing care work also means talking about resistance in relation to different forms of destruction that the current GDP-based economic model causes in social, political, cultural and natural environments as well as in people's mental and physical health. Developed as a wartime metric, GDP aligns with the imperatives of the current economic framework tracing capital circulation regardless of its source (Hickel, 2021). GDP is silent on past and ongoing oppressions and injustices like racism, colonialism and heteropatriarchy, ignores Indigenous knowledges, and centres white, male supremacy in all its manifestations. Meanwhile, it attributes factors like weapons manufacture, extractive industries, and illicit practices like smuggling and drug dealing.

Furthermore, when evaluating human well-being, GDP is not a meaningful measure. What truly impacts well-being is provisioning – essentially, people's access to the resources necessary for long, healthy and fulfilling lives. GDP is an inadequate metric because it only reflects a limited aspect of economic activity, specifically that related to commodity exchange value. It overlooks many forms of provisioning, including those that are essential yet completely excluded from GDP calculations. Emerging evidence has further illuminated the problematics of GDP in terms of inequality, injustice, climate change and environmental degradation and its possible and necessary abandonment (Hickel and Kallis, 2020; Vogel and Hickel, 2023; Slameršak et al, 2024).

GDP ratifies the very structures feminist economics seeks to undo. So why continue to use it to accommodate care work, even 'in a dashboard of indicators'? Jacinda Ardern, the former prime minister of New Zealand, for example, captured headlines in 2019 with her promise to abandon GDP and economic growth as an objective in favour of well-being. Nicola Sturgeon, the former First Minister of Scotland, followed suit, along with the former prime minister of Iceland, Katrín Jakobsdóttir. Going beyond GDP, however, should mean not only to devise better gender indicators to measure human welfare and equality, but also to go beyond the single imperative of economic growth in the high-income countries. For instance, the Sustainable Development Index was created to update the Human Development Index, which neglects ecological concerns and continues to prioritize high income levels despite their strong correlation with ecological impact, thus violating sustainability principles (Hickel, 2020). The Sustainable Development Index aims to better reflect the ecological realities of the Anthropocene, shifting focus from growth to sustainability.[5]

Imagining women only as capitalist and aspiring to modernity via the world of paid labour and committed to growth-based economic development are 'better understood as ideological projections than as knowledge about specific people and places' (Charusheela, 2009: 1). These Western-centric modernist discourses accommodate neoliberal ideology and impose Western moral authority. They assume an isolated growth-based capitalist economy, where in its simplest version, only capitalists and workers exist, with the state ensuring law and order and the rules of the game of the economic system are followed. We must imagine the possibility of the economic beyond the institutional structures of the growth-based economy, nation-state, the market and the unquestioned 'ethics of work' in our lives. As Maria Galindo (2023: np) claims, 'in the face of power, you rebel; not empower'.

To avoid depersonalization and depoliticization, feminist economics must view unpaid work through the lens of various forms of violence – heteropatriarchal, colonialist, extractivist, productivist and individualist. A crucial aspect of this paradigm shift is the rejection of growth-centric ideology, allowing for the cultivation of a communal imagination that vigorously resists Westernized hegemonic representations of being and becoming. This decolonizing approach can help mitigate the cultural bias in feminist economics.

The problem of equal opportunities and gender equality

The economy, despite its commitment to equality – specifically the notion that women do not have a socially defined relationship of equality to men – hierarchizes existences and distributes futures based on who can become what. In this framework, the economy is seen as a distributor of life options, expanding or restricting them based on social mobility and context, governed by a codified system of expectations. Within the current economic system's opportunistic game, a reduction in the possibilities of being has emerged from three major equality fictions: the idea of equal opportunities between men and women; the notion of *potency* in gender equality and women's empowerment; and the affirmation that gender equality is a universal human right.

First fiction. Equal opportunities between men and women are often regarded as a liberal fiction, turning individuals into formal subjects of rights within a supposedly neutral market of life options. Consequently, the state intervenes to neutralize these conditions, enabling individuals to exercise their options freely. Michael Sandel (2020: 85) argues that 'true equality of opportunity requires more than rooting out discrimination', suggesting that even genuine equality of opportunity falls short as a socio-economic and political ideal. Simply levelling the playing field between men and women is insufficient, as it may still permit significant inequalities based on differences in individuals' efforts and talents, thereby hindering those less fortunate from living dignified lives.

In the ideal of equal opportunities, gender-skewed outcomes are attributed not to inherent individual differences but to the oppression of men and the exclusion of women from the capitalist economy. If women do not make the same choices and achieve identical outcomes as men when given the chance, this is ascribed to socialization within a culture that has shaped gender differences in individual preferences and aspirations, disadvantaging women. The removal of this culture is expected to allow the underlying substratum of universal being to take over, leading to the disappearance of systematic differences in outcomes between men and women. The idea is that if we create equality of opportunities, then we do not have to worry much about inequality because mobility (competition) can allow people to move up from jobs with stagnant wages to better ones.

Some feminist economists, particularly within the gender and development discourse, have offered the rhetoric of upward mobility rather than directly responding to inequality. I am not saying we should abandon the equal opportunities project. I believe this is a very important project, morally and politically. The mistake is to assume that creating more equality of opportunities is a sufficient response to the enormous inequalities of income and wealth that neoliberal globalization has caused. Can we envision worlds where women act differently from men, where not all men or women aim to be successful, productive capitalists or champions of development, achieving diverse outcomes based on criteria we may not agree with, yet doing so as autonomous beings expressing a desired identity for themselves and striving for liveable, just futures?

Second fiction. The notion of *potency* in gender equality and women's empowerment discourses is neoliberal, conceptualizing each individual as a unique and distinct resource defined by their latent potential (*empowerment*). A good economy, according to this perspective, is one that provides the tools to unlock and extract the maximum performance from this potential. In both instances, the individual becomes the central figure on the chessboard of possibilities, transitioning from the individualism of opportunity to the individualism of capacity.

The new identity of the individual, in a system based on the intensive exploitation of resources, is their *potential*. This word, if we look carefully, is today at the centre of the most heard human-rights based discourses on gender and the economy. The United Nations (nd, np; emphasis added), for example, says that '[w]omen and girls represent half of the world's population and, therefore, also half of its *potential*. Gender equality, besides being a fundamental human right, is essential to achieve peaceful societies, with full human *potential* and sustainable development'. Here, potential (repeated twice!) represents the unique qualities of each individual existence and the uncertainty that shapes its potential economic relationships.

In that sense, a good economy based on gender equality and human rights would therefore, as Canada's Feminist International Assistance Policy states, 'make sure that women and girls are empowered to reach their *full potential* so they can earn their own livelihoods, which will benefit families as well as the economic growth of their communities and countries' (Government of Canada, 2017: ii; emphasis added). And here we go again: this economic potential is synonymous with economic growth. The idea posits that gender equality results in productivity gains; when women, historically excluded from the formal economy, become active participants (realizing their *full potential*), their economic empowerment triggers a ripple effect contributing to overall economic growth. In light of this approach, a question arises: what happens when the potential is deemed insufficient, inadequately developed, or simply resists conforming to established economic norms, opting for an antithetical trajectory such as being unproductive, degrowth or post-extractivist living practices?

The cultivation of one's potential, spanning the entirety of one's life journey, may bear fruit or may falter – an endeavour replete with uncertainty regarding discernible and actionable outcomes. The economic structure and mainstreaming empowerment rhetoric mandate uniformity in behaviour, irrespective of individual aspirations, staunchly adhering to a single imperative – growth. The bedrock of this paradigm rests upon the relentless pursuit of unbridled potential. Subsequently, life, even as an economic index, becomes inextricably linked to an incessant rhythm of economic expansion, perpetually oscillating between augmentation, extension and amelioration. A contrary trajectory, if detected, invariably furnishes fertile grounds for the assertion that women, owing to cultural inertia, internalized subjugation or a fragmented comprehension of their authentic aspirations, lack the requisite self-awareness (empowerment) indispensable for sound decision-making conducive to their potential realization. Unfortunately for feminist economists working on these issues, such an assertion of inadequate or inappropriate consciousness for women 'elsewhere' is subject to sharp challenge, given the historical baggage of ethnocentric racial ideology and colonial heritage permeating Western perceptions of 'Others'.

Feminist economics, which addresses a contemporary global audience, must transcend the limitations imposed by the dominance of Western-centric modernity and its claimed supremacy. This requires a fundamental reconfiguration – a conceptual shift that recognizes the economy and economic agents as contextually and culturally embedded entities. By doing so, feminist economics needs to open the door to economic paradigms and rationalities that do not rely solely on Western-centric and capitalist constructs of empowerment, labour or productivity.

There are many reasons for falling outside this ideal of continuous growth (or potency/empowerment), ranging from the absence of identifiable potential to the lack of, inability to find, or disinterest in creating, the necessary conditions for its cultivation. On the other side of the spectrum of potential lies the residue – the marginalized, the 'left behind'. They represent the unaddressed aspects of the 'leave no one behind' principle championed by Agenda 2030's sustainable development policies. The very system that transforms every individual into a potential contributor is the same one responsible for generating increasing amounts of residual existence. This system fosters an economy built on individualistic competition, resulting in disparate, unequal and competitive future trajectories.

What if the question is not merely about what individuals must do or who they must become to integrate into the economy, but rather: what direction should the economy take to benefit the greatest number of people possible? In this context, the focal point is not a growth-based economy (or sustainable development, viewed as synonymous) but a people and planet-centred economy. Economics is here founded on the radical idea of solidarity, where futures are collectively shared with society at large, demonstrating more care, concern and genuine interest in the weak and vulnerable rather than the strong and powerful.

Third fiction. The defence of gender equality often rests on the assertion that it is a fundamental human right.[6] Feminist economics have critiqued, for example, the 'Smart Economics' development narratives and their association with gender equality (Chant and Sweetman, 2012; Esquivel, 2017; Prügl, 2021). The critique primarily centres on the argument that 'Smart Economics' not only perpetuates and reinforces patriarchal norms while disregarding long-standing gender inequalities but also instrumentalizes gender equality for neoliberal purposes over its *intrinsic value as an inherent human right.* From my point of view, this appeal (that gender equality is a human right and should not be instrumentalized) is overly abstract. It treats human rights as a natural and uncontested endpoint, thereby prematurely closing an analysis that I think could be more profound and offer possibilities for concrete and transformative answers.

Human rights often carry different meanings for different people, particularly failing to resonate with those in the global South who are supposed to be the beneficiaries. Human rights are not universally neutral tools for achieving gender justice and human dignity; rather, they have a dual genealogy. Since the 16th century, human rights have both legitimized Eurocentric, capitalist and colonial oppression and supported resistance against such subjugation. The gendered and Western rhetoric framing the 'war on terror' as a 'fight for the rights and dignity of women' is a stark example. In this instance, human rights have been instrumentalized to justify terror and violent actions in the name of gender equality and human rights values.

The conventional human rights discourse often excludes the contributions of anti-colonial movements and figures from the global South. It insists on universal applicability regardless of social, political, economic or cultural contexts, rooted in a Western notion of human nature as individualistic and distinct from more-than-human nature. This approach diminishes non-Western knowledge systems to mere local peculiarities without truly impacting the universal norms of human rights.

However, despite their flaws and history of violence, human rights remain indispensable in the struggle against oppression. Acknowledging these limitations does not necessarily advocate for their dismissal; instead, it emphasizes the urgent need to reconsider and reshape human rights within broader movements of resistance. It is, therefore, crucial to recognize that these ideas originate from Western modernity and require substantial rethinking.

A critical perspective on human rights, when freed from Eurocentrism and capitalist influences, can emerge as a potential vehicle for cross-cultural dialogue and emancipation, contributing to a broader global strategy for transformation (Spivak, 2005; Santos, 2015; see also, de Jong, 2022). This perspective challenges the claims of human rights' universality and completeness, creating space for alternative conceptions of justice.

The danger for feminist economics lies in uncritically adopting the human rights framework. In striving for global ethical standards, feminist economics may overemphasize legal frameworks similar to Western models, potentially limiting our imagination of justice in diverse forms. Instead, as stated by Gayatri C. Spivak (2005), we should salvage elements of human rights while critically acknowledging their problematic history and exploitation for imperial purposes.

The problem of imagination and feminist contradictions

In 2018, during the final stages of my PhD in the Netherlands, I attended a public lecture in Amsterdam by feminist economist Professor Naila Kabeer. Titled 'Locked out and left behind? Gender, intersecting inequalities and the SDGs', the lecture, sponsored by the KIT (Koninklijk Instituut voor de Tropen) Royal Tropical Institute and UN Women, delved into intersecting inequalities as it plays out in different regions of the world and how certain sections of the poor in these countries were systematically 'locked out and left behind'. Kabeer, renowned for her influential works in both feminist economics and development, has been highly regarded by academics and development practitioners alike.

Having utilized Kabeer's work in both academic and non-academic settings, I was interested to hear her insights in person. During the lecture, she explored the nuances of intersecting inequalities across different regions and the SDGs, offering an assessment of their evolution from the Millennium Development Goals (MDGs). As Professor of Gender and Development at the London School of Economics and Political Science, Kabeer's expertise in feminist economics and gender and development, particularly in South Asia, and at that moment involved in an ERSC-DFID (Economic and Social Research Council and Department for International Development, UK government) funded research project on gender and labour market dynamics in Bangladesh and India, promised a stimulating perspective.

During the Q&A session, concerns were raised about her exclusion of critical elements such as growth, capitalism, ecological issues and corporate dominance in the Agenda 2030 and SDGs. Kabeer acknowledged the limitations of her lecture, recognized 'some' omissions in the Agenda 2030, and conceded the heightened corporate influence in the SDGs compared to the MDGs. However, it was her response to a question about the feasibility of achieving goals within the Agenda 2030, given these critiques, that resonated deeply and unveiled, in my opinion, a significant issue in feminist economics thinking. She stated, 'For me, the question is: Is there anything that can be achieved within [the Agenda 2030], or does one turn back on it and say, you know … I am depressed' (Kabeer, 2018: 1:34:39).

Kabeer expressed here a false dilemma: either work within the confines of the Agenda 2030 or succumb to a sense of despair. This highlights what I identify as two broader problems in feminist economic thinking – a lack of economic imagination and feminist contradictions. The inability to envision alternatives on the current economic paradigm (that includes the Agenda 2030) contributes to an apocalyptic outlook on the future. As explored in Chapter 7 of this book, imagination is not about the boundless or the unattainable; rather, it is the capacity to perceive the limits of the possible critically. Imagination allows us to bring forth what is absent, question what is unquestionable, and envision alternative possible futures. In that sense, the critical role of feminist economics lies in its ability to question the type of economies we want. The intersection of criticism and imagination becomes, therefore, vital in envisioning transformative economic paradigms. Can imagination serve as a catalyst for feminist economic transformation? The challenge lies in overcoming the current deficit of economic imagination in feminist economics to navigate towards more sustainable and just futures.

While the Agenda 2030 and its SDGs may serve as strategic tools for researchers and collectives advocating for feminist, human rights and social justice issues, a potential pitfall arises when these pursuits clash with the agenda's foundational principles rooted in economic growth. The risk of succumbing to opportunism – exploiting contradictions for personal gain – and cynicism – engaging in the game without ethical consideration – looms large.

Rather than falling into the trap of opportunistic contradictions or easily becoming cynical, what if we embraced the paradox?[7] Can we transform paradoxes into dynamic situations rather than viewing contradictions merely as opportunities? Embracing the paradox involves making it a lived experience, enabling us to navigate through complexities without succumbing to despair. This approach allows for an active, transformative and imaginative engagement, pushing the boundaries and tensions inherent in the multidimensional aspects of our existence.

In the realm of the Agenda 2030, working within its framework might present an opportunistic contradiction such as 'let's participate as long as there's financial benefit'. Contrarily, a paradoxical exploration involves a critical examination of the consequences. Maybe this 'yes' of working within the Agenda is not only about taking advantage but also changes the subject/the collective that said 'yes' and knows it is inside a paradox. But also, I/we can say 'no' and this opens up a different set of consequences. Breaking free from binary thinking, the paradox liberates us from the confines of either-or choices.

In this perspective, saying 'yes' does not necessarily imply opportunism, nor does saying 'no' suggest an outright rejection. Both responses coexist in a dynamic relationship, offering a more profound understanding of the complexity at hand. The paradox creates an alive, critical and imaginative space where our interactions with 'yes' and 'no' become intertwined, fostering a continuous exploration of possibilities from a critical perspective. Instead of being trapped in a rigid dichotomy, the acknowledgement of both answers allows us to navigate the intricate landscape of the Agenda 2030 with a sense of freedom – albeit not in the neoliberal sense but having in a way the 'yes' and the 'no' in our hands – and a commitment to thoughtful and transformative feminist action.

3

Should We Use the Word 'Decolonizing' in Our Pursuit of a Better Feminist Economics?

Introduction: Travelling ideas

Decolonizing is a hot topic today. Numerous meetings, books, calls for papers and conferences around Europe and globally gives us the impression that we are now going towards several calls to decolonizing. More and more scholars are now revisiting, also retrospectively, their methodologies, and exploring alternative views inside and outside academia. This book is also doing that. This chapter, however, starts with the observation that such appeal should perhaps give us pause. What happens to the project of decolonizing, not originated in academia but, very explicitly, from Indigenous movements, when it moves from one place to another?

In his essay 'Travelling theory', Edward Said (1983) explores the circulation of theories and ideas across different cultures and societies, highlighting their transformation through these travels. Said (1983: 226) states, '[l]ike people and schools of criticism, ideas and theories travel'. However, the metaphor of travel carries cultural and political implications, as it reflects the 'privileges accorded to "cosmopolitan intellectuals" within Western academy' and the unequal freedoms within Western intellectual culture in the global production and dissemination of ideas (Gregory, 2000: 860; see also Braidotti, 1994). A closer look at Said's travel theory also reveals a striking emphasis on a linear progression towards an end point. Travel, it could be argued, involves not just a departure from one place to another (from A to B) but also a return. Despite the associated baggage, I retain this metaphor for the same reason as Rosi Braidotti (1994), James Clifford (1997) and Vera Vicenzotti and Mattias Qviström (2018): it conveys a sense of worldly, mapped movement that alternative terms may overlook, capturing the mundane and taken-for-granted routes and directions of movement.

Said suggests four stages in the 'travel' of theories, describing them as follows:

> First, there is a point of origin, or what seems like one, a set of initial circumstances in which the idea came to birth or entered discourse. Second, there is a distance traversed, a passage through the pressure of various contexts as the idea moves from an earlier point to another time and place where it will come into a new prominence. Third, there is a set of conditions – call them conditions of acceptance or, as an inevitable part of acceptance, resistances – which then confronts the transplanted theory or idea, making possible its introduction or toleration, however alien it might appear to be. Fourth, the now full (or partly) accommodated (or even incorporated) idea is to some extent transformed by its new uses, its new position in a new time and place. (Said, 1983: 26)

Building on Said (1983) and Derek Gregory (2011), we can categorize these four stages into three critical moments. The first moment is the origination, emphasizing the importance of understanding an idea's birth or emergence within its specific historical and cultural context. As Gregory (2011) emphasizes, Said does not assume the existence of one single point of origin for an idea, as indicated by the qualifying phrase 'or what seems like one'. Further, Said does not regard ideas as free-floating constructions; rather, their analysis requires a contextual history. Thus, a theory or idea must always be understood in the place and time from which it emerges. The second and third critical moments represent two possible effects of the travels of theory and concepts: (2) the institutionalization of the travelling idea and its 'theoretical closure' or co-optation that mutates its political potential, or (3) a process where the theory is strengthened and reinvigorated through its travels.

First moment: origination

Said's emphasis on the point of origin aligns with feminist scholars who have critically and influentially explored the concept of location. These feminists have invoked location to shed light on the unequal distribution of knowledge, as well as the production of knowledge across the globe. They also highlight the entanglements of theory-building with heteropatriarchal, racist, colonialist and capitalist geopolitics, as well as power relations that shape and inform knowledge production (Rich, 1987; Haraway, 1988; Mohanty, 1991, 1995; Smith, 1999; Wynter, 2003; Rivera Cusicanqui, 2012).

For example, Donna Haraway (1988: 590) cautions against adopting a singular feminist standpoint and advocates for a politics of location that remains 'insatiably curious about the webs of differential positioning'.

Similar to Said, Haraway rejects fixation, finality and closure in favour of embracing vulnerability. Silvia Rivera Cusicanqui (2012), firmly rooted in the political economy of knowledge production in Latin America, critiques statist ideologies regarding the emergence of hybridity and multiculturalism used to manage difference, particularly Indigenous difference. She introduces the notion of 'chi'xi', which encompasses the complexities of *mestizas* and *mestizos*, defying reduction to colonial governmentalizing manoeuvres. Rivera explains that 'chi'xi' captures the parallel coexistence of multiple cultural differences that both antagonize and complement each other, each one reproducing itself from the depths of the past. Likewise, Gloria Anzaldúa's (1999 [1987]) conceptual offering of borderlands, located in the borderlands of Mexico and the south-west of the United States, represents a specific geography of origination. Yet, *Borderlands/la Frontera* (Anzaldúa, 1999 [1987]) encompasses specific border geographies, imperial histories, racialized political economies and psycho-sexual socialities, reflecting the complexities of loss, marginality, struggles for belonging, displacement and perpetual transition that exist in the origin of ideas.

Rejecting the politics of authenticity in claiming an 'origin', Sharmila Rege (1998) argues for a Dalit feminist standpoint that is liberatory, multiple, heterogeneous and open to dialogue with other liberatory projects. Rege writes about the Dalit feminist standpoint, originating from Dalit women's struggles but not relying solely on an authentic well of Dalit women's difference or experience. Further, Patricia Hill Collins (2000: 269), highlighting specific and diverse feminist standpoints, discusses the Black feminist standpoint as a 'subjugated knowledge' situated in a point of origin rooted in the context of racialized and gendered economic and political domination. She explains that this standpoint emerges from the interdependence between the everyday knowledge of Black African American women and the specialized knowledge of Black women intellectuals. Patricia McFadden (2018) also emphasizes the politics of struggle as a central factor in the origination of ideas. She draws on conflicting feminist struggles across various African locations and conceptualizes 'contemporarity' as a novel framework for Black resistances (McFadden, 2018: 417). Contemporarity challenges both neoliberal extractive capitalism and gendered nationalisms, presenting itself as an innovative feminist sensibility and an epistemology situated within radical imaginaries and just futures that sustain relationships between the self, feminist politics and the ecological universe.

These feminist conceptual interventions of origination highlight the rich possibilities that emerge when attention is paid to a critical reflexive feminist politics of location, including in economics. Thus, theories and ideas are always contextual and shaped by historical, political, socio-economic, cultural and disciplinary factors. These conditions include factors such as racialization, gender, class, ethnicity and other forms of social identities and related systems of oppression, domination or discrimination as well as its resistances that influence how ideas are birthed and enter discourse. Recognizing these power dynamics inherent in knowledge production is, therefore, crucial, as it encourages critical engagement with the ways in which ideas are used to shape economic and social relations and hierarchies.

The questioning of an idea or project's location is not limited to feminist thinking alone. However, what distinguishes feminist scholarship on location is its insistence on the point of origin as a critical reflexive ethics. This attentiveness to a critical reflexive politics of origination reveals the lack of conceptual diversity and the inadequacy of existing ideas and conceptual repertoires in capturing the complexity of life-worlds in most of the world. For feminist scholarship, similar to Said, recognizing the situatedness of an idea or movement is a crucial step in developing a new model of responsible, accountable and locatable science.

When delving into the study of anti-colonialism and decolonization, in this sense, it is crucial to recognize that Indigenous peoples, since the initial contact with Europeans, have actively contested colonialism and engaged in the process of decolonization (Fanon, 1963; LaRocque, 2010). Hence, it is necessary to understand that the origins of decolonizing and anti-colonialism lie with Indigenous peoples.

In this regard, the approach to decolonizing must explicitly acknowledge its roots in Indigenous movements, struggles and peoples, underscoring the profound influence of origin and context in shaping theories and ideas as well as their fundamental questions. In this regard, Leanne Betasamosake Simpson (2013: 9:40–9:43) asserts that the core issue of the colonial problem is and has always been 'the dispossession of Indigenous Peoples from our homeland', thereby highlighting that the essence of decolonizing is located on 'land and how we're going to share it' (Simpson, 2013: 9:45–9:47). Likewise, Eve Tuck and Wayne Yang (2012) remind us that decolonization without emphasizing the centrality of land, water and air is a shell game.

Second moment: institutionalization

In the process of institutionalization of a travelling idea, Said expressed concerns about the loss of criticality and the commodification of ideas resulting from their widespread adoption. Said (1983: 247) cautions that while the movement of ideas enables intellectual activity, they tend to lose their critical edge when they transition from theoretical margins to a mainstream paradigm or what he calls 'cultural dogma'.

> Appropriated to schools or organizations, they [the kinds of theory gaining the status of cultural dogma] quickly acquire the status of

> authority within the cultural group, guild or affiliative family. … [T]hey are insidious in that their original provenance – their history of adversarial, oppositional derivation – dulls the critical consciousness, convincing it that a once insurgent theory is still insurgent, lively, responsive to history. (Said, 1983: 247)

Said laments the appropriation, institutionalization and dilution of once powerful and revolutionary theories, not as a misinterpretation of the theories, but as a consequence of their dissemination. This is the case, for instance, of intersectionality, the radical feminist idea that centred around the Black female body, which has become invisible in its trajectory.

Mieke Bal (2002) argues that individual concepts are more susceptible to detachment from their original contexts than fully developed theories. In this sense, single concepts, such as decolonizing, are at an even greater risk of being domesticated and institutionalized compared to comprehensive theories. They often travel as fragmented elements – selective discourses, nascent ideas and synthesized models (Peck and Theodore, 2010). Will decolonizing render Indigenous knowledges and struggles invisible in its trajectory? Facile appeals to 'decolonization' seem to evade the question of land, economic sovereignty and the genocidal violence against Indigenous people that maintaining colonial state control over Indigenous land bases entails. Eve Tuck and Wayne Yang (2012: 3) observe 'with growing apprehension' a metaphorical use of 'decolonization' as a synonym for a range of social-justice projects, a use that serves to 'domesticate' the concept. In this regard, it is crucial to exercise caution when radical ideas enter various political and economic projects, especially in academia.

In the context of institutionalization, Said emphasizes the significance of power dynamics and their influence on the widespread dissemination of ideas, as well as the selective attention given to certain ideas while others remain unheard or marginalized. Power differentials in citation practices, academic hierarchies, and the notion of 'scientific knowledge', for example, create favourable conditions for some ideas to gain traction more easily than others. Furthermore, the trajectory of ideas often follows a pattern where they originate from the 'margins' and gradually extend towards the 'margins', rather than the reverse (Susam-Sarajeva, 2006; Cerwonka, 2008; Costa and Alvarez, 2014). Consequently, instead of unrestricted and equitable mobility of ideas and concepts, there are blocks, barriers and disparities in access to dissemination, particularly in academia. In the following, I identify four blocks to the dissemination of decolonizing ideas, particularly within economics, and propose feminist possibilities to overcome these impediments.

Block 1: Politics of citation

The uneven politics of citation exemplify unequal access to mobility. Within academic circles, there is a tendency to cite more renowned scholars, even if their contributions appropriate subordinate or oppressed ways of knowing, struggles and contributions. Rubén Gaztambide-Fernández, Eve Tuck and Wayne Yang (2015: 1) assert that '[w]e also often cite those who frame problems in ways that speak against us. Over time, our citation practices become repetitive; we cite the same people we cited as newcomers to a conversation'. Consequently, these citation practices persist without sufficient consideration of the politics involved in the circulation of ideas and projects, resulting in reference lists that often reinforce existing power dynamics. Feminist scholars have brought attention to the problematic nature of citation practices, particularly within academia, and have proposed politics of citation as a decolonizing feminist practice to disrupt the unidirectional flow of theory or idea dissemination.

Citations are much more than mere mentions, they denote those ideas that we want to bring along with us, and that resonate (or not) with our own positioning. Engaging in politics of citation requires acknowledging that citations are not neutral nor objective acts of referencing; they are influenced by various political factors. One such factor is gatekeeping and authority. Citations can reflect and perpetuate existing power structures within academia. The most cited articles are typically regarded as the most authoritative, leading to their further citation. On a practical level, this creates significant barriers for new or outsider voices to be heard and respected. As long as citations remain the primary indicator of influence for tenure-track faculty, they will perpetuate a 'have' and 'have-not' situation for early-career scholars, researchers or 'non-experts'. Senior scholars, research groups and influential institutions, including those engaged in heterodox economics, postcolonial and decolonial thought, tend to receive more frequent citations, sometimes utilizing citation as a reproductive mechanism of power to promote and validate their own work.

This reinforces unethical hierarchies of knowledge production while potentially neglecting or appropriating the work of marginalized or underrepresented voices and ideas (Indigenous, feminist, queer, non-capitalist, students, non-academic, non-scientific). Consequently, this perpetuates inequalities, exploitation, including cognitive extraction – that is, the conversion of ideas, particularly from Indigenous communities, into economic or symbolic capital without acknowledging the people who produced them to depoliticize and re-signify these ideas from Western-centric logics through 'assimilation' (see Leanne Betasamosake Simpson in Simpson and Klein, 2013; Galindo, 2021) – and limits the diversity of perspectives within academic discourse.

Additionally, unconscious biases, prejudices and career considerations can influence citations. Researchers may unintentionally appropriate, overlook or undervalue the work of scholars and thinkers from underrepresented groups, contributing to the perpetuation of bias and discrimination in academia. Furthermore, citations often exhibit a bias towards English-language sources and research from English-speaking Western countries, thereby hindering and excluding valuable contributions from non-English-speaking scholars and thinkers. This bias restricts the movement of ideas and reinforces existing power imbalances between different regions and linguistic communities.

Despite important advances made by feminist economists and anti-racist scholars, economics remains overwhelmingly dominated by white, Western(ized), male, cisnormative-heterosexual voices and a narrow set of epistemological approaches favouring Anglo-centric systems of knowledge. This perpetuates a cycle of exclusion and discrimination, further entrenching systemic inequities within the field. Therefore, there is an urgent need to strive towards citation politics in economics that is feminist, and by extension, anti-racist. This is not about counting citations or using other neoliberal metrics that imprecisely approximate measures of impact, influence and academic excellence. Citation can also be a feminist, decolonizing and anti-racist tool of resistance that demonstrates critical engagement with the authors and voices we wish to foreground. It involves recognizing 'non-experts' as having a legitimate role in shaping economic research and understanding.

The point is not to establish prescriptive rules for citation politics but to support strategies that challenge established hierarchies in economics – both heterodox and orthodox – and how knowledge is reproduced. Citation is not merely a passive representation of what we write or read but an active interrogation: Who do I choose to link and re-circulate through my work? Who should I stop citing? Who gets erased? Why? Engaging with these questions as a 'form of conscientious engagement with the politics of citation' (Mott and Cockayne, 2017: 956) serves as a feminist decolonizing practice, recognizing how we cite (and how we read) can be a tool either for the reification of or resistance to unethical hierarchies of knowledge production and movement.

Block 2: The 'non-scientific'

In overcoming obstacles to recognizing diverse knowledge systems, particularly those labelled as 'non-scientific', it's essential to address how institutionalization can marginalize or dismiss certain knowledge systems within mainstream academic traditions. By labelling them as 'non-scientific', institutions often silence their transformative potential. 'Non-scientific' knowledge refers here to knowledge that is not produced in isolation as separate knowledge-practices detached from other social practices. This encompasses diverse forms of empirical knowledge, popular knowledges, *saberes lentos* and vernacular knowledges (Rivera Cusicanqui, 2012; Santos, 2018; Varon and Egaña Rojas, 2024).

It is important to note that a significant portion of knowledge circulating in the world and directly relevant to people's lives is transmitted orally and falls under the category of 'non-scientific'. Yet, universities and research centres primarily prioritize written and scientific knowledge, often overlooking other forms of knowledge and research methods. Storytelling, crafting, and oral life histories, as explicitly Black, African, Indigenous, and decolonizing feminist methods, are powerful tools for creating and sharing knowledge. However, due to their incompatibility with dominant 'scientific' knowledge systems, these methods have often been dismissed as 'invalid' or relegated to the status of 'traditions' (Smith, 2012). Despite this marginalization, these methods simultaneously generate and analyze knowledge, often making traditional 'scientific' data analysis unnecessary.

Indigenous oral histories, for instance, serve as privileged spaces for exploring profound perceptions of the colonial order, collective memory, and diverse forms of resistance to economic dispossession (Rivera Cusicanqui, 1987, 2012). They also provide invaluable historical perspectives on past climatic changes and climate baselines (Reyes-García et al, 2024). Similarly, practices such as weaving, widely recognized as a predominantly female activity in many societies, hold significant potential as decolonizing methods (Galindo, 2020). Weaving often encodes stories, symbols, and traditions into its patterns, serving as a form of cultural preservation and resistance to colonial and patriarchal systems. Furthermore, it is frequently a collective activity, fostering collaboration, intergenerational knowledge exchange, and the reinforcement of communal values that counter the individualism promoted by capitalism.

Oral, artisanal, conversational, and story-making extend far beyond the confines of conventional 'participatory' or 'action-research' methodologies, which often place the researcher in control of both the action and the modalities of participation. Instead, they constitute a collective exercise in de-alienation, fostering mutual transformation for both the researcher and their interlocutor (Rivera Cusicanqui, 1987; Smith, 1999).

Block 3: Objectivity

One of the key obstacles in the institutionalization process is the emphasis on objectivity, which often serves as a barrier to the recognition and utilization of other knowledge systems. Within mainstream academic traditions, objectivity is highly regarded as a crucial aspect of rigorous knowledge, and particularly within the field of economics, where it is often associated with abstract and mathematical inquiry. Mainstream economists argue that a quantitative approach ensures objectivity and rigour, setting economics apart from 'softer' fields such as gender studies and political science.

However, the reliance on mathematical modelling obscures underlying interests and values, including the embedded gender, sexuality, ethnic and race dynamics. The question of objectivity in economics is closely linked to the question of neutrality, although these two aspects are distinct. Objectivity primarily pertains to methods and epistemic values such as simplicity, consistency, explanatory power and predictive capacity, while neutrality specifically relates to the results and contextual values, encompassing moral, social and political considerations.

Given that economics is a social science intrinsically connected to society and its complexities, suggesting neutrality in economics, as well as in the work of economists, becomes both impossible and immoral. Neutrality in economics assumes that markets are inherently efficient and self-regulating, but markets are not neutral instruments. As discussed in Chapter 1, questions of equity, morality and justice arise when considering who benefits from markets or the economy, and these questions are value-laden. Michael Sandel (2013, 2020) argues that the prevailing view of market neutrality, which avoids moral judgements about the value of goods being exchanged, has led to a lack of public debate regarding the moral limitations of markets. This has perpetuated inequalities and corruption while maintaining the market's centrality as the only viable economic model. In this way, neutrality hinders the travel of alternative economic ideas that offer non-market perspectives and plural, non-dogmatic understanding of economies.

The concept of objectivity itself, however, is subject to ongoing debate. Sandra Harding (1995) contends that the prevailing notion of objectivity, which assumes knowledge to be neutral, unbiased and independent of social context, is inherently flawed as it reflects and perpetuates existing power imbalances and social inequalities. Harding, along with feminist economists, argues that traditional notions of objectivity in economics, largely shaped by dominant male-centric perspectives, are not truly objective but rather shaped by specific cultural, social and historical contexts. Consequently, Harding (1995: 56) proposes an alternative framework called 'strong objectivity', rooted in feminist epistemology, which emphasizes actively including the perspectives and experiences of marginalized groups in the knowledge production process to attain a more comprehensive and accurate understanding of the world. Strong objectivity acknowledges that bias and subjectivity are inherent in human perception and interpretation, challenging the traditional goal of eliminating bias and calling for a shift in knowledge production and the questions being asked. This approach also highlights the importance of reflexivity, involving critical reflection on one's own biases, assumptions and positionality in the research process (it is, however, important that reflexivity is not mistaken here for self-referentiality).

In this context, Harding underscores the imperative to commence thinking from marginalized lives and advocates for the necessity of strong objectivity in critically evaluating which social situations generate the most objective claims. Donna Haraway (1988: 583) also contributes to this dialogue through the concept of 'feminist objectivity', urging acknowledgement of one's perspective limitations and active engagement with situated knowledge emerging from specific contexts. Both frameworks, strong objectivity and feminist objectivity, disrupt and reshape the traditional understanding of objectivity in economics, fostering a more equitable circulation of notions and ideas that deepen our comprehension of societies and their intricacies. They emphasize the crucial step of recognizing the origins of knowledge, in our case economic knowledge, considering the influence of social, cultural and historical contexts on economic theories, policies and practices to achieve a more objective economics.

Moreover, these feminist frameworks encourage economists to engage with decolonization and other disciplines, including sociology, anthropology, gender studies, postcolonial studies, anti-colonial and decolonial thought. Fields like economics often uphold conservative systems of knowledge production, relying on positivist categorizations rooted in colonial notions of people and space (McKittrick, 2021; Nasong'o and Ikpe, 2022). By embracing anti-disciplinary, transdisciplinary, or counter-disciplinary methods, we can break down restrictive disciplinary boundaries (Charusheela and Zein-Elabdin, 2003). This approach enables feminist economics, along with other heterodox and radical perspectives, to gain a fuller understanding of economic processes.

Transdisciplinary engagement offers insights into the social, cultural and political factors shaping our economies. Rather than perceiving diverse economic knowledges as mere manifestations of a single form of knowledge (for example, under the section 'case studies') or cultural dogma, these feminist approaches on objectivity advocate for unblocking and valuing the movement of ideas, including within and beyond disciplines. They facilitate intellectual activity throughout the emergence and self-presentation of knowledges that may otherwise be overlooked.

Block 4: Translation

When examining the travel of theories, it is crucial to consider translation both in its literal and metaphorical senses. In a broad and metaphorical understanding, translation encompasses all the changes and transformations that a theory undergoes when it is received in a different context. This translation extends beyond linguistic aspects to include economic, cultural and political dimensions. Edward Said (1978) explores the intercultural translations of Western ideas in new historical contexts. This notion of travelling applies to Said's (1978) concept of Orientalism[1] as well. According to the author, the Western perception and representation of the 'Other' are not isolated phenomena but are part of a larger network of circulating and influencing ideas. Similarly, Allaine Cerwonka (2008) and Katrine Smiet (2021) suggest that the travels of ideas do not occur on an equal footing, as power/knowledge differentials are always at play.

However, what types of economic knowledge relationships, if any, are possible between different locations? To address this question, I draw on Judith Butler (2000) and Boaventura de Sousa Santos (2008) and propose intercultural translation as a tool to overcome obstacles in the travel of decolonizing when blockages arise due to cultural differences and mutual unintelligibility. Ideas not only speak different languages and emerge from different historical trajectories but also possess distinct economic-cultural premises and symbolic universes. In this sense, Butler (2000) sees translation eminently as a political practice by which resistance movements from different cultures (not necessarily different languages) can be combined, avoiding the pitfalls of both particularism and monocultural universalism. Thus, Butler (2000: 38) sees translation as part of an 'open-ended hegemonic struggle'. Yet, the author alerts us that translation is not intrinsically emancipatory, as it can work and has worked in the past to further the goals of colonial expansion. To counter this, and following Gayatri C. Spivak, Butler (2000: 36) suggests we can reclaim the role of cultural translation 'as both a theory and practice of political responsibility'.

Intercultural translation is, therefore, concerned with both the importance of translation and the power relations involved in the translation process of an idea or project. Thus, intercultural translation is not merely an act of intellectual curiosity or cultural dilettantism; it is an imperative driven by the need to expand an idea beyond the confines of a particular locale or culture without institutionalizing it. It challenges the reified dichotomies among alternative knowledges (for example, Indigenous knowledges versus scientific knowledge) and the unequal abstract status assigned to different forms of knowledge (for example, Indigenous knowledges as a valid claim of identity versus scientific knowledge as a valid claim of truth) (Santos, 2018). The work of translation, therefore, allows us to navigate diversity, intersectionality and power in the absence of a general universalizing theory.

One example of this obstruction can be observed in the current scientific debate on the climate crisis, which perpetuates modernist dichotomies such as Indigenous/traditional versus science, often overlooking and folklorizing Indigenous knowledges. However, research highlights that lands inhabited by Indigenous peoples contain 80 per cent of the world's remaining biodiversity and emphasizes that integrating their knowledge and practices into policy is crucial for achieving transformative and sustainable futures (IPCC, 2023; Reyes-García et al, 2024). Victoria Reyes-García (ICTA-UAB, 2023: np; translation mine) explains that '[c]onnected with their natural environment across generations, [Indigenous people] have a holistic understanding of the cascading effects of climate change impacts, from changes in atmospheric, physical, and biological systems to impacts on their livelihoods'.

Findings underscore that the adaptive responses of Indigenous peoples and local communities to the climate crisis are diverse and can serve as inspiration for effective adaptation pathways in other populations. Therefore, international environmental negotiations need to move beyond tokenistic participation of Indigenous peoples to genuinely dialogue with their cosmologies and knowledge systems in favour of intercultural translation with Western science (see Reyes-García et al, 2024).

Ideally, intercultural translation should occur within equal power relations, characterized by shared authority, as this fosters reciprocity among distinct locations. This ideal serves as a normative standard against which concrete translation practices of ideas should be evaluated (Santos, 2008, 2014, 2018). As a living process, intercultural translation aims for reciprocity rather than focusing on source cultures and target cultures or engaging in cross-sourcing and cross-targeting. However, decolonizing does not always entail the mere coexistence of knowledges or knowledge synthesis, which would inevitably reproduce colonial logic (Tuck and Yang, 2012). Western-centric modernism does not harmoniously coexist with other perspectives but rather fragments and marginalizes them. Therefore, we must question coexistence at what cost and for whose benefit.

When theories from the 'margins' travel to the 'centre,' they often lose their radical edge, becoming domesticated within the academy. This suggests that the real battle is not merely against reigning hegemonies, but on the terrain of those hegemonies – appropriating, interrupting and deconstructing them in new contexts.

Decolonizing inherently disrupts existing structures while resiting institutionalization. At the core of this encounter is *discomfort economics*, which involves a willingness to embrace and propose discomfort in order to question and destabilize the status quo upheld by institutionalization. This perspective is crucial for a decolonizing approach to feminist economics and one of the reasons why I turn to Said's work: to acknowledge that ideas inevitably transform as they travel without succumbing to a postmodern 'anything goes'.

Third moment: reinvigoration

In his later essay, Said (2000) presents a more optimistic perspective, introducing the concept of reinvigoration as a third critical movement, distinct from the processes of institutionalization discussed earlier. According to Said, theories can be revitalized as they travel. Central to this idea is the role of critical consciousness, which he distinguishes from theory itself. Said describes critical consciousness as 'sort of spatial sense, a sort of measuring faculty for locating or situating theory' (Said, 1983: 241). In Said's view, critical consciousness should encompass an awareness of the historical and geographical circumstances that give rise to particular theories and to which they respond, as well as 'resistances to theory' (Said, 1983: 242). This consciousness must consider the contextual differences between the theory's place of origin and its subsequent destinations, as no theory can fully capture the context from which it emerges or to which it is transported. A feminist perspective enriches this: Rosi Braidotti (1994) suggests a *nomadic consciousness* that is not defined by literal travel but by a critical awareness and resistance to socially encoded ways of thinking and being. This consciousness fosters 'an acute awareness of the nonfixity of boundaries' (Braidotti, 1994: 36). It opposes all strategies of fixation, absoluteness and normativity, while maintaining a position of political resistance and agency. Through this move, decolonizing is therefore transformed and strengthened by travel, but yet the radicality of the project remains intact. Hence, the recovery, revalorization and strengthening of Indigenous life and knowledge, power, community, resurgence, as well as an Indigenous future, are honoured and revitalized while invoking decolonizing.

It is not surprising that Said does not provide a universal benchmark to determine when an idea has travelled too far or when it has become overly institutionalized. This task, he maintains, falls to the critic on a case-by-case basis. However, there are hints regarding the criteria that should be considered. Said suggests that the critic's role is to open up a theory 'toward historical reality, toward society, toward human needs and interests' (Said, 1983: 242).

In other words, theories and concepts should serve not only to advance knowledge or specialized theories but, above all, to contribute to the betterment of humanity. In a similar vein, Aimé Césaire (1955), Frantz Fanon (1963), Amílcar Cabral (1979) and Ngũgĩ wa Thiong'o, (1986) envision the ultimate goal of decolonization as the construction of a new humanity – a collective 'we' – capable of breaking free from the cycle of perpetual colonization. Linda Tuhiwai Smith (1999) guides this inquiry, clarifying that the assertion of humanity, this experience of 'we', should be understood within an anti-colonial framework that examines the dehumanizing imperatives of colonialism (and heteropatriarchy, capitalism and ecological degradation) and the resistances against it.

Invoking decolonization

Decolonizing cannot exist without a framework that acknowledges and values Indigenous life, community, epistemology, and envisions an Indigenous future. However, the definitions of 'decolonization' and 'Indigenous' remain open and, to some extent, unknown despite their necessary role in the decolonizing project. This is not entirely unexpected, as Aman Sium, Chandni Desai and Eric Ritskes (2012) argue, Indigenous knowledges and, consequently, decolonization are deeply embedded in the everyday lives of communities and individuals to the extent that they cannot be codified or precisely defined. Decolonization and Indigenous knowledges and struggles that sustain it are diverse and unique to specific contexts and geographies due to their embedded nature.

Nevertheless, it is important to clarify that decolonizing is not 'everything' we want to change. 'Decolonial' is used too much to mean too little (Dar et al, 2018) or as Eve Tuck and Wayne Yang (2012) have emphasized, decolonization is not a metaphor or an all-encompassing term for any social justice movement. Instead, it is a living and breathing movement that aims to ensure Indigenous futurity and sovereignty by dismantling the broad structures of oppression that have historically and presently hindered Indigenous well-being. Consequently, decolonizing necessitates action across all sectors of society, particularly the deconstruction of prevailing power structures, from economics to popular culture.

The process of decoloniz*ing*, as a gerund, recognizes that decolonization is not simply a state or condition that can be arrived at or completed, but is rather an ongoing process, which will always be subject to further review and interrogation (Le Grange, 2016). Herein lies the revitalizing effect of the idea's travel. Decolonizing, therefore, involves the deconstruction of colonial ideologies that propagate the superiority and privilege of Western growth-based modern thought and approaches. On one hand, it entails dismantling structures that perpetuate the status quo and addressing unbalanced power dynamics. On the other hand, decolonizing entails revitalizing, valuing and acknowledging Indigenous knowledges, practices, peoples, struggles and lands, while removing settler biases or assumptions that have impacted Indigenous ways of being and living.

In these contestations, decolonizing is not merely a reactionary force or in a binary relationship with colonial power. While decolonizing opposes colonial ways of thinking and acting, it demands an Indigenous starting point and an articulation of what decolonization means for Indigenous peoples worldwide. In various declarations, such as the Anchorage Declaration (2009), the People's Agreement of Cochabamba (2010), the Managua Declaration (2018) or the Red Deal (Red Nation, 2021), Indigenous peoples have asserted that Indigenous identity encompasses multiple dimensions that extend beyond mere ancestry or ethnicity. It encompasses a revolutionary proposal with a profound connection to specific lands, territories and waters that Indigenous peoples have inhabited since time immemorial and the urgent and global responsibility to care for this connection. As indicated in the People's Agreement of Cochabamba (2010: np):

> It is imperative that we forge a new system that restores harmony with nature and among human beings. And in order for there to be balance with nature, there must first be equity among human beings. We propose to the peoples of the world the recovery, revalorization, and strengthening of the knowledge, wisdom, and ancestral practices of Indigenous

> Peoples, which are affirmed in the thought and practices of 'Living Well', recognizing Mother Earth as a living being with which we have an indivisible, interdependent, complementary and spiritual relationship.

Indigenous identity is rooted in a holistic understanding of relationships with nature, ancestors, community, language and cultural practices, including their economies. It is often intertwined with a shared history of colonization, resistance and resilience in the face of ongoing challenges related to extractivism, climate colonialism, capitalism, climate crisis, genocide, heteropatriarchy, gender violence, economic exploitation and epistemicide, while simultaneously asserting rights, autonomy, ways of knowing, languages, liberation, environmental justice, cultures, economies, governance systems, sovereignty and self-determination to decide their own destinies.

In the Red Deal, for example, it states:

> [Indigenous peoples] belong to long traditions of Indigenous resistance. We claim our rightful place among all freedom fighters around the world. ... We seek not just challenge power, but to build power. We are not simply a negation of the nightmarish colonial present – colonialism, capitalism, heteropatriarchy, imperialism, and white supremacy – we are the embodiment and affirmation of coming Indigenous future, a future in which many worlds fit. (Red Nation, 2021: 1)

It is not, therefore, about just recognizing the problems but working towards economic sovereignty, distributive justice, reparations, land return and restitution. Indigenous knowledges serve as the starting point for resurgence, and decolonizing acts as the process through which both Indigenous and non-Indigenous peoples engage in the present and envision the possibility of just futures for all, an Indigenous future. As Aman Sium et al (2012: iv) astutely notes, 'without this power base, decolonization becomes a domesticated industry of ideas'.

Decolonizing is not intersectionality nor postcolonialism, decolonial turn or epistemologies of the South

We must respect the intellectual and political projects of Indigenous scholars, resistances and thinkers who have chosen the term 'decolonial' in conversation with and against other terms such as intersectionality, postcolonial, the decolonial turn or epistemologies of the South. Teasing apart nuances of intellectual and political alignment that generate new terminologies in distinction to previous ones is in itself a work of respect for the travel of projects behind the terms. This section reflects on ongoing intersectionality and anti-colonial debates within academia – here anti-colonial debates in academia are referred to as these studies that interrogate the logic of colonial domination and subordination and explore the relationship between colonialism and knowledge production – primarily focusing on intersectionality, decolonial and postcolonial theory, their challenges and their potential contributions to the process of decolonizing.

Overcoming academic boundaries: intersectionality

The roots of the intersectionality framework can be traced back to Black feminist activists in the United States, notably those within the Combahee River Collective. This framework also appears in Indigenous feminisms, third world feminism, Chicana feminism, anti-colonial feminist thought, and considerations of the intersection of gender with class. These groups articulate a profound discomfort in their pursuit of a life free from fear, where their rights to justice, equality and freedom are respected. They confront racism and class prejudice within the women's rights movement, while also grappling with sexism within civil rights, nationalist and anti-colonial movements.

In 1977, a Boston-based feminist group called the Combahee River Collective produced *A Black Feminist Statement*. This important document highlights, among other critical issues, their commitment to 'those struggles in which race, sex and class are *simultaneous factors* in oppression' (Combahee River Collective, 1977: 279; emphasis added). By describing the distinct experiences of Black women who were lesbians, the Combahee River Collective pioneered what would eventually become known as 'intersectionality'. They insisted that the experiences of Black lesbians could not be reduced to gender, race, class or sexuality alone. The Collective demanded politics that could account for all aspects of their identity. They understood that no political movement could be organized 'without responding to the particular forms of oppression experienced by Black women, Chicana women, lesbians, single mothers, and so many other groups' (Taylor, 2020: np). Their conviction relies on their previous contention that the liberation of all peoples will be delivered with the destruction of capitalism, imperialism and patriarchy.

Over ten years later, in 1989, Kimberlé Crenshaw introduced the concept of 'intersectionality' in the social sciences through her seminal article 'Demarginalizing the intersection of race and sex: A Black feminist critique of antidiscrimination doctrine, feminist theory, and antiracist politics' (1989). Intersectionality was 'intended to address the fact that the experiences and struggles of women of colour fell between the cracks of both feminism and anti-racist discourse' (Davis, 2008: 68). Crenshaw's conception of intersectionality extends beyond the mere combination of racism and sexism. She underscored that while her initial focus was on the intersection between gender and 'race', the concept of intersectionality is far broader. She argued that intersectionality should encompass other factors such as class, sexual orientation, age and colour.

Intersectionality is not merely a concept that adds while fragmenting the component parts of identification (such as being a woman, Black, lesbian, and so forth). Rather, it offers a more nuanced understanding that gender does not exist in isolation; instead, it configures gendered experiences through interactions between various systems of power in society. By embracing an intersectional perspective, we can scrutinize the simultaneous impact of and resistance to various systems and structures of oppression and domination, encompassing racism, classism, heterosexism, patriarchy, ableism, colonialism and capitalism.

In this regard, intersectionality and decolonizing feminisms have many things in common: both challenge white-dominated feminist discourses within gender, sexuality and women's studies, resist hegemonic feminism, and their analysis includes multiple oppressions. Their theoretical frameworks analyse systems of power which implicate all subjects and social groups, both approaches work towards solidarity and crafting alliances, and both emphasize the importance of coalition to collective struggle against a matrix of systems of oppression. Deep resonances exist between intersectionality and decolonizing feminisms due, in large part, to a shared commitment to an intersectional approach that critically interrogates the relationship between central categories to the history of feminist theorizing: for example, 'woman', 'gender', 'race', 'ethnicity' and 'sexuality'. Both frameworks are compatible but they are not the same.

As Maria Lugones (2008, 2010), Rita Kaur Dhamoon (2015), Anna Carastathis (2016) and Emma D. Velez (2019), among others, have argued, colonialism, particularly settler colonialism, remains undertheorized within intersectionality scholarship. Intersectionality, however, has the potential to address the coloniality of categories still widely employed in social-justice projects. While this approach alone cannot be equated with decolonizing, it is a necessary step towards decolonization by centring land, sovereignty and Indigenous futurity. Nonetheless, for intersectionality to align with decolonizing politics, it must move 'beyond narrow forms of identity and left-liberal discourse', in which it is often currently entrenched (Dhamoon, 2015: 33; Christoffersen and Emejulu, 2023). It remains to be seen whether the gender–race–class framework will shift from an abstract theme or if the current reliance on 'race' as a catch-all category, alongside gender and class, will adequately address colonialism and develop a 'different logic'.

It is important to recognize that while 'intersectionality' and 'decolonizing' have different origins, they travel in similar ways within academic circles. Both terms are often invoked to validate the ethical or political commitments of intellectual projects or to ensure the 'inclusiveness' of curricula, academic disciplines and institutions. However, such usage can sometimes serve as a superficial justification, potentially overlooking the more radical implications of these concepts – the normative claims they carry – and the complicity of individuals with colonial power structures.

Overcoming academic boundaries: postcolonial and decolonial studies

The rise of interdisciplinary studies in the 20th century has led to a complex array of designations, exemplified by postcolonial and decolonial studies. The reasons behind this diversity are not always clear but can be attributed to theoretical and political differences, as well as academic allegiances, lineages or even mundane rivalries within or between departments. It is evident that what may hold significance for some can be regarded as trivial by others, depending on the conceptual or political frameworks employed. Moreover, the issue arises when interdisciplinary approaches eventually transition into disciplinary frameworks, potentially giving rise to new disciplines. According to Boaventura de Sousa Santos (2021) these commonalities and differences are primarily observed in academic contexts within the global North.

Scholarly work on postcolonialism and decoloniality uses anti-colonial literature and revolves around examining the consequences of European colonialism on contemporary social, economic, political and cultural modes of thought and action. However, these consequences are articulated in various ways. Ania Loomba (2002) cautions against oversimplification, schematization or summarization of complex histories and debates, which often leads to reductionism – a vulnerability, she warns, particularly relevant in the study of colonialism.

Some scholars perceive the differences between postcolonial and decolonial studies as primarily rooted in their geopolitical and intellectual traditions. Postcolonial studies emerged in the wake of the independence movements of the 1960s, questioning the cultural foundations of Eurocentrism and asserting local and national contributions to global knowledge. The Modernity/Coloniality group (part of, but not synonymous with, decolonial thought), emerging later, represent a response to perceived shortcomings within postcolonial studies. Originating in Latin America during the 1990s, the Modernity/Coloniality group focus on exposing the hierarchical racial, political and social orders imposed by modern European colonialism on Latin America. They also analyse the enduring legacy of colonialism, which manifests as power structures and knowledge systems based on race and gender that have persisted beyond historical colonialism and integrated into 21st-century social orders. The differences between postcolonial and decolonial studies can also be seen in their focus on distinct forms of modern colonialism: postcolonial studies primarily address colonialism in Africa and Asia, while decolonial studies predominantly concentrate on the colonial experiences of the Americas.

From another perspective, scholars associated with the Modernity/Coloniality group, such as Walter Mignolo and Ramón Grosfoguel, have elaborated on the distinctions between postcolonial and decolonial studies. They argue that while postcolonial studies draw heavily on Eurocentric intellectuals like Jacques Lacan, Michel Foucault and Jacques Derrida to critique colonial legacies in knowledge and politics (for example, Gayatri C. Spivak and Homi Bhabha), decolonial studies and epistemologies of the South, though influenced by Marxism, aim to amplify subaltern voices. This focus, they state, allows decolonial studies to undertake epistemological interventions that are often absent in postcolonial scholarship. However, feminist and queer scholars have pointed out the limited engagement with feminist and queer perspectives within the Modernity/Coloniality group. Despite significant contributions such as María Lugones' (2008) work on the coloniality of gender, the feminist analysis within this approach remains tokenistic and androcentric (Curiel, 2007; Rivera Cusicanqui, 2012; Mendoza, 2016).

When delimiting academic territories, two considerations are necessary. Firstly, critical and transformative studies existed prior to the classification of postcolonial or decolonial, highlighting the need to contextualize these designations (Cumes and Iñigo, 2017). Secondly, across the Americas, the Caribbean, the Middle East, Asia, Australasia, Africa and Europe, there exists and has existed a vast field of anti-colonial studies and thinkers that can be categorized as either postcolonial or decolonial. This suggests the importance of relative distinctions. We need to further acknowledge that the debate regarding the differences between postcolonial and decolonial studies has largely been confined to academic institutions in the global North without practically any impact or resonance within Indigenous and/or social movements (Curiel, 2007; Rivera Cusicanqui, 2012; Santos, 2021).

Shared elements

Designating intellectual traditions often becomes an exercise in academic power, which can unintentionally obscure differences or similarities. Instead of positioning postcolonial theory, decolonial theory and epistemologies of the South against each other, it is essential to explore their potential complementary contributions (see, for example, Colpani et al, 2022; de Jong, 2022). Gurminder K. Bhambra (2014) notes that 'there has been little work, thus far, bringing together the various trajectories of [these fields]'. Similarly, Gianmaria Colpani et al (2022) and Sara de Jong (2022) observe that each has established distinct citational circles with minimal overlap, where interactions are often marked by silence rather than engagement. This pattern suggests a masculinist approach to knowledge production within these scholarly domains.

Thus, rather than engaging in endless attempts to decolonize postcolonialism or decoloniality, it is crucial to recognize and share common concerns and struggles during these turbulent times, both within academia and beyond. Emphasizing Priti Ramamurthy and Ashwini Tambe's (2017: 503) perspective, attention should be given to 'how [postcolonial studies, decolonial studies and epistemologies of the South] speak about each other, and how they can speak to each other' to effectively act towards the end of colonization and contribute to a better future for all. Thus, the common threads uniting these studies include the aspiration for radical change (which necessarily includes an anti-patriarchal approach), the challenge to hegemonic Western-centric ways of knowing, being and perceiving the world.

Challenges

As follows, I identify four significant challenges within anti-colonial studies in academia today and offer possibilities for addressing them:

- *Connecting with social struggles, not just theory*: A crucial challenge for anti-colonial studies in the present context is to connect with social struggles, particularly Indigenous ones, rather than focusing solely on theory. Unlike the early generations of anti-colonial intellectuals who actively participated in economic, social and political movements against colonialism, contemporary representatives of postcolonial and decolonial studies have often remained limited within the confines of academia (Santos, 2021). While these studies have provided insightful theoretical, epistemological and political critiques of Eurocentrism, they have sometimes neglected the urgent need for practical engagement with real-life Indigenous struggles (Rivera Cusicanqui, 2012; Santos 2021). This issue is especially pressing in our current academic context, where tactics to suppress critical discourse are becoming more common around the world. Silencing tactics related to genocide and settler colonialism are not new, but in recent years, there has been a marked intensification of the response from Western academic institutions to the genocidal violence in Gaza. This response has been aimed at silencing Palestinian voices and pro-Palestinian activism.[2] Anti-colonial studies should extend their reach beyond the academic realm and actively involve themselves in the broader social, economic, political and cultural spheres where struggles against colonial legacies persist. By integrating and mobilizing knowledge that deviates from traditional scientific paradigms, anti-colonial scholars can contribute meaningfully to transformative social change and offer alternative visions and approaches to address the pressing challenges faced by Indigenous communities worldwide. As Frantz Fanon (1963) emphasized, the goal is not merely to understand the world, but to actively transform it.
- *Environmentalism and growth logic*: Despite the clear link between colonialism and ecological degradation, anti-colonial studies have yet to make a significant contribution to addressing environmental issues. While crucial effors have been made by postcolonalism and

environmental humanites and ecological and degrowth economists using a decolonizing approach and supporting Indigenous movements (Hickel, 2021; Schmelzer et al, 2022; De Capitani and Bassi, 2023), more work is needed to integrate environmental concerns into anti-colonial studies and develop effective strategies for environmental justice. Recognizing the interdependence of colonialism, growth-based capitalism, heteropatriarchy and environmental issues offers a more nuanced perspective for understanding and addressing ecological challenges. While there must be space for non-destructive growth in the global South, it remains essential to continually ask, both in the global North and South: growth of what, and for whose benefit?

- *Spirituality*: Many anti-colonial scholars encounter limitations when it comes to exploring spirituality, but this is not the case for studies conducted by authors from outside Western-centric contexts, particularly third world feminisms, anti-colonial feminism, communitarian feminisms, *feminismos del Sur*, Afro-ecofeminism and decolonial feminisms, among others. The exploration of spirituality within anti-colonial studies remains underdeveloped, and there is a need to broaden the understanding of spirituality beyond modern Eurocentric frameworks that label it as 'non-scientific', infantilizing or directly rejecting it. Elsewhere, I have coined the term 'coloniality of secularism' to describe the peculiar premise that the cosmologies, spiritualities and religions of the overwhelming non-Western/non-Christian majority are ontologically inferior, thus confirming the superiority of our present modern secular European outlook (Carrasco-Miró, 2020b: 3).

Examining the coloniality of secularism through a decolonizing approach reveals the problematic and misleading essentialist construction of a modern secular Europe that fails to recognize Christianity as a foundational part of the past and present of Western/European-centric modernity, including its economic approach. In this regard, Giorgos Kallis (2019) explains the secret to understanding Malthus, the first professor of political economy, and his theory of exponential population and arithmetic food supply growth – developed in his famous essay *An Essay on the Principle of Population* (1798) – is to remember that he was both a priest and an economist. In his book, Kallis revels how Malthus' influence on subsequent economists and economics is much stronger than we often realize: he turned the Christian mantra to go forth and multiply into an economic principle. Population growth in Malthus' model was the greatest possible good for humanity, its God-given mission. Malthus translated this expansionary logic into a foundational assumption of economics. In economics, Kallis (2019) states, the religious dimension disappears but the assumption that our duty as humans is to expand, multiply and colonize the Earth's surface (and beyond) remains.

In my proposal, the point is not to rehabilitate 'religion' nor to prove the benign or progressive character of spirituality, but rather to open up the implicit religious aspects in the Western European debate so that we can have more nuanced and complex decolonizing analysis and political and economic evaluations without hastily subsuming them beneath instances of religious fundamentalism or patriarchal reactions. By incorporating diverse spiritual traditions and perspectives, anti-colonial studies can provide a more comprehensive analysis of the impacts of colonialism and offer alternative ways of knowing and being.

- *Feminisms/anti-patriarchy*: François Vergés (2021) highlights the insufficient intellectual articulation between anti-colonial studies and anti-capitalist and anti-patriarchal/feminist studies. This contrasts with anti-colonial struggles, she explains, which have demonstrated acute awareness of the deep interconnections between capitalism, colonialism and patriarchy. Similarly, Brendy Mendoza (2016), jointly with other Indigenous, queer Indigenous and Afro-descendant feminists in Latin America and the Caribbean, has pointed out the lack of acknowledgement of feminist theory in decolonial studies, particularly the Modernity/Coloniality group, despite being 'inspired' by it. Likewise, Deirdre Byrne (2020: 44) points that 'decolonial theorists such as Mbembe and Ndlovu-Gatsheni unaccountably ignore' African feminism in the decolonial project.

To address this challenge, it is essential for anti-colonial studies to engage in meaningful dialogue and collaboration (not just citing) with feminist, and anti-patriarchal perspectives. Recognizing and incorporating feminist theories and insights enriches and strengthens the overall framework of anti-colonial thought and action.

PART II

4

Extractivist Economies and Productivist Logic

Introduction: An impossible equation

The concept of extractivism has evolved beyond its original focus on natural resource extraction, both theoretically and geographically (Bruna, 2022; Chagnon et al, 2022). While still central to discussions on rural peripheries, extractivist practices now extend into new domains. These include the digital and intellectual realms (data extractivism), urban areas (urban extractivism), tourism, finance (financial extractivism) and even the global economy's transition to renewable energy (for example, 'green' or 'aeolian' extractivism). Today, nearly anything – be it mineral resources, labour, data or cultural assets – can be extracted to generate financial value.

International development organizations such as the World Bank (Cameron and Stanley, 2017) and the United Nations (UN, 2021) increasingly present extractive activities as opportunities for 'sustainable development' and poverty reduction. Yet, who benefits from these extractivist practices, and who bears the costs? If extractivism represents a deliberate transformation of landscapes, what are the economic, social and political implications for natural ecosystems, economic sustainability and the communities living in these areas?

Extractivism is a development model that encompasses historical and contemporary methods of accumulating wealth based on the 'metaphor of production', which fosters the belief that increased production is essential for well-being (Colectivo Miradas críticas del territorio desde el feminismo, 2014: 13). From this perspective, achieving better conditions and 'development' requires 'progress' through the extraction of resources. The fallacy of this metaphor is that extractivism is not producing anything new; it is merely transforming resources extracted from the biosphere into commodities.

In a system that prioritizes the production of commodities over life itself, it is crucial to recognize that infinite growth on a planet with finite resources is an impossible equation. Extractivism involves a complex network of beliefs, self-reinforcing practices, mentalities and power imbalances that support and justify economic and socio-ecologically damaging ways of organizing life through subjugation, depletion and non-reciprocity (Chagnon et al, 2022). Extractivism, thus, stands in stark opposition to the principles and practices of economic sustainability – stewardship, reciprocity, regeneration and ensuring life for future generations (Klein, 2014). Part II contrasts extractivism with sustainability principles, highlighting the inherent contradictions in current economic practices and pointing towards transformative practices and policies for more just, sustainable, futures.

Driven by the pursuit of continual growth and production (productivism), extractivism is closely tied to capitalist processes and has become a defining force in shaping modern societies. It represents a fundamental expression of global capitalism, particularly evident in the rural realities of the global South (Mezzandra and Neilson, 2017; Ye et al, 2019). However, the dynamics behind extractivism extend beyond mere capitalism. While capital accumulation is a key premise, extractivism also relies on processes of centralization and monopolization. It encompasses diverse sector-specific developments and resistance dynamics (Chagnon et al, 2022).

Asymmetrical power structures and a history of exploitation such as patriarchy and colonialism are widely acknowledged as fundamental aspects of contemporary large-scale extractivism (Gago and Mezzadra, 2017; Blaser and de la Cadena, 2018). These dynamics disproportionately affect women's and girls' bodies, often in racialized and gendered ways (Murrey and Mollett, 2023). Works by scholars like Dai Ra (2022), Natcha Bruna (2022), Amber Murrey and Sharlene Mollett (2023) and Siddharth Kara (2023) shed light on the foundational ties of extractivist and productivist capitalist systems to enclosures, colonialism, heteropatriarchy, racism, sexism, industrialization and globalization.

The people most directly impacted by extractivist paradigms – Indigenous, Black, working-class, rural women – demonstrate that 'the impacts of extractivism-based development are deeply sex-gendered' (Hargreaves, 2019: 63) and racialized. Historical evidence reveals that extractivist economies and the relentless pursuit of growth result in widespread poverty, increased inequality, violence, gender-based violence, economic crises, land-grabbing, and the destruction of other economies and social networks, particularly in the global South (Gudynas, 2004, 2018; Hickel et al, 2021). The pursuit of limitless growth and the exploitation of nature as 'natural resources' or 'natural capital' have notably impacted Indigenous lands, rich in oil, gas, minerals, forests and rivers (Gudynas, 2004, 2018). In extractivist conflicts, Indigenous peoples face severe consequences, including loss of livelihoods and land dispossession (Dell'Angelo et al, 2021), environmental pollution (Fernández-Llamazares et al, 2020), threats to their knowledge systems (Fernández-Llamazares et al, 2021), racial- and gender-based violence (Deonandan et al, 2017; Altamirano-Jiménez, 2021), as well as intimidations and assassinations (Estes, 2019). Global reports on Indigenous rights violations extensively document these impacts, compiling data as well as local testimonies and narratives from diverse case studies (see, for example, Global Witness, 2022 and 2023).

A recent study (Scheidel et al, 2023) analyses 3,081 environmental conflicts related to development projects. The study quantifies Indigenous people's exposure to 11 reported social-environmental impacts that jeopardize the United Nations Declaration on the Rights of Indigenous Peoples. The findings reveal that Indigenous peoples are affected in at least 34 per cent of all documented environmental conflicts worldwide, with more than three-quarters of these conflicts attributed to dam projects, fossil fuels, mining, and the agriculture, forestry, fisheries and livestock sector. The most frequent global impacts are landscape loss (56 per cent of cases), livelihood loss (52 per cent) and land dispossession (50 per cent), with significantly higher rates in the agriculture, forestry, fisheries and livestock sector. These burdens jeopardize Indigenous rights and their way of life, hindering global environmental and economic justice.

Nevertheless, extractivism has sparked long-standing resistance on the ground, especially from Indigenous communities and often led by women and youth, despite the violence they face. Indigenous activists, thinkers and healers are engaged in lasting political battles to defend their right to live in harmony with the land. Their worldviews, their worldsenses, which include principles of sustainability and deep relationality with lands, waters and other beings, provide a direct challenge to extractivism and its logics.

Extractive and productivist logics

Understanding the broad scope of extractivist economic practices allows for a deeper exploration of their impacts on people, ecosystems, societies and economies. To grasp the essence of extractivism and productivism, it is essential to understand their ontological underpinnings, as these practices are fundamentally shaped by the contexts from which they emerge. Extractivism, as an intertwined set of logics and material actions, actively prevents and restricts certain futures, creating a socio-economic environment where individuals are coerced into accepting extractivism as the only possible future.

Scholars such as Ramón Grosfoguel (2016), Anna Willow (2018), Hamza Hamouchene (2019), Sharon R. Krause (2020), Christopher Wetherell Chagnon et al (2022) and Amber Murrey and Sharlene Mollett (2023) argue that extractivism and the pursuit of growth represent more than mere exploitation of the Earth. They embody specific mentalities or logics that sustain enduring structures and relationships of extraction, destruction and dehumanization. To effectively address these issues and avoid falling into abstract and politically paralysing discussions, it is crucial to understand the underlying logic of global extractivism and its historical development.

In this context, I identify five main characteristics of extractivist and productivist economic logics and draw from real-life experiences of resistance movements to explore possibilities for subversion.

A violent, colonialist mentality

Research on the impact of extractive industries consistently reveals a recurring pattern of violence accompanying this economic activity (Holz and Pavez, 2022; Ra, 2022; Kara, 2023). Extractive capital, as a form of accumulation, involves 'non-economic' mechanisms of value extraction, including violence and coercive political and legal strategies. Economically, extractivism generates violence by destructively altering the Earth, the livelihoods and essential economic resources of people. This includes land appropriation, crop destruction, forest access restrictions, non-payment of wages, human trafficking, slavery, and the exploitation of domestic and reproductive labour. Furthermore, extractivism has eroded economic, cultural and knowledge diversity, inflicting severe damage on people and the environment and jeopardizing the well-being of future generations.

Much of the intrinsic violence of extractivism remains largely unpunished, allowing it to continue mostly unquestioned. This is not to undermine or overlook the significant and ongoing efforts of those resisting extractivism but rather to highlight the discontent and frustration that impunity generates within movements defending territory and life (see, for example, González-Hidalgo, 2021).The logic of extractivism embodies cruelty (the deliberate infliction of pain and suffering) and violence, even though these often go unnoticed. This normalization of violence and its underlying logic has been termed 'pedagogies of cruelty' by Rita Segato (2018). Drawing on Hannah Arendt's analysis in *The Origins of Totalitarianism* and her exploration of the link between violence and capitalism, Segato uses the term 'pedagogies of cruelty' to describe how acts of violence are learned, internalized and perpetuated through socialization and education. These practices are then manifested in our actions, mentalities and behaviours, leading us to view suffering, cruelty and death as natural, and perhaps unavoidable, aspects of contemporary life. This rationale undermines solidarity and empathy, leaving us feeling powerless and impotent.

Segato understands the current form of what she calls the 'capitalism of cruelty' as a system that teaches, accustoms and programmes people to capture life and maintain the edifice of the system. In her words, the pedagogy of cruelty is the system's reproduction strategy for 'the sterility of inanimate things that are measurable, saleable, purchasable in ways that are very convenient to the apocalyptic current phase of capitalism' (Segato, 2018: 13). These pedagogies of cruelty are supported by the current capitalist system in its extractivist form, which, according to Segato, is based on teaching us to view life, nature and even our own bodies from an external standpoint. From that position of exteriority, we then colonize, dominate, extort and plunder life in a new way.

Segato's work re-centres patriarchy in the discussion about extractivism. She argues that these pedagogies of cruelty both stem from and reinforce patriarchy, which Segato (2016) views as the primary defining characteristic of modernity. In this regard, her approach differs from that of María Lugones (see Lugones, 2008). While Lugones contends that colonizers imposed gendered structures upon Indigenous peoples of Latin America, Segato asserts that they imposed a more intense patriarchy, replacing the existing, lower-intensity patriarchy. This more intense patriarchy, Segato states, comes with a 'mandate of masculinity'.

According to Segato, this violent logic based on exteriority introduces new, warlike forms of masculinity and adds a new expressive character to violence, different from earlier 'utilitarian' manifestations. However, violence is not inherently male or masculine. It does not originate from the depths of men, nor is it an essential part of masculinity. Instead, we should consider the structures of masculine domination or heteropatriarchy – a system that also oppresses (heterosexual) men. It is these social structures and their histories that need dismantling. I agree with Segato that, due to these pedagogies of cruelty, violence and its logic have become a language through which messages of impunity and the power of domination over bodies and territories are communicated. This is particularly evident in the context of extractivism.

While the impact of extractivism affects entire communities, racialized individuals, mainly Indigenous women and girls, are disproportionately affected. Kathryn Yusoff (2018: 59) refers to these logics as 'geologics' of extraction, establishing 'particular bodies and subject positions … as disposable in the shadow economy of extraction'. Feminist research in the context of extractivism highlights specific focus on women and girls for three reasons (Holz and Pavez, 2022; Kara, 2023; Murrey and Mollett, 2023). Firstly, many large-scale mining companies have adopted the recruitment of women and girls as a key corporate strategy. Secondly, gender-specific issues facing women and girls in extractive industries highlight experiences of sexual harassment, unequal wages and poor working conditions of a racial/gender-specific nature in the mines (WoMin, 2020; Kara, 2023), aligning here with Segato's pedagogies of cruelty hypothesis. Thirdly, women and girls who defend land and the environment against extractivism constitute one of the groups at the highest risk. The attacks and criminalization they face take on specific characteristics due to their race/gender, impacting them differently.

The forms of violence against women unleashed in contexts of extractivism target everything lacking the market rationality of a *Homo economicus*: nature, female and non-normative bodies and sexualities, Indigenous peoples, the community and the popular. This violent logic is directed against the ways of life and community networks that resist and create amidst the colonial and capitalist hurricane of dispossession, super-exploitation and death. The defence of territories and ways of life against the expansion of extractive projects, particularly on resource frontiers, predominantly rests on Indigenous and rural communities (Svampa, 2019; Tilley, 2020; Holz and Pavez, 2022). According to Global Witness's 2022 report (Global Witness, 2022), a shocking total of 1,733 defenders lost their lives over the past decade, averaging one person killed every two days. In 2021 alone, there were 54 reported killings, an increase from 30 the previous year. Over 40 per cent of those killed were Indigenous people.

The report underscores that land and territory control are central issues in countries where defenders face threats. The increasing violence, including killings and repression, is intrinsically tied to territorial conflicts and the pursuit of economic growth through the extraction of natural resources. In the preface of the report, Vandana Shiva (Global Witness, 2022: 6) states that 'nearly all of the murdered environmental and land defenders are from the Global South, and yet it is not the Global South that reaps the supposed economic "rewards" of all this violence'. This highlights the inequities and complexities of the extractive, unlimited growth-driven economic system that perpetuates violence against those who dare to protect their lands, livelihoods and environments.

Women who work to defend the environment from extractivism often face significant harm rooted in deep-seated structural oppression with a long history of colonial, heteropatriarchal and racialized violence. Despite the risks to their lives and well-being, women environmental defenders play powerful and diverse roles in uniting communities while resisting exploitation and violence. Violating women's bodies is a way of destroying that sense of community. A paradigmatic case of this violent extractivist logic and its pedagogies of cruelty and impunity is the murder of the environmentalist and defender of Indigenous Lenca rights in Honduras, Berta Cáceres. Eight years after her murder, justice and reparations are still awaited, and Honduras remains one of the deadliest countries in the world for human rights defenders.

Berta Cáceres, a leader of the Council of Popular and Indigenous Organizations of Honduras (COPINH), became one of many activists who fell victim to violence in a country marked by the 2009 US-supported removal of democratically elected President Manuel Zelaya. In her last interview before being murdered, Berta Cáceres stated:

> Energy is not just a technical issue; it's a political issue to do with life, territories, sovereignty and the right to community self-determination.

> We believe this is the moment to profoundly debate capitalism and how energy is part of the domination of Indigenous communities and violation of their rights. … That's what Lenca communities like Río Blanco are living through right now. (Lakhani, 2020)

Her story is part of an alarming global trend where environmentalists, Indigenous activists and independent journalists opposing extractivism's economic world order encounter escalating levels of violence and repression orchestrated by states and corporations around the world.

Since the 2009 coup, Honduras has witnessed an explosive growth in extractive megaprojects that displace Indigenous communities. Nearly 30 per cent of the country's land was allocated for mining concessions, driving a demand for inexpensive energy to support future mining operations. In response, the government sanctioned hundreds of dam projects nationwide, effectively privatizing rivers and land while displacing communities. Berta Cáceres joined forces with the Indigenous Lenca people in Río Blanco to lead a grassroots campaign that successfully pressured a joint project of Honduran company Desarrollos Energéticos SA and Chinese state-owned Sinohydro, the world's largest dam builder, to withdraw from the Agua Zarca Dam project. Among the financiers and collaborators of the project were the Central American Bank for Economic Integration, the United States Agency for International Development, the Dutch Development Bank, FinnFund (owned by the state of Finland with a 93.4 per cent stake) and Desarrollos Energéticos SA (Nuñez et al, 2018). Agua Zarca, slated for construction on the sacred Gualcarque River, was pushed through without consulting the Indigenous Lenca people – a violation of international treaties governing Indigenous people's rights (Nuñez et al, 2018). The dam threatened to disrupt the water, food and medicine supply for hundreds of Lenca people, infringing upon their rights to sustainably manage and live off their land.

After Berta Cáceres' death, national, regional and international human rights organizations and women's groups activated their networks denouncing her assassination and demanding justice. United Nations Special Rapporteurs and the Inter-American Commission on Human Rights condemned the killing and requested an impartial investigation (OHCHR, 2016). The Honduran government was pressured to abandon its original line of inquiry, which portrayed her killing as a 'crime of passion', and look into the likely possibility of corporate and military involvement in the assassination. Following the killing of another COPINH member, Nelson Garcia, 12 days after Berta's assassination, the Dutch Development Bank and FinnFund eventually announced the suspension their financing of the hydroelectric project.

As in the case of Honduran leaders such as Berta Cáceres and Lesbia Yaneth Urquía from the COPINH, the death of women who fight against extractivist projects in their territories has become a tragic reality that affects the global South. Various forms of resistance against extractivism have resulted in the systematic and systemic assassination of women defending their territories and the environment. This has been called 'extractivist feminicides' (Timm Hidalgo, 2018: 93), whose perpetrator is not specifically a male individual, *per se*, but rather the entire capitalist, colonialist and heteropatriarchal machinery that, through a mafia-like association, perpetrates acts of violence and inevitably culminates in the death of women defenders. According to this approach, these are crimes that can be understood as 'spectacular forms of punishment' (Holz and Pavez, 2022: 123), and following Segato's (2018) pedagogy of cruelty, a way to transmit a message of impunity and power of dominance over bodies and territories.

The same sense of exemplary punishment operates as a pedagogy of cruelty in sexual violence or the threat of it. In the pedagogy of cruelty, 'sexual attack and sexual exploitation of women', Segato (2018: 11; translation mine) says, 'are today acts of plunder and consumption of the body that constitute the most precise language with which the reification of life is expressed'. Historically, sexual violence and threats of rape are part of the repertoire against women who oppose extractive projects (Global Witness, 2023). Raúl Holz and Paulina Pavez (2022) has documented how sexual violence cases have increased in mining areas, especially through networks of human trafficking, sexual exploitation and forced prostitution. Such is the case, for instance, in the Colombian mining context, where Rosa Bermúdez Rico et al (2011) identified an intensification of physical and sexual assaults on women. The increase in rape cases and the growth of the sex market in these areas are indicators of women's social deterioration and pedagogies of cruelty with the expansion of extractive projects and the appropriation of life. In some cases, sexual abuse, including rape, perpetrated by security forces hired by extractive companies, has also been reported (see Oxfam International, 2017). Similar cases have been presented in a group of Indigenous Maya Q'eqchi' women from Guatemala, accusing the Hudbay Minerals company of group sexual violations perpetrated by agents in charge of harassing Indigenous communities and repressing anti-mining activists (Holz and Pavez, 2022). These tragic and violent events have been decisive in displacing Indigenous peoples from their ancestral territories.

Epistemic violence – the different ways in which violence is exercised in relation to the production, circulation and recognition of knowledge – directly impacts communities and Indigenous people. Despite its magnitude and persistence, epistemic violence continues to be relatively marginal in economic analysis of extractivism and feminist economics in general. However, these are forms of economic violence that can be central to the experience of marginalized individuals and communities, not only because they affect them in their epistemic exchanges, but also because the imbalance they cause in the social system feeds other types of violence and exclusion. On the other hand, epistemic violence as a structural phenomenon is a key factor, though unrecognized, in systems of privilege such as racism and sexism, and as such its logic is strengthened by its own imperceptibility.

Epistemic violence can escalate, especially for individuals situated at the intersection of various oppressive axes, such as racialized women. Illustrated in the Human Rights Watch report (2019) researched and written by Juliana Nnoko-Mewanu, this form of violence is evident in the erosion of identity, as highlighted by community leaders in Begkayang regency, West Kalimantan, Indonesia. The report discusses the impact on Iban women in Semunying Jaya village, where the loss of the forest has adversely affected traditional handicrafts with deep intergenerational significance. According to the report's interviews, Indigenous women explained that the scarcity of materials, such as panda leaves for mats and various tree leaves for weaving ropes, resulted from the clearance of land for an oil palm plantation operated by an Indonesian company. Women's identity and role as protectors of life in many Indigenous communities – such as in food provision, as protectors of seeds, ancestral medicines, healers, and several other roles connected with the transmission of ancestral knowledge about the health of nature – are crucial to the continuity of the communities and their economies as part of their harmonious interaction with nature. However, under the violence of extractivism these knowledges are devaluated, silenced or directly removed, contributing to the ongoing epistemicide that Indigenous communities are suffering and fighting against.

Epistemic violence is further manifested in the contamination caused by extractive projects. The pollution of land, air and water affects biodiversity and agrobiodiversity and the exercise of food sovereignty (Romero Epiayú and Barón Romero, 2013; Carvajal, 2016). This is especially serious for women in many Indigenous contexts who prepare the food for self-consumption and participate in the healing rituals through traditional medicine. As guardians of native seeds, the negative impact of contamination on biodiversity affects women's ability to protect local knowledge and life (Carvajal, 2016; Holz and Pavez, 2022). Moreover, the gendered power dynamics and women's autonomy are deeply affected, as economic violence targeting women diminishes their role in economic practices and their ability to participate in communal decision-making.

As a pedagogy of cruelty, violent logics of extractivism aim at depleting any source of solidarity and any form of connection between people, people with more-than-human animals, and the Earth. However, inspiring movements against this logic are emerging. Resistance shows that extractivism logic has not and is not being passively endured by dispossessed communities. 'Why are we not the beneficiaries of the oil wealth that is lying under our feet?' asks Karim, one of the unemployed movement leaders in Ourgla, Algeria

(Hamouchene, 2019: 8). Armine, another leader, expressed his dismay when they learned that some French companies (including Total and GDF Suez) could be fracking in Algeria after they were banned from doing so in France: 'This is just another form of colonialism and it angers me to see our decision-makers going down this path' (Hamouchene, 2019: 9).

In Kenya, women are uniting to confront one of the largest development projects in East Africa. Nestled on a 40-acre expanse, Lamu Old Town stands as a quaint island town on Kenya's coastline, adorned with white sandy beaches and embraced by mangrove forests. Established in 1370 by Arab settlers who engaged with Bantu traders, Lamu Old Town embodies the rich Swahili culture and holds the status of a United Nations Educational, Scientific and Cultural Organization World Heritage Site. Despite its natural allure and appeal to tourists, the area has borne the brunt of various development extractivist projects, disrupting the lives of residents and causing irreversible damage to the environment.

In 2009, the Lamu Environmental Protection and Conservation organization launched a campaign to unite various groups and individuals in advocating for community resource rights, spurred by the implementation of the Lamu Port South Sudan, Ethiopia Transport Corridor. The Corridor, an ambitious infrastructure project spanning three countries, involves constructing highways, railroads and oil pipelines connecting Kenya, South Sudan and Ethiopia. It also encompasses the development of three international airports, resort cities and a dam along the Tana River.

From this initiative emerged the Save Lamu coalition, comprising members from over 40 local and national organizations. Frustrated by years of being disregarded in their individual efforts to assert their rights, these groups joined forces. Save Lamu has been at the forefront of advocating for economic sustainability, championing causes such as coal, oil and gas, and land rights. Its members have campaigned for the compensation of farmers whose land was acquired for construction purposes, organized forums to engage government leaders and stakeholders, written petitions, and participated in demonstrations.

Ramya Famau, a board member at Save Lamu, explained:

> We have 12 groups represented in the management, including members from women's groups, youth groups, farmers, fisherfolk, people living with disabilities, human rights organizations, and many others. We did this because we observed that in the past, when everyone worked individually without collaboration, the government easily ignored us. However, through our collective efforts, the government is compelled to listen. (Kirui, 2021: np)

Within Save Lamu, Famau represents a women's group called Voice of Women. Lamu, she notes, is not just a religious and cultural town; it's also a place where women struggle to have their voices heard (Kirui, 2021). This realization led to the formation of a women's group back in 2005. They have been able to amplify women's voices in the community by informing them about their rights and about government plans in their area, and seeking their opinions.

Save Lamu gained prominence for its strong opposition to the Kenyan government's decision to build a predominantly Chinese-financed coal plant. For decades, Lamu has thrived with minimal emissions, relying on donkeys and motorbikes for transport and preserving a simple way of life. However, the proposed coal plant threatened to pollute the island's air and disrupt this lifestyle with smoke from a 210-metre stack, which would have been East Africa's tallest structure.

Proponents of the plant argued it would deliver electrification and stimulate economic growth, lifting many from poverty. In contrast, the Institute for Energy Economics and Financial Analysis (IEEFA) highlights that Kenyans would bear up to $9 billion in losses, locked into a 25-year commitment costing $360 million annually, even if no power was produced (Schlissel, 2019). David Schlissel, IEEFA's Director and lead researcher of the report, states that 'Kenya does not need a coal plant. Kenya has abundant sources of renewable energy, and we expect by 2029, the costs of producing renewable energy will have declined' (Murikira, 2019, n.p). Further, coal combustion releases harmful pollutants such as carbon, sulfur, and nitrogen into the atmosphere, posing significant health risks to humans. These emissions contribute to respiratory diseases and other health problems. The resulting acidic rain alters the composition of groundwater and seawater, creating hazardous conditions for both human and aquatic life, potentially leading to toxic contamination and ecosystem disruption.

A legal challenge by Save Lamu and the Decoalonize Kenya movement delayed the construction of the coal plant, and the recent ruling to halt the project has been celebrated as a significant victory in Africa's fight against coal. Omar Elmawi, coordinator for Decoalonize Kenya, remarked: 'Our fight will not stop at the courts. We are seeking to ensure that the policy in Kenya is changed so that we can get coal out of the picture completely and focus more on renewable energy. We will stand in solidarity with other African countries trying to stop the establishment of coal plants' (Murikira, 2019, n.p).

Expansionist universalism

The assertion of universality inherent in the extractivist and productivist logic is expansive in nature. This means that it rests upon the projection of a particular cultural model (growth-based) on other cultures, legitimating assimilation. Over the past 500 years, the processes of extractivism and capitalist growth have unfolded as a continuum of enclosure, exploitation and dispossession, guided by an expansionary territorial logic. Importantly, extractivism is not exclusively dependent on or synonymous with global capitalism; as previously discussed, it is deeply embedded in other systems as colonialism, heteropatriarchy, racism, industrialization and individualism. These processes are intricately linked with expansive politico-economic and socio-technological systems dedicated to facilitating extractive operations.

Globalization has ushered in a new economic era where extractive practices are not confined to the global South but have become a widespread phenomenon. These practices now operate across diverse geographical areas, deeply ingrained within the contemporary capitalist system focused on continuous growth. This phenomenon shapes not only global economic structures but also physical environments, social relationships, human and more-than-human entities, and even time itself (Ye et al, 2019). This offers a nuanced understanding of global colonial dynamics that extends beyond traditional North–South frameworks. For instance, the Arctic has seen a surge in extractive activities, while countries in the global North like Finland have expanded raw material extraction to meet global demand. Christopher Chagnon et al (2022: 761) introduce the term 'global extractivism' to highlight the planetary significance of this trend.

In this context, several authors have been warning about the spread of extractivism throughout Europe, where natural resources such as water, energy or land are being harnessed through land grabs (Franquesa, 2018; Ye et al, 2020). In recent years, the mining industry has begun a resurgence in the mountains of Europe. This expansion adds to the established presence of extractive industries that predominantly affect rural areas in Europe, focusing primarily on construction and industrial minerals (EIP, 2018). This shift is partly due to changes in the European Union's regulatory framework for mineral extraction, influenced by various governmental interventions aimed at reshaping international trade in raw materials. These interventions include export taxes, price-fixing, subsidies, dual pricing, quotas and restrictive investment rules. These regulatory adjustments prioritize the promotion of domestic production of critical minerals, thereby reshaping the legislative and political landscape for rural areas.

At a time of evident climate change, Europe is embarking on the race for metal ores in its quest to increase self-sufficiency. The current expansion of metal mineral mining across Europe, together with the established extraction of industrial and construction minerals, is bringing about far-reaching changes in rural development. In contrast to former trends on natural protection, this new wave of extractivism is sweeping European rural areas, exploring the land for critical minerals. Many prospecting projects and mines are attempting to seize rural landscapes that, so far, had been developing within a framework dominated by conservation policies and tourism promotion. This is happening even within the jurisdiction of actual protected areas, as in the case of the Catalan Pyrenees, in a dramatic mountain pass between

France and Spain that is currently being prospected by an international corporation searching for tungsten (del Mármol and Vaccaro, 2020). The emergence of this refractory metal prospecting has led to an escalation of social movements and platforms opposing (or supporting) the initiative on both sides of the mountain range. Numerous local inhabitants, however, are deeply concerned by the way in which mining has come back into their lives. The same is happening in Malmberget (literally 'ore mountain') in Sápmi in the north of Sweden, which will ultimately disappear as a result of the expansion of mining ore. Similarly, Eisenerz at the foot of the mountain Erzberg (also meaning 'ore mountain'), in the Austrian Alps is 'in a crisis of identification, over-ageing, and shrinking, because mining requires a diminishing human workforce'(Reisenberg, 2022: 66).

As capital continues to draw vast portions of nature into circuits of accumulation and privatization in global extractivism, it colonizes lands, forests, seas and even the atmosphere. This capitalist promise of 'progress' and 'development' often leaves behind nothing but waste, disease and death. This is the universalist expansionist nature of extractivism: its horizon is private. It creates a world without a common dimension, visible only through our fragmented perspectives and as the surface of our economic exchanges. The roots of this universalism lie in the aggressive and unprecedented privatization of our existence. Extractivist capitalism thrives on individualism to expand and function. How do we move beyond this?

By embracing postcolonial and decolonial critiques, but going further, we must affirm that universalism can be the way to come together in the era of individualism. In this sense, the commitment to decolonizing feminist economics opposes a privatized destiny while not denying a common horizon. In the planetary era, beyond an expansive, invasive and dominating universality, there is an opportunity to embrace a reciprocal and welcoming universality. Critiquing the colonialist and expansionist universalism of the extractivist economy should not erase the ability to connect with the common ground of human experience. This common ground does not exclusively refer to a single economic model or everything non-Western; rather, it encompasses the capacity to share fundamental life experiences such as dignity, justice, care, and more. What paths can we explore to find these proximities and develop the meaning of human experience without imposing one economic model onto another?

Around the world today, many movements oppose extractivist logics and experiment with different possibilities with a common horizon. Though imperfect, these efforts offer hope. One example is the *zone à défendre* (Zone-to-Defend [ZAD]) movement originated in France as opposition to the construction of an international airport near Notre Dame des Landes, where protestors occupied land designated for the project for ten years (Mauvaise Troupe, 2018).

Over time, the resistance strategy of inhabiting transformed the ZAD into an experimental space for different futures rebelling against the extractivist logic (Despentes, 2018). The inhabitants put emphasis on the value of local communities and their territory, creating a 'new commune for the 21st century' (Jordan, 2018: np). Despite state efforts to suppress it, the ZAD movement advocates communal living in harmony with ecosystems, defending against police and corporate intrusions. The ZAD, a collective autonomous zone, emerged, featuring housing collectives, cooperatives, a bakery, and more, reflecting a non-growth anti-capitalist society based on shared participation and collective ownership. Despite the constant threat of eviction, ZAD residents lived with the goal of limiting their connection to capitalism. In 2018, the state cancelled the airport project, but ZADistes faced expulsion orders. A massive eviction operation in 2018 led to the destruction of buildings and injuries, causing some to leave while others vowed to rebuild.

The relevance of the ZAD came to transcend its territory. An edited volume by Jade Lindgaard (2018), with contributions from Vandana Shiva, Kristine Ross, Bruno Latour and Virgine Despentes, among others, praised the ZAD and its potential for helping to create alternative futures against extractivist projects and logics. However, in the same volume, Amandine Gay (2018: 140) writes of the 'crisis of a white utopia', pointing out the ways in which French leftist movements have remained blind to the dynamics of racial domination, no matter how deep their political commitments run. Drawing on her involvement in leftist ecological movements and personal experience visiting the ZAD, Gay observes a notable absence of connections with communities of colour in neighbouring towns. Furthermore, Gay explains, there is a lack of attention within the ZAD itself towards Black agricultural workers from Martinique and Guadeloupe, as well as Indigenous land struggles in French Guiana. The result is an 'expression of another violence, diffuse and ancestral' (Gay, 2018: 142; translation mine). To be sure, ZADistes express support for, and endeavour to aid, diverse struggles from Rojava to Palestine, and they embrace undocumented migrants from North and sub-Saharan Africa (Lindgaard, 2018). But there is much work to be done in terms of actively undermining white privilege and whiteness more broadly.

Decolonizing feminist economics opposes extractivist logics; however, it should not merely defend the local but aspire to construct new, future-oriented economies capable of challenging racist, capitalist, colonial and patriarchal extractivism on broader scales. This pursuit involves creating spaces that are emancipatory, receptive, experimental and attentive. This effort requires not only criticism but also moving beyond both expansive extractive universalism and defensive particularism, aiming to develop reciprocal universals in a liberatory way. Therefore, a decolonizing feminist economy must unmask the pseudo-universality of extractivist social relations and reclaim the meaning of the future – one that is shared: reclaiming our collective power to make decisions about what is common.

Commodification of nature

Arising from a dualist ontology that positions human dominance over 'nature' – often conceptualized as '*terra nullis*', 'inert space', 'resources' or 'capital' to be acquired – the extractivist and productivist economic logic objectifies nature, reducing its value to a singular economic metric: price. This narrow focus on monetary measurements creates the illusion that economic estimations alone offer a comprehensive indicator of nature's value, supposedly guiding sound decision-making for the economy. However, economic estimation is just one of many ways to assess the value of nature. By exclusively measuring nature in monetary terms, this logic oversimplifies its diverse values, turning them into mere technical instruments and stifling public dialogue about the various forms of valuation.

In this reduction to price, diverse perspectives on the significance of nature – whether for its ecological richness, the beauty of landscapes, cultural cosmovisions or sacred importance – are homogenized. Consequently, environmental protection is framed as a form of investment, and the biodiversity of ecosystems is not valued for the intrinsic worth of each life form and its role within communities of mutual support. Instead, it is assessed solely as a means to serve the interests of a few companies or states. This approach imposes cultural and economic values of efficiency and profit while disregarding ecological, cultural, religious, sacred or aesthetic values.

The concept of the Capitalocene (Haraway, 2016; Moore, 2016) – understood as a system of power, profit and re/production in the web of life – becomes relevant here, providing a framework to better describe this rationality. Jason W. Moore (2016) emphasizes that the Capitalocene does not only represent capitalism as an economic and social system but signifies the current economic system as a way of organizing nature – a multispecies, situated, capitalist world-ecology. Adopting this perspective allows us to comprehend extractivism and productivism and its logic as a colonial discourse within the Capitalocene, exercising power through hierarchical articulations of racial or cultural difference, rather than relying solely on an economic analysis starting with an undifferentiated humanity and a culturally neutral path towards 'prosperity'.

The triad of economy, science and technology has been fundamental in the colonization of nature. Through the introduction of nature into the market, economic extractivism disarticulates and replaces the concept of nature with capital, services, products or resources. As Moore (2016: 112) argues, 'the genius of capitalism … has been to treat nature as a "free gift" … to make the whole of nature work on the cheap'. If ecosystems are (ab)used to the point of collapse, then all life in the planetary community is diminished (Klein,

2014). Acknowledging that ecocide entails all-encompassing diminishment would already mark a departure from the current unsustainability of the economic system. The process of assigning prices to nature is not innocent or neutral; it reflects the *Homo economicus* rationality based on aspects such as the maximization of benefits, the utilitarian use of resources and consumerism. Recognizing these dynamics is essential for locating economies, sustainable just futures, decolonizing and transformative environmental practices in the 21st century. It calls for embracing a broader economic understanding of value, one that encompasses ecological, cultural and social dimensions beyond the confines of the extractivist and productivist logic.

When assessing the value of nature, ethical and moral public discussions and assessments should prevail. However, as mentioned at the beginning of this chapter, a defining characteristic of the extractivist and productivist logic is an imbalance, a non-reciprocity in the relationship. It does not align with the visions, goals and aspirations of the people rooted in political communities within the territories from which extraction occurs.

Despite this incongruence with local visions for the future, extraction proceeds. Thus, when price becomes the sole measure to allocate value without open and informed discussions about the value and meaning of nature, this estimation is colonial, ethnocentric, anthropocentric and capitalogenic. To defend nature or land does not mean to sacralize it, but rather to reconstruct it so that it can encompass all beings and objects in their myriad diversity, including ourselves.

One way to critically examine the extractivist logic and challenge its commodification of nature is to question the assumed primacy of 'economic value' over other dimensions such as political, cultural, symbolic and spiritual values. In the extractivist and productivist logic, there is no room for debate or contestation about what holds value or what constitutes true wealth. While economic valuation and market considerations may be relevant aspects of sustainable strategies, they alone are insufficient. It is essential to elevate the economic question of 'the value of the value' from diverse perspectives and lived realities. This was the case of the Hambach Forest protests in Germany.

The Hambach Forest (Hambacher Forst), which is over 12,000 years old, was once the largest forest in North Rhine-Westphalia, Germany. It was a biodiversity hotspot, home to 142 species considered crucial for conservation (Greenpeace, 2018). Described as 'the last remnant of a sylvan ecosystem' that has existed in the Rhine River plain between Aachen and Cologne since the end of the last ice age (*National Geographic*, 2018), the forest has been dramatically reduced to just 10 per cent of its original size. The remaining forest faces severe threats from mining activities for brown coal, or lignite, which is known for its high carbon dioxide emissions. The German energy company Rheinisch-Westfälisches Elektrizitätswerk AG planned to clear the forest as part of the Hambach surface mine operation.

Because coal power as a form of energy supply is extremely climate-intensive, the Hambach Forest rapidly became a symbol of the fight against climate change and the ongoing destruction of nature for its 'economic value' (Henseleit et al, 2022). In 2012, activists from around the world occupied the Hambach Forest with tree houses to avoid the forest's clearing by Rheinisch-Westfälisches Elektrizitätswerk AG. Over more than ten years, the Hambach Forest occupation aimed to protect the Hambach Forest from the migrating and largest coal mine in Europe. 'We're fighting capitalism and the big companies who are ruling the world and destroying it for profit', says Jim, a German activist, and Peter, who is originally from Kenya, but now works in Bonn, states that 'Germany should take a more active role in stopping fossil fuels' (Mansel, 2019: np).

While the struggle has had ebbs and flows, it has mostly been a forest occupation, where people lived in tree houses to protect the forest for its *symbolic value*. Kathrin Henneberger, a climate justice activist, said:

> [T]he forest is a symbol of what is wrong with our society and our economy. We need to protect it, not destroy it for the profit of just one big company. The climate crisis is a reality and we have to act on [it] now. … As people of the global north, we should finally take responsibility. This is where the climate crisis begins so this is where we stand and say: No more! (Quoted in Sharma, nd)

In 2020 a law was passed to preserve the forest.

As seen in the case of the Hambach Forest, when we view nature as a subject separate from human assessment, it reveals itself as multifaceted and can be evaluated from various perspectives. This plurality challenges the epistemicide and ecocide inherent in extractivist and productivist logic. However, different approaches to understanding nature often remain incommensurable (though not necessarily incompatible) due to the diverse values attributed to it. Consequently, efforts to measure and quantify nature will always be partial and incomplete. While economic estimation can serve as one of many approaches, its application should be limited, acknowledging the complexity and richness of nature's values. Engaging in open, public deliberations about these issues, rather than leaving decisions solely to the market and its extractivist and productivist logic, forces us to confront competing conceptions of what constitutes a life worth living.

Racialized cheap labour

Extractivism demands not only natural resources but also labour. As exploitation persists, it heavily relies on racialized cheap labour under the guise of 'development'. Those forced to work as 'super-humans' are often compelled to live as 'sub-humans' (Roi, 2022). The relentless drive towards commodification within the extractive system is directly based on the appropriation of both natural resources and labour power from these territories. Kwame Nkrumah's (1965) analysis highlighted how the compromise between capital and labour in the global North has historically been facilitated by the ruthless exploitation of colonies. He noted that '[t]he struggle against neo-colonialism is not aimed at excluding the capital of the developed world from operating in less developed countries. It is aimed at preventing the financial power of the developed countries from being used in such a way as to impoverish the less developed' (Nkrumah, 1965: np). This dynamic persists today. Yet, often overlooked in extractivist discourses is that women disproportionately bear the costs of reproducing community life and contribute, through low or unpaid work, to a greater accumulation of extractive capital (Federici, 2012; WoMin, 2015, 2020). Following Gayatri C. Spivak (1999), it can be argued that the burden of sustaining the extractive system falls predominantly on the bodies of racialized women and girls.

Examining the economic impact on women and girls, particularly racialized women and girls, and evolving labour–land relations reveals the entwined nature of production, reproduction, exploitation of wage-labour and dispossession. These aspects are unified, though unevenly and dynamically, making disentanglement challenging. A comprehensive study by SAGE Fund (Anderson and Real, 2023), based on nearly 100 interviews with women leaders and allies across Africa, Asia and Latin America within diverse social movements, underscores the disproportionate exclusion of women from the economic benefits of extractive projects. This includes the loss of women's access to and control over land and employment within the sector. Women are often omitted from compensation agreements, frequently denied payment for their land and labour.

Extractive projects perpetuate gendered, racialized, exploitative and perilous working conditions, often disregarding workers' fundamental rights to life, safety, health and fair labour standards (Schrecker et al, 2018). The plight of miners in the Democratic Republic of the Congo (DRC) epitomizes the global challenges faced by extractive industry workers, characterized by the conflict between health, the environment and economic opportunities. In Congolese mines, both adults and children toil as cobalt[1] miners, enduring gruelling shifts exceeding 12 hours without adequate protective gear (Achiume, 2019). These harsh conditions have grave implications for miners' long-term well-being, with fatal accidents commonplace among cobalt miners, who have earned the grim moniker *cobalt riders*.

The Katanga region in south-western DRC possesses more cobalt reserves than the rest of the world combined, making it essential for the West's energy transition. For instance, the production of electric vehicles requires over a thousand times more cobalt than a mobile phone. However, this demand comes at the expense of the local people and environment in one of the world's most impoverished areas. Siddharth Kara (2023) reports that much of the cobalt from the DRC is extracted by artisanal miners – freelance workers who endure extremely hazardous conditions for just a few dollars a day. These miners, operating without formal contracts, earn meagre compensation based on piecework while assuming all associated risks. After extracting minerals in deplorable conditions, they sell their yields to opportunistic buyers, who funnel them through various intermediaries until they reach multinational technology corporations. Kara (2023) describes these conditions as subhuman and degrading, with workers using pickaxes, shovels and rebar to dig in trenches and tunnels to collect cobalt for the global supply chain. This opaque supply chain allows these corporations to maintain strict control measures and claim commitments to human rights and zero-tolerance policies against child labour (Kara, 2023). In this context, Kara suggests that instead of eliminating cobalt altogether – given its crucial role in technology and the sustainable energy transition – the focus should be on improving the supply chain to ensure fairer practices and better conditions for workers.

The technical demands of mining, coupled with limited employment opportunities, create an oversupply of local labour, intensifying competition for jobs – even among children. Tragically, boys as young as ten suffer from accidents and exposure to toxic substances in hazardous tunnels, while girls face not only dangerous working conditions but also sexual violence (Kara, 2023). As Elliott Prasse-Freeman (2022) aptly describes, this dire situation epitomizes a necroeconomy, where individuals' worth is only recognized when they are submerged beneath the earth. Extractivism commodifies both land and people, reducing them to mere factors of production or consumers for the global North and the elites of the global South.

In the realm of oil extraction, expatriates and migrant contract workers dominate the workforce. Annually, half a million men traverse Southern Africa to toil in South African mines, with local communities contributing only a fraction of skilled labour (Khumalo, 2015). This influx marginalizes local and impoverished migrant workers, exacerbating ethnic and racial divisions in countries like Nigeria, where expatriates and migrant workers receive preferential treatment over locals (Achiume, 2019).

Under the current extractive economic model, territories are identified for exploitation, displacing Indigenous populations and reshaping entire economic and social structures to accommodate monoculture. This transition from coercion to purported consent disregards the fact that artisanal miners have no viable alternatives once their economic systems are decimated – their only recourse is to flee. Hence, managing migration flows necessitates addressing root issues within countries of origin.

Amidst these struggles, Henchir Jemna, nestled in the southern region of Kebili, emerges as a beacon of resistance against unjust Tunisian state policies and extractive practices. This oasis, with its excellent quality date plants, situated in the south-west corner of Tunisia within the Sahara, once belonged to the communal property of the Jemna community. However, during the colonial period, it fell prey to seizure, transitioning into the private possession of French settler-colonists. Following Tunisia's independence in 1956, the nation faced a pivotal moment regarding land distribution. Instead of restoring the land to its rightful owners and redistributing it among landless peasants, the ruling elite opted to nationalize the land, perpetuating a colonial model of intensive, mechanized agriculture over traditional practices (Hamouchene, 2019).

Efforts to create agricultural cooperatives and the sale of land to individuals close to decision-makers ensued, perpetuating historical injustice and leaving many small-scale and subsistence farmers, including those in Jemna, as landless peasants in the post-colonial period. The liberalization of the agricultural sector in the 1980s (with the International Monetary Fund Adjustment Programmes), coupled with corruption and cronyism, led to the bankruptcy of the public company managing Jemna's oasis in 2002. Seizing this opportunity, private investors with ties to the ousted dictator Ben Ali profited, paying minimal rent costs to the state (Hamouchene, 2019).

Change only came with the 2010–2011 Tunisian revolution. The 'Revolutionary Committee' successfully reclaimed confiscated land, expelling profiteers just days before Ben Ali fled. After a century-long battle, they achieved victory through self-management and voluntarism, highlighting the significance of labour rights, the peasant question, land rights and natural resources.

Jemna's oasis became a symbol of people mastering their material existence, emphasizing that the revolution extended beyond political rights to include economic sovereignty and values of solidarity, dignity and freedom, resonating with the early Tunisian revolution's slogans. The formation of the Association for the Protection of Jemna's Oases (APJO) was pivotal. Under its leadership, the community redirected profits towards agricultural management, developmental projects and public welfare, showcasing collective management that significantly increased employment, offering stable contracts and higher salaries.

The results have been inspiring. Between 2011 and 2014, production doubled, and the oasis now employs around 300 workers – a significant increase from the pre-2011 period (Hamouchene, 2019). Jemna challenges exploitative extractivism and counter-revolutionary elites, offering an alternative to extractivist logics. According to Taher Etahri, president of the APJO, '[t]he experience is rich in lessons. We are no longer under the tutelage of the state; we act for the public good. Everybody is looking up at Jemna, which makes us stronger and more united' (Hamouchene, 2019: 15).

While significant in their own right, Dhouha Djerbi (2024) argues, Jemna's experiences and their respective analyses provide an incomplete picture of how gender relations shape the trajectories and modalities of dissent. Djerbi emphasizes that 'a granular examination of social reproduction as a site of recurrent, micro struggles, as encapsulated by its labors, is especially helpful not only in tracing lineages of popular discontent induced by dispossession and depletion but also in understanding where and how peasant women … are situated in these processes' (Djerbi, 2024: 11).

Jemna currently faces challenges such as state threats to impose cooperative management of land and production, as well as growing tensions between agricultural workers and the APJO. But 'Jemna's experience', as locals call it, also reveals that at the margins, the revolution meant reclaiming history, economic sovereignty, land, solidarity, and revisiting a past marked by domination and oppression.

Denial of most existences

Extractivism relies on epistemological and ontological processes of negating, overlooking, subjugating or directly denying most existences, narrowing the scope of beings who can exist in a place, while often introducing a very limited array of life in place of the beings that are eradicated (Kröger, 2021; Chagnon et al, 2022). Marisol de la Cadena et al (2015) contend that extractive destruction occurs when more-than-human beings are devalued and landscapes are not recognized as living entities. More-than-human nature is therefore denied and only made available to be conquered, subjugated and exploited because it is first defined as 'empty', 'potential' or 'uncultivated' lands and nature as either wasteful or inefficient, a resource without its own purposes or meanings (Plumwood, 1993; Carrasco-Miró, 2017, 2018a). Similarly, Verónica Gago and Sandro Mezzadra (2017) note that colonial and modern 'territorial advances' rely on specific forms of political and economic violence upon the lands to render them 'available', generating benefits for distant entities at the expense of Indigenous and local peoples, economies and ecosystems.

This has clear links to colonialist narratives of settler invasion. Eve Tuck and Wayne Yang (2012: 5) argue that, in settler colonialism, 'human relationships to land are restricted to the relationship of the owner to his property. Epistemological, ontological and cosmological relationships to land are … made pre-modern and backward. Made savage'. Such a framework reveals how settler colonialism not only alienates Indigenous peoples from their lands but also perpetuates systems of racism and ecological exploitation. Understanding these relationships disrupts the status quo by exposing complicity in ongoing colonial projects against Indigenous lives, knowledges, and ecosystems. Leanne Betasamosake Simpson explains that this itself exposes part of an extractivist and productivist mentality, since, in extractivism:

> My land is seen as a resource. My relatives in the plant and animal worlds are seen as resources. My culture and knowledge is a resource.

> My body is a resource and my children are a resource because they are the potential to grow, maintain, and uphold the [extractivist and productivist mentality]. … [Indigenous peoples] are not seen as peoples – they are seen as resources. (Simpson and Klein, 2013: np)

Within the extractivist and productivist mindset, Indigenous people, the Earth, and its animal and plant inhabitants are viewed as inferior and reduced to mere resources. This reinforces the narrative that the Indigenous are less developed or disempowered, supporting the idea that the seizure of 'potential'land is justified or even destined to happen. However, we are now witnessing the consequences of this treatment of the Earth. Climate change and environmental degradation are resulting in countless wildfires, catastrophic storms, polluted water and collapsing fisheries worldwide. These events are not isolated but form a systemic pattern, linked to human-induced global warming, as science has consistently shown.

I write these lines in the midst of the disaster caused by the DANA storm in Valencia, Spain, near where I live. Official sources report that, as of now, 223 lives have been lost. Ten days after the storm, 78 people are still missing.[2] These are not just numbers. They are people with stories, dreams, people who have loved and been loved, whose lives have been brutally interrupted. There were failures, negligence and incompetence. The disaster is the result of an economic model driven by real estate speculation, tourism and the rising temperatures of the Mediterranean Sea due to human-induced climate change. Those responsible must be held accountable for the deaths in Valencia. Thus, it is imperative to identify the immediate parties responsible, to demand stronger prevention against climate change effects, and to call for more adaptation measures to reduce future casualties. But this is far from enough. A monumental silence persists in speeches, articles and discussions among those with the most responsibility for this catastrophe.

The primary entities responsible for the collapse making extreme weather events more frequent and severe – not just in Valencia but globally – are fossil fuel corporations (oil, coal and natural gas) (Romanello et al, 2024). Why are fossil fuel corporations not being held accountable? These corporations generate profits for a minority of ultra-wealthy individuals who, in recent years, have amassed even greater fortunes. This minority, backed by most of the world's governments and parliaments, is increasing fossil fuel production rather than reducing it. The 2024 report from the Lancet Countdown, created with the expertise of 122 leading researchers on climate change and health from UN agencies and academic institutions worldwide, reveals 'the most concerning findings yet in the collaboration's 8 years of monitoring' (Romanello et al, 2024: 1847). They warn that 'far from declining, global energy-related CO_2 emissions reached an all-time high in 2023. … Oil and gas companies are reinforcing global dependence on fossil fuels and – partly fueled by high energy prices and the windfall profits of the global energy crisis – most are further expanding their fossil fuel production plans' (Romanello et al, 2024: 1846–1848). The authors analysed the plans of the world's 114 largest oil and gas companies, which account for 80 per cent of global oil and gas production. They conclude that the gap is widening: based on data from March 2024 on new fossil projects, researchers estimate these companies' emissions in 2040 will be 189 per cent higher. Many of these oil companies are publicly funded, meaning that governments are behind these expansionist and disastrous strategies. If we continue to remain silent, we will remain trapped in the horror of counting the dead.

With life tied to profit, what becomes viewed as inefficiency and against mutual benefit is antithetical to 'proper' economic logic (that is, extractivist capitalism). In the face of climate collapse and accelerating biodiversity loss, Eliane Brum (2024) argues that only a radical shift in perception can halt the corrosion of our Earth. Brum asserts the need to upend capitalist ideas of centre and periphery. According to her, the true centres of the Earth are not in Washington, Madrid, London, Frankfurt, São Paulo, Beijing, or other major capitals that drive stock markets and wield political power. Rather, they lie in the resilient enclaves of nature that continue to survive despite relentless attacks from an economics logic based on corporations extracting oil, minerals, soy, meat or palm. For Brum, the centres of the world are wherever nature resists.

In this view, we must uphold the Indigenous perspective that life is an interconnected web and embrace a reciprocal relationship with nature, rather than viewing every connection through the lens of denial of most existences – that is of domination and subordination. This involves recognizing and valuing the principles and ways of life of peoples who remain close to nature and who coexist with others – human and more-than-human – without exploiting or degrading the Earth, that is, life itself.

In this context, the political concept of 'resistance as re-existence' emerges as both a practice and an actionable idea deeply rooted in the enduring struggle of Black and Indigenous communities. Adolfo Albán Achinte (2013) defines re-existence as the strategies developed by Indigenous and Afro-descendant communities to confront the reality imposed by hegemonic forces that have marginalized and silenced their existence, often portraying them negatively. Thus, re-existence seeks to decentralize established norms by delving into the depths of Indigenous and Afro-descendant cultures, uncovering 'the organizational, productive, nutritional, ritual, and aesthetic elements that dignify life and enable its reinvention for the purpose of ongoing transformation' (Albán Achinte, 2013: 455).

A powerful example is the work of Ehuana Yaira Yanomami, an artist, researcher and member of the Yanomami community in the Brazilian Amazon. As an illustrator, writer and activist, Yaira has reflected on the concept of *body-territory* (this concept is discussed later, in Chapter 7) from the perspective of women in the forest and on the genocide currently faced by the Yanomami people, who are threatened by illegal mining. In the face of this extractivist threat, Yaira uses her art as both resistance and re-existence, bearing witness to the daily violence suffered by her community and highlighting the strength of the 'feminine forest'. She is the co-author of *Yïpïmuwi thëã oni* (Words about Menstruation), the first book written by a Yahomani woman in her language, which describes menstruation rituals and the role of women in her community (Yaira Yanomami and Pawë Yanomami, 2017). Alongside preserving and transmitting ancestral traditions, Yaira's art denounces deforestation, land pollution, community destruction and sexual violence against women by *garimpeiros* (illegal gold miners). In this way, we see 're-existence' promoting thinking, recognizing and validating the alternative forms of existing that the colonized communities construct beyond those imposed on them. That is, the ways that people are sowing and resowing life, cultivating the possibilities of an otherwise economic, social, cultural, political, epistemic, ethical and existence-based affirmation (Walsh, 2023). In the context of 're-existence', as Yaira demonstrates, resistance is not just about denying oppressive power, but also about *creating ways of existence.* This includes forms of creating, feeling, thinking and acting in a world that is itself being constructed through various insurgencies and interruptions aimed at building more just futures. Decolonizing feminist economics, in this sense, can be understood as processes of 're-existence as resistance' encompassing economic, social and political trajectories, as well as possibilities that radically deviate from the prevailing extractivist and productivist rationality and offer better futures for all.

5

The Scar Sands

In contrast to dominant economic perspectives that emphasize technocratic views of nature, society and the future, this chapter explores how art, as a form of 're-existence', can disrupt extractivist and productivist logics and action and radically challenge and reshape our perceptions. Specifically, it examines the video-essay *Deep Weather* (2013: 9m) by Swiss postcolonial feminist artist Ursula Biemann and the poems of Canadian decolonial feminist poet-activist Rita Wong. These artworks present decolonizing, post-extractivist feminist analysis and proposals, focusing on the Tar Sands of Alberta. The Tar Sands, or the 'Scar Sands' as Wong metaphorically refers to them in her poems, represent the world's largest (and expanding) industrial project, known for producing the most destructive, carbon-intensive and toxic fuels on the Earth. Recent measurements have revealed that emissions from the Tar Sands were up to 6,300 per cent greater than what the oil industry was reporting (He et al, 2024).

The mining activities in the Tar Sands have had profound impacts on both Indigenous communities and more-than-human ecosystems, leading to the designation of the region as one of global capitalism's most distinctive fossil fuel 'sacrifice zones' (Klein, 2014: 169). Naomi Klein describes such zones as inevitable outcomes of capitalist extractivism and its economic logic, revealing a mindset that equates progress and fossil fuels with a coercive notion of freedom. This politico-economic mentality views certain people, places and landscapes that 'somehow don't count and therefore can be poisoned, drained, or otherwise destroyed for the supposed greater good of economic progress' (Klein, 2014: 169–170). It follows the logics of extractivism and productivism, simplifying the complex web of life and treating both organic and inorganic entities as either resources to exploit or waste to discard. In this context, Ursula Biemann and Rita Wong critically examine the extensive oil extraction processes in the Northern Alberta sands and their profound impacts on Indigenous communities and the climate. Their works underscore forms of resistance and movement-building against extractivist and productivist mentalities and practices, opening possibilities for better futures for all.

Deep Weather (2013) by Ursula Biemann immerses the audience in two remote landscapes, one in the global North and the other in the global South. First, we witness aerial images of the extraction sites of heavy oil called bitumen, in the Tar Sands in northern Canada (see Figure 5.1). The video is narrated by the artist in a whispered – 'intimate and viceral' (Biemann, 2015: 11) – voice-over speculating about the geological impacts of these corporate activities both locally and globally. In a visual shift, the narrative transports us to the Ganges-Brahmaputra delta in Bangladesh (see Figure 5.2). Here, the

Figure 5.1: Athabasca Oil Sands in Alberta, Canada

Source: Photograph from *Deep Weather* (2013) by Ursula Biemann, used with permission of the author

Figure 5.2: Ganges-Brahmaputra delta in Bangladesh

Source: Photograph from *Deep Weather* (2013) by Ursula Biemann, used with permission of the author

camera descends to ground level, revealing the collective efforts of coastal communities working tirelessly to construct barriers against the encroaching seas. Volunteers are seen hand-packing sandbags with mud, determined to protect their homes and communities from submersion.

Biemann connects these seemingly disparate locations through their atmospheric chemistry, revealing their underlying interconnectedness bound together by the overarching economic logic of extraction and its impact on climate disruption. The video emphasizes the fragility of human territories and civilization in the face of planetary atmospheric systems' power. In doing so, it demonstrates that the expansionist dream of human superiority over 'nature' is ultimately precarious: the unbridled consumption of fossil fuels unleashes power far beyond the control of *Homo economicus*, ultimately leading to ruin.

Throughout the video, profound insights into the dynamics of extractive logic unfold, revealing two-directional movements. On one hand, fossil and mineral materials, once extracted, undergo a transformative process, losing their original context and histories. Stripped of their social narratives of labour and displacement, as well as the natural histories of local ecologies and landscapes, they are reduced to mere exchangeable commodities. In this commodification of nature, a homogenizing temporal dimension takes hold. On the other hand, the video also sheds light on a distinct dynamic – one that arises not during extraction but at the exhaustive end of fossil fuel production. Here, the focus shifts to the emissions released into the air during consumption, leaving a lasting and undesirable impact on the planet's future.

Through this powerful geographical confrontation, the film embodies the unforeseen repercussions of massive resource exploitation, its expansionist universalist character and the unpredictable future shaped by extractivist actions on the other side of the world. As Biemann (2015: 11) notes in a short text of the short video: '[f]or what becomes increasingly evident is that the passage from a diffused soft cause to hard consequences is what defines the contemporary planetary condition'.

The collective labour undertaken by Bangladeshi communities to construct barriers against encroaching seas stands as a testament to the human cost of the oil industry – a consequence that corporations and governments often deny or disavow, disproportionately placing the burden on racialized cheap labour. The result is a system of climate colonialism, wherein those least responsible for contributing to climate breakdown bear a more acute impact over extended periods. This socio-spatial differentiation, indicative of a colonial pattern, determines who bears the brunt, who is deemed expendable, and who is temporarily spared, leading inexorably towards a climate apartheid. This reality is palpable for individuals situated at the intersection of race, ethnicity, gender and class as they confront ecological harms and toxic environments across various locations.

It is evident that Bangladeshi villages deep in the Bengal delta, devoid of access to fossil fuels, have made zero contributions to global warming and rising sea levels. In envisioning a future of environmental and economic justice, one cannot help but question what form of ecological debt could ever adequately redress the immense impacts inflicted upon these vulnerable communities (Warlenius et al, 2015; Demos, 2020; Paul, 2021).

In both geographies, there is a manipulation of mud, symbolizing the transformative and often violent interactions between humans and the Earth. However, the two geographies express radically different perspectives and attitudes towards the Earth. In Canada, the burtal extraction of heavy fuel, the deployment of vast machinery and the vertical desire of extraction into the depths of time; in Bangladesh, the drowning of communities of the delta, the manual labour of millions, and the submerged expansion into the horizontality of a rising ocean (Biemann, 2020). As Canada strives for exhaustive accumulation, the video gives a sense that in Bangladesh they are truly investing in a future, however precarious it may be. These different economic models are the expression of profoundly different ethical attitudes towards the Earth and our future: seen as either a utilitarian planet providing material resources for humans or a living entity in its own right.

Amidst the devastating loss of territory caused by resource extraction and climate change, the unregulated market system perceives these catastrophes as 'empty'; opportunities to intensify its extractivist and productivist logic of scarcity denying most existences. As land becomes scarcer, its value increases, perpetuating a cycle that seems indifferent to the human and environmental costs involved. However, Ursula Biemann's thought-provoking analysis challenges such fatalistic narratives in *Deep Weather*. She portrays not only the collective efforts to fortify geographical defences but also delves into the root causes and showcases the building of collective agency for resistance and re-existence.

Biemann (2015: 11) notes '[t]he open questions documentary viewers might have about labour conditions or social realities of first nation communities in Alberta or populations in the Ganges delta remain unanswered'. However, they are not ignored. While the First Nations community living in the Athabasca region is absent from the visual imagery, their legendary collective space, on the verge of disaster, is evoked in *Deep Weather*. In a whispered voice-over, the video conjures: 'The wildlife has retreated / the traplines are empty / the elders call the spirits / the young ones sing rap songs / and the acid wind's hissing / Evolution isn't fast enough. Mutate!'

This whispering voice, in sync with the aerial video footage, transcends the immediate physical and political reality, activating a time-space beyond. For First Nations people, the damage caused by extractive industries goes beyond just blocking ancestral knowledge and hunting practices. Their land is intricately intertwined with local mythologies and spiritual entities and each Nation has its own unique relationship with the land. 'If we don't have land and we don't have anywhere to carry out our traditional lifestyles, we lose who we are as a people. So, if there's no land, then it's equivalent in our estimation to genocide of a people', says George Poitras of the Mikisew Cree First Nation (Robins, 2020). Shiv Visvanathan (1997: 42) tells us that what politicians and technocrats fail to understand is that, for Indigenous people, 'land is not real estate or a space over which people are moved like objects. Land is memory, a map of one's world, a way of life for which people are willing to die'.

Thus, the Tar Sands landscape contains both worlds, it is a psycho-socio-economic habitat. The noise, subterranean sonar waves and vibrations, and the invisible toxic juices seeping into lakes and rivers affect not only the biological but also the psychic ecologic of contamination. The aggressive extractive mining, steam processing and transportation of Tar Sands have had severe repercussions on both the environment and the human rights of First Nations communities (Nikiforuk, 2010). These destructive economic activities not only obliterate biodiverse ecologies, derogatively referred to as 'overburden', but also leave vast, lifeless scars on the landscape, transforming it into carbon geologies. Extraction companies like ConocoPhillips, Petro-Canada and ExxonMobil have played a significant role in this environmental devastation, leading to ruinous consequences for nearby First Nations populations (Demos, 2020) and for the future of all of us.

The consequences of these practices are evident in the rising health issues within these communities. Cases of cancer, asthma, diabetes and mental illness caused by air and water pollution have dramatically increased over the past decade among the affected populations (Westman Clinton and Joly, 2019). Toxic waste, an inevitable byproduct of bitumen processing, is stored in open-tailing lakes that now cover vast areas once inhabited by ancient spruce forests – the living spaces and hunting territories of First Nations communities and hundreds of species.

In response to these destructive practices, First Nations communities in the Athabasca region have taken action. They have filed grievances against Shell for engaging in ecocide and have held the Canadian government accountable for breaching historical treaties and failing to protect the health of Indigenous populations though so far these lawsuits have been without success (Demos, 2020).

Canadian poet-activist Rita Wong (2015: 17–18), drawing inspiration from her first-hand experiences during the Tar Sands Healing Walks – founded by a coalition of Indigenous women from First Nations communities impacted by Tar Sands projects organized annually by local First Nations groups from 2010 to 2014,[1] which brought together Indigenous peoples and environmental activists across Canada to traverse a 14-kilometre loop around the mines and tailings ponds near Fort McMurray (Ellman, 2013; Leahy, 2014) – writes in 'Fresh Ancient Ground'*:

> those who don't respect the magic of ice
> are doomed to melt it for their descendants
> as miles of living medicines made by rivers over millennia
> are unceremoniously eradicated, annihilated, wasted
> everything leaking everywhere it wasn't meant to go
> rainbow in the sky or on slick oil
> […]
> we walk for healing the scar sands, in a living pact with the bears, the
> eagles,
> the muzzled scientists, the beavers who've built dams you can see from
> outer space'
>
> step by step, we conduct ceremony for those who don't know
> any better or don't care, broken whole, waiting for our sisters &
> brothers to catch up with wind, sun & water.

In my reading, these lines imply a ramifying series of environmental impacts issuing from the violent destructiveness of bitumen mining, where leaking pipelines and tailings ponds not only pollute the Athabasca River but also annihilate the 'living medicines' (native plants) it might use to heal itself. The poem, as in Biemann's video-essay, reminds readers the interconnectedness of the Earth offering a way of imagining the complex interaction of extractivist economic activities with the planet's climate systems and the future.

In both art works, the Tar Sands region emerges as a landscape of negation and emptiness. Wong's poem, in its portrayal of the area's Indigenous inhabitants and knowledge, captures the effects of what Rob Nixon (2011: 19) terms 'displacement without moving'. This phenomenon occurs when corporations and state authorities induce 'the loss of the land and resources beneath them, a loss that leaves communities stranded in a place stripped of the very characteristics that made it inhabitable'. This resonates with Biemann's *Deep Weather*, where Bangladeshi people, despite their mass efforts to build flood defences, find themselves facing the relentless rise of sea levels, rendering the land an ever-shifting and precarious entity.

In the last verse of Wong's poem, 'we' initially refers simply to the human participants in the Tar Sands Healing Walks but throughout the act of

* 'Fresh Ancient Ground' by Rita Wong from *undercurrent* (Nightwood Editions, 2015). Reproduced with permission of the publisher.

walking the 'we' is transformed and expands acknowledging the interlinks among and beyond humans. For the local and Indigenous people, walking becomes a powerful act, a ceremony, of joint remembrance and healing, a way to honour the places that have been obliterated by bitumen extraction. However, this act of remembering is bittersweet, as it confronts them with painful 'absences' and losses – the remembered places no longer exist.

In the works of Wong and other Canadian poet-activists representing the Alberta Tar Sands, like Stephen Collins, walking becomes a collective, political act rather than a solitary or merely personal one (Alexander, 2022). It is closely aligned not only with the struggles of local and Indigenous communities but also with the rights of all living and non-living beings threatened by the extractive and productive logic of the economy and its industries. This collective mobilization emphasizes the interconnectedness of life on Earth and the shared responsibility to protect it. As Rebecca Solnit (2002: 217) remarks, there is a long tradition of parades and protest marches in which walking functions as 'a bodily demonstration of political or cultural conviction and one of the most universally available forms of public expression', symbolizing the power of unity and collective action. In the context of the Tar Sands and the global environmental crisis, walking becomes a symbolic act of resistance against destructive economic extractive practices and a call for a more economically sustainable and ecologically responsible future.

Walking embodies a mode of bodily engagement with the more-than-human world and stands in direct opposition to the core principles of the extractivist and productivist logic of the economy. These principles are embedded in self-perpetuating cycles of extraction, combustion and consumption, fundamental to modern transportation, energy generation and manufacturing. For Wong – who does not write from a position outside of or beyond the extractivist economy but from within its structures of exploitation and exchange – walking through a polluted and brutalized landscape becomes both a form of resistance and a spatial practice that concretely expresses ecological, feminist, and anti-capitalist politics. That is a form of re-existence.

Similarly, the earth movers in *Deep Weather* are at the frontiers of earth revolution unfolding across geographies, in making continuous territorial claims as the sea encroaches upon their land. Their collective and creative struggle unfolds on ground that is increasingly becoming negative space (Biemann, 2015). As their communities confront and resist the violent impacts of climate change and extractive economic practices, the evolving, marginalized landscape they shape serves as tangible evidence of this reconceptualization of territoriality – living on the edge of land and water, in a future that is rapidly approaching.

Through the artistic works of Rita Wong and Ursula Biemann, we see how the walkers in the Tar Sands and the earth movers in the Bangla delta both challenge the dominant extractivist and productivist logic and enact modes of re-existence. They provide a glimpse of an alternative, sustainable way of relating to the land and the beings that inhabit it – a future-oriented perspective that acknowledges the interconnectedness of all life and ecosystems and the urgent need to resist destructive economies. By confronting the reality of their respective environments, these works highlight the imperative of building economies that are collectively organized around ecological sustainability and regeneration rather than around fossil fuels and extractivism.

6

Life at the Centre and the Oil Underground

Introduction: Fighting climate colonialism

Brianna Fruean, a Samoan climate justice activist and member of the Pacific Climate Warriors delegation at COP26 (Conference of the Parties) in 2021, delivered a powerful speech at the UN climate convention in Glasgow, Scotland:

> I am from Samoa, one of the regions that contributes the least, and yet is one of the most threatened by climate breakdown. I became a climate activist at age 11 and have led citizen climate justice movements for most of my life. … For hundreds of years, my people have shown great resilience. We have fought against our colonizers and made them change. Now that the rest of the world begins to suffer the effects of climate change, as we already do in the Pacific Islands, we can teach them to fight like us.
>
> From the very moment the United States, Germany, and Great Britain began trying to colonize Samoa, they tried to strip us of our culture. In a sense, the colonizers recognized that our knowledge, beliefs, and way of doing things were our source of *mana*, our power. Therefore, one of our main messages in the Youth 4 Pacific declaration that we brought to the COP [Conference of the Parties] is that Indigenous knowledge must be respected as a form of climate science.
>
> We fought against the colonizers who sought to eradicate our culture, and we achieved independence. However, we are now facing a different revolution. Now we face climate colonialism: rich and polluting companies profit from our destruction.
>
> All of these struggles are connected. The climate crisis and social inequalities are symptoms of a world shaped by colonialism and capitalism, both forms of social organization that prioritize the

> comfort of one group over the lives of another. (Fruean, 2021, np; translation mine)

Two years after Fruean's speech, the 2023 Intergovernmental Panel on Climate Change (IPCC) Report (IPCC, 2023: 12) has mentioned for the first time the term colonialism, recognizing the connection of the climate crisis with 'historical and ongoing patterns of inequity such as colonialism, especially for many Indigenous Peoples and local communities'. The IPCC Report (2023: 52) clarifies that the inequitable impacts of the colonialism–climate crisis relationship 'are worsened by compounding and cascading risks (high confidence) and are socially differentiated. For example, low-income, young, poor, and female-headed households face greater livelihood risks from climate hazards'. In this regard, the Report points towards an intersectional approach and the urgent need, as Fruean states, to unite forces against the systems of domination attacking life.

Climate change issues have the same systemic root causes of colonialism, capitalism and patriarchy, and can and should be worked on together. As Fruean explains, for many Indigenous people, climate change is not a new emergency; it is a long-standing, unfolding catastrophe. However, if climate change is now an emergency, it is because it is becoming an emergency for the beneficiaries of colonial-capitalism-patriarchy. Like Fruean, many Indigenous people have been on the frontlines of struggles against environmental harm for centuries, from the beginning of their dispossession. Kyle Powys Whyte argues that:

> [C]limate injustice is a recent episode of a cyclical history of colonialism inciting anthropogenic (human-caused) environmental change on Indigenous peoples. Indigenous peoples face climate risks largely because of how colonialism, in conjunction with capitalist economics, shapes the geographic spaces they live in and their socio-economic conditions. … Climate injustice, for Indigenous peoples, is less about the specter of a new future and more like the experience of déjà vu. (Whyte, 2017: 88)

In that sense, if we are not attentive to the colonial dimensions of climate breakdown, we are missing the point. Global North–South inequality in climate crisis responsibility and impact is intrinsically linked to discriminatory social and structural processes produced during colonialism. These processes continue today through mechanisms such as corporate land destruction, excessive emissions, and the frequent exclusion of people from the global South and Indigenous peoples from international climate-related decision-making. Additionally, the burden is often placed on marginalized communities 'to develop' less, 'progress' slowly, or restrict their population growth to mitigate climate change. We have previously analysed these issues by exploring extractivism and its links with the climate crisis in *Deep Weather* (2013), particularly focusing on the effects of the Tar Sands on Bangladeshi communities (see Figure 5.2). This phenomenon has been called climate colonialism.

Climate colonialism initiates a process of re-embodiment and relocation, altering our understanding of how, why and who is at fault or responsible. The climate is not merely undergoing change; it is being colonized, compelled to modify and, as evident in catastrophes, engaging in rebellion and resistance against the assault upon it. Farhana Sultana (2023; see also Sultana, 2024) explains that climate coloniality is

> experienced through continued ecological degradations that are both overt and covert, episodic and creeping – for example, pollution, toxic waste, mining, disasters, desertification, deforestation, land erosion, and more – whereby global capitalism, via development and economic growth ideologies, reproduces various forms of colonial racial harms to entire countries in the Global South and communities of color in the Global North. (Sultana, 2023: 80)

Climate change is ultimately an effect of the economic system: capitalism, which aims to exponential growth and maximizes profits by cheapening labour and resource inputs, often through processes of extractivism and exploitation, through historical and ongoing processes of colonization, dispossession and coercion. Racism and other forms of oppression have long been used to justify these processes.

Stopping climate change is likely going to require constraints on energy use. Will the burden of constraints fall on the working classes and the poor (as is typical under capitalism), or will it be placed on the wealthy and corporations? Colonial-capitalist-patriarchal dynamics have produced severe global inequalities, where centers of wealth and capital accumulation – such as private company data centers with their high (and increasing) consumption and energy use – exist alongside energy poverty, which continues to affect millions of people worldwide.

Discourses on sustainable energy and the green energy transition rarely interrogate the mode of production underpinning so-called green technologies. However, as long as these technologies are developed within a capitalist framework, they will inevitably rely on the cheapening of nature and labour, perpetuating colonial dynamics. The green energy transition is heavily dependent on metals, making it far from straightforward as it drives increased material demand, market pressures, and geopolitical competition. This is particularly evident in the case of lithium, a critical resource in this transition. The lithium extracted from Argentina, Bolivia and Chile – together referred as the 'Lithium Triangle' – plays a pivotal role in producing batteries for electric cars, a key component in the global North's strategy to decarbonize its economy. While lithium extraction is relatively cost-effective,[1] the pressing question arises regarding its sustainability and long-term impact. Will lithium mining contribute to global well-being, or will it perpetuate societal and environmental harm? When doing the maths, the three South American countries find themselves with minimal job opportunities for unskilled, women, Indigenous workers, scarce well-paid positions, water shortages, displaced communities, and the degradation of both livelihoods and ecosystems. The promised economic development from this extraction fails to materialize again. Moreover, lithium mining has additional environmental consequences, including soil damage, air contamination and the depletion of already limited water supplies. In Tibet, for instance, Chinese lithium mining has resulted in chemical leaks into the Liqi River, leading to the poisoning of fish and livestock – a scenario mirrored in the Lithium Triangle (Ahmad, 2020).

Despite these environmental and social urgent problematics, proponents of lithium mining argue that lithium-ion batteries are indispensable in combating the adverse effects of global warming. Electric vehicle manufacturers, such as Tesla, advocate for the widespread adoption of clean, battery-powered alternatives to combustion engines. They contend that increasing the number of electric cars on the road will significantly reduce greenhouse gas emissions, with the United States Department of Energy estimating a 60 per cent lower carbon pollution level compared to gasoline-powered vehicles. In a clean-energy state like California, this reduction could be as high as 80 per cent (Nuccitelli, 2018). However, saving the Earth should not come at the expense of people and the destruction of fragile ecosystems. Lithium mining, therefore, cannot be viewed as a sustainable or just long-term solution for the green energy transition; instead, it clearly reflects climate colonialism.

We see over and over again, countries in the global North leveraging their geopolitical and commercial dominance to drive down prices for resources and labour provided by the global South. Jason Hickel et al explain that:

> As a result, for every unit of embodied resources and labour that the South imports from the North, they have to export many more units to pay for it, enabling the North to achieve a net appropriation through trade. This dynamic was theorized by Emmanuel (1972) and Amin (1978) as a process of 'unequal exchange'. (Hickel et al, 2022: 2)

In a similar vein, other anti-colonialist thinkers like Walter Rodney (1972) have critiqued the development rhetoric of 'developed', 'developing' and 'underdeveloped' nations, arguing that it overlooks the dynamics of exploitation. Over 50 years ago, Rodney already contended that resource-rich yet finance-poor countries are being aggressively underdeveloped by the global North. He asserts: Africa is not 'underdeveloped' abstractly; *Europe underdeveloped Africa*, actively and concretely.

The results of Jason Hickel et al's (2022) study demonstrate that the general pattern of appropriation that characterized the colonial period has been maintained and indeed expanded into the post-colonial era through the mechanism of unequal exchange and dynamics of exploitation, despite significant changes in the structure of the global economy.

> In an equitable world, the resource trade deficit that the North sustains in relation to the South would be financed with a parallel monetary trade deficit. But in reality, the monetary trade deficit is very small, equivalent to only about 1% of global trade revenues, and fluctuates between North and South. In effect, this means that the North achieves its large net appropriation of resources and labour from the South *gratis*. (Hickel et al, 2022: 5)

In this regard, extractivism propagated by global capital and state-sanctioned interventions perpetuates colonialism and geopolitical climate necropolitics within and beyond borders.

If we misunderstand and misrepresent the economic causes of climate change, we are likely to reinscribe the systems and relations that caused the climate crisis, even in our efforts to address it. Consequently, settler-colonial nation-states may exploit these periods of crisis and disaster to perpetuate racist and gender violence and dispossession. Racism, colonialism, patriarchy and capitalism, coupled with the displacement of Indigenous peoples from their ancestral lands and the disruption of their long-standing ways of life, economies, governance and thought, stands as a fundamental driver of climate change and the collapse of ecological systems. It is essential to recognize that alterations to Earth's systems are not incidental or inevitable outcomes, but rather the result of deliberate, often violent, interventions (pedagogy of cruelty). The pursuit of 'climatic improvement' and the exertion of dominance over and transformation of 'wild' lands and waters have historically been, and continue to be, central tenets of colonial ideology.

In the last decade, there has been a massive expansion of climate international commitments. These commitments have been designed, supported and executed through multilateral financial cooperation and foreign policy strategies, as well as robust civil advocacy schemes. An example of this is all the commitments conceived and driven through the United Nations. However, these commitments have drawn attention for their incremental tendency, financing strategies through foreign investment and external debt, and because they have largely allowed the blurring of the scope of derived interventions, limiting the governance and influence of communities and local governments in the face of climate action. Why should voters in high-income countries have the right to poison the air, the sea, the soil, and the rivers of the entire Earth? The carbon emitted in the United States and Europe wreaks havoc in Brazil, Mozambique, and the Philippines, yet the inhabitants of those countries have no right to vote in United States or European elections.

These commitments have been accused of perpetuating colonial strategies of domination and dispossession, as well as establishing goals that depend on the continuity of the current political and financial power scenarios. For example, existing climate mitigation scenarios maintain energy use in the global North at a per capita level two to three times higher than the global South. These scenarios also hinge on the advancement of expensive technologies like negative emissions technologies (such as greenhouse gas capture and sequestration methods like deforestation and reforestation projects), which frequently lead to land-grabbing in the global South. Indeed, diverse anti-colonial movements, civil society organizations, activist groups, environmental and human rights collectives, social leaders and academics from various regions have issued calls to the international community to reassess and scrutinize the frameworks underpinning the development of international climate policies. These calls primarily focus on three key issues that have yet to be addressed by the international community. First, there is a need to assess the extent to which the alternatives and solutions promoted by the global climate agenda have reinforced heteropatriarchal and colonial legacies. Second, it is crucial to understand how climate action has contributed to the creation of new patterns of North–South domination. Third, there is a need to examine how climate action has influenced inequality and the distribution of wealth.

Feminist scholars and activists have long demonstrated how climate justice will not be as effective or equitable without feminist perspectives and insights, as these integrate various feminist strands of scholarship, as well as anti-racist, anti-colonial, anti-patriarchal, postcolonial and decolonial scholarship, and struggles to advance justice-oriented praxis and futures. Feminist insights often inform critical climate justice scholarship and activism exposing interconnected inequities and harms. Indeed, it was at the 2007 COP where 'No climate justice without gender justice' became a rallying cry among feminist climate activists and social movements. Further, women, particularly young women, have been at the forefront of climate justice movements around the world. Feminist scholars and activists have raised awareness of the importance of paying attention to the differential gendered burdens and harms worldwide. They have also shown that increased intersectional gendered marginalization, inequality and vulnerability result from climate change.

However, feminist analysis of climate justice extends beyond gender considerations to address colonialism, capitalism and racism. Structural inequalities and power relations inherent in capitalism and heteropatriarchy manifest across various levels – household, community, state and internationally. A scalar analysis incorporating feminist insights reveals both barriers and opportunities in configuring climate justice pathways. Anti-racist, anti-capitalist, anti-patriarchal feminist praxis fosters more nuanced understandings of climate injustices and the resulting possibilities for people to cope, adapt and renew.

Advocates of feminist ethics of care and solidarity promote care and commoning over endless growth, addressing the structural inequities exacerbated by climate change (see, for example, Fraser, 2008, 2021). In the context of climate colonialism and decolonizing feminist economics, I further the conversation by advocating for radical solidarity and I propose ecoSImies of care as a critical approach that reflects contemporary awareness of how we live our lives and how to die well. This proposal emphasizes the importance of mutual care, sustainability and the recognition of interconnectedness in addressing the profound challenges posed by climate change.

Radical solidarity

'Solidarity' is a term often used in conversations about climate and social justice. However, two distinct approaches to mobilizing solidarity can be identified. One approach centres on solidarity in its radical sense – a recognition that your problem is also mine, emphasizing our shared involvement. It is crucial to underline that this does not arise from identical experiences with the threats of climate change. Instead, it signifies that I am engaged in this problem that affects both me and us. In essence, radical solidarity binds us to a situation, rendering us simultaneously singular and plural: the singular does not function as a mere component (individual parts cannot be rescued); rather, it responds for the whole (and each one, for all the others). To be in radical solidarity is, therefore, to learn to say 'we' (Garcés, 2013; Carrasco-Miró, 2025b). It is not about one fighting for the future, but fighting *with* accomplices, friends, and comrades.

In contrast, another form of solidarity emerges from the understanding that if things do not go well for you, it will have repercussions for me. This version of solidarity views the 'Other' as a potential threat, driven by fears of resource scarcity, wealth inequality, and competition for privileges. It is grounded in a rational calculation of self-interest (efficiency), often framed as mutual benefit.

These narratives are shaped by an interest in shared advantages, sometimes presented under the guise of similarity, exemplified by South–South cooperation initiatives, and a shared destiny, particularly in the pursuit of sustainable development (economic growth) (Carrasco-Miró, 2017). This type of solidarity is prevalent in economic development narratives, extending to discussions on the climate crisis such as the COP.

The UN General Assembly, for example, has adopted, for the first time, a resolution on the social and solidarity economy:

> [T]he social and solidarity economy contributes to more inclusive and sustainable economic growth by finding a new balance between economic efficiency and social and environmental resilience that fosters

> economic dynamism ... the social and solidarity economy can play a key role in eliminating poverty and catalysing social transformation, thus helping to achieve the objective of leaving no one behind and to achieve the 2030 Agenda and its Sustainable Development Goals. (UN General Assembly, 2023: 2–3)

These narratives, in fact, are not new at all. They are growth-based and continue to fail to recognize that the ecological crisis is not caused by everyone equally while employing a neutralizing rhetoric that absolves settlers of their responsibility, allowing them to continue enjoying privilege. Although the ecological crisis is a common problem, it is overwhelmingly driven by a small handful of high-income countries. Research indicates that the high-income nations of the global North bear the primary responsibility for exceeding the planetary boundary of 350ppm concentration of CO_2 in the atmosphere – essentially the emissions fuelling the climate crisis (Hickel, 2020). Collectively, the global North, encompassing the United States, Europe, Canada, Australia, New Zealand, Israel and Japan, is responsible for a staggering 92 per cent of excess emissions. In stark contrast, Africa, Asia and Latin America, hosting the majority of the global population, shoulder a mere 8 per cent of the excess emissions burden (Hickel, 2022). Notably, numerous countries in the global South, including populous nations such as India, Indonesia and Nigeria, remain well within their equitable share of the planetary boundary and have not contributed to the problem at all (Hickel, 2022). Expressions of economic 'solidarity' (or rather egoistic altruism) that largely ignore the conflict between life and capital work to exculpate, exonerate or ignore complicity in ongoing climate colonialism and racism.

Returning to the first definition of (radical) solidarity, in what way can we elaborate on the meaning of common problems? Solidarity, in its radical sense, has to do with possible reciprocities. It is precisely in this learning, this awareness, that we are part of a bond, even as unequal, that asks us to understand each other as reciprocal in a common problem. Instead of saying 'do as I do', radical solidarity extends a hand that invites 'do it *with* me'. In this sense, understanding life as premised on the relationship between *difference* and *interdependency*, rather than similarity and the rational calculation of self-interests (efficiency), defines economic solidarity in the radical sense of it. It means, therefore, recognizing that economics is itself a site for the production of difference and not simply a point of reception and mediation through which multiple cultures are brought into contact with each other. An economy based on radical solidarity sustains life and opposes expressions of solidarity that largely work to exculpate, exonerate or ignore complicity in ongoing climate colonization, colonialism, capitalism, heteropatriarchy and racism, thus deepening inequalities and reinforcing economic and social injustice. In other words, solidarity entails rejecting projects that attack life and at the same time is about the politics of (re-)imagining the future.

However, solidarity is an 'uneasy, reserved, and unsettled matter that neither reconciles present grievances nor forecloses future conflict' (Tuck and Yang, 2012: 3). But this does not mean it is unnecessary. Even amidst the incommensurability of alliances and solidarities, they can evolve into a shared arena for experimentation.[2] Contrary to being a rigid, homogeneous and tightly organized endeavour in practice, radical solidarity is inherently messy, unstable and dispersed. And yet, it holds promise for ecologically just futures.

EcoSImies of care

Creating generative, sustainable economics and alliances means casting our lives with some and not others. As the Earth heats up and as intra-human and interspecies divergences speed up, we need words that world worlds, to 'make a much hotter compost pile for still possible pasts, presents, and futures' (Haraway, 2016: 57). As Donna Haraway (2016) has stated, it matters what thoughts, knowledge or stories are marshalled to theorize and transform a profoundly damaged world. Words play a significant role in shaping specific political outcomes and new economic imaginaries.

In this context, I have proposed elsewhere ecoSImies of care (Carrasco-Miró, 2017) to suggest economic emancipatory possibilities in times of extractivist and productivist logic. EcoSImies of care are not meant to be a recipe for economic policies, but rather a path to open our economic perspective and imagination and think economics while identifying and freeing ourselves from the destructive extractivist, colonialist, heteropatriarchal, authoritarian, anthropocentric and abstract burden that permeates current global economy and its economic theories. EcoSImies of care ask how to collectively envision emancipatory, radical solidarity, sustainable economies in the mist of climate colonialism. In that sense, it contributes to decolonizing economic knowledge and pushes the transition from an extractive economy to a more generative and imaginative sustainable economic paradigm.

I owe the term ecoSImies in its Spanish version (*ecoSImias*) to Miguel Guaira Calapy, an Indigenous leader from Cotacachi, Ecuador. He proposed '*ecoSImias*' as a term, an analytical category, and a potential tool to conceptualize and explore subaltern knowledges (referenced in the book *Posibles y Plurales. Analíticas para no perder el acontecimiento* by Olver Quijano Valencia [2008]) and economies. The term's significance is linked to a popular etymology that interprets ecoNOmy as the negation of what is mine and/or what is ours, emphasizing that not only capitalism but all forms of ecoNOmy involve accumulation by dispossession. In this context, *ecoSImias* refer to processes of (re)appropriation from the global South – along with numerous and meaningful vital exchanges facilitated through various forms of cooperation that are situated and contextual. This approach encourages dialogue through difference, singularity and heterogeneity (Quijano Valencia, 2008, 2016).

Drawing from this, ecoSImies of care are a concept that opens a communitarian dimension of autonomy, radical solidarity and collective self-organization that expands alternatives for thinking about the feminist politics of care. It shows the radical affirmation that we, all humans, are already interdependent and ecodependent, and situates 'taking care of life' at the very centre of the economy and economics. The fundamental question posed here is: what kind of life do we aspire to live together, acknowledging that life is inherently life in common and our existence is inseparable from a living and non-living environment? In this context, ecoSImies of care act from the awareness that living is not survival, but that life brings into play a common sense of dignity. By taking seriously this radical affirmation of our lives, economy and economics only makes sense from the sustainability of life (that is, taking care of our vulnerabilities, managing inter-ecodependence, inhabiting a living surrounding, understanding land as a place where beings live, and imagining possible futures), which is in direct antagonism with the extractivist and productivist colonial ideal where life is under attack (ecoNOmy).

However, it's important to clarify what ecoSImies of care do not imply. Firstly, they do not refer to ideological, gender, ethnic or racial plurality; nor do they refer to the incorporation or inclusion of marked differences into a multicultural economics. Secondly, they are not an issue of reporting differences among contexts ('case studies') that present people facing similar 'economic' situations and behaving more or less the same – thus, confirming already defined (Western modernist) universals or cultural dogmas. Thirdly, ecoSImies of care do not mean Indigenous. They are about the sustainability of life (Eco) and life in common (SImia of care), knowing that, in each notion of ecoSImy, there is a notion of good life. As such, they seek to redefine economics from a framework that views it solely as power struggles within a singular world (ecoNOmy) to one that acknowledges the potential for cooperative relationships across diverse worlds (ecoSImies of care).

By so doing, it questions the *Homo economicus* and growth as the basic units of economic analysis contesting everything that seems self-evident, unified, present and inescapable and force the epistemological and ontological pluralization of economies. EcoSImies of care allow us to encounter among ourselves, embrace, transform, decolonize and create meaning, fostering connections and radical solidarities that do not eradicate the unfamiliar but welcomes it. In that sense, ecoSImies of care is the reconfiguration of the economics as a feminist decolonizing reaction to the violence of the expansionist universalist logic of extractivism and productivism, its pedagogies of cruelty and climate colonialism. EcoSImies of care are, therefore, about the re-existence and resistance of currently devalued and silenced economies based on the sustainability of life. As such, they aim to account for economic difference affirming the epistemic rights of the racially devaluated 'Other' cultures or non-economies – that is, diverse modes of social and material organization with diverse forms of subjectification that enunciate fundamentally different, yet always entangled, worlds.

In ecoSImies of care, sustainability does not equal growth nor slowness and durability; it tells the story of how everything we do around the world is interconnected here and now. As shown in *Deep Weather* (2013), how the Western lifestyle, known to have an effect on climate disruption (see Klein, 2014), also has an impact on Bangladeshi communities (see Figure 5.2). A way of thinking about sustainable economies through ecoSImies of care, then, is to generate images that do not exhaust the possibilities of others by fixing them in a place when their potential for a fuller life is likely to be realized in a distant country.

Therefore, ecoSImies of care challenge the conventional notion of wealth, aiming to liberate the richness of the world: What holds value in this shared space where we all exist and eventually pass away? Situated concepts of value and living well, such as *suma qamaña* in Bolivia, *sumak kawsay* or *buen vivir* in Ecuador, *Ubuntu* in South Africa or *vida digna* in Spain, are economic epistemologies capable of inspiring another way of being and being in the world, contributing to the global debate about environmental sustainability and which kind of economies do we want to support that.

As follows, I suggest three workable emancipatory criteria of ecoSImies of care: an ecocentric approach, uncertainty and dialogue, and not-knowing to facilitate economic analysis and action in contemporary economies and solidarities.

Ecocentric worldview

An ecocentric approach in ecoSImies of care places nature and the environment at the centre of economic decision-making and evaluations of planetary well-being. Unlike anthropocentrism, which prioritizes human interests and needs above all else, this worldview emphasizes the intrinsic value of nature and the interconnectedness of all living and not-living beings and ecosystems. Under this criterion, economic strategies and 'solidarities' that exploit the generative powers of women, racialized people, Indigenous peoples, animals, plants, genes and cells, or support countries in exporting food when that same country suffers from malnutrition, are enacting violence.

Ecocentrism encourages long-term economic planning and decision-making that consider the potential consequences of actions on the environment over extended periods, rather than focusing solely on short-term gains. Thinking ecoSImies of care under this principle helps us shift away from the extractivist goal of material affluence, which rejects and attacks life, and allows us to decentre extractivist and productivist logic (ecoNOmy).

This shift enables us to enunciate the diverse existing ecoSImies of care (beyond markets, the state and households) that sustain and care for life in common, and thus envision possible just futures.

Ecocentrism, however, is not new. As a worldview it has been with humanity since we evolved. Many Indigenous cultures reflect an ecocentric view of the world. At the international level, significant recognition of ecocentric principles has been evident. For instance, the visionary Earth Charter of 2000 prominently advocated for an ecocentric worldview, emphasizing in Principle 1a the importance to '[r]ecognize that all beings are interdependent and every form of life has value regardless of its worth to human beings'. In 2008, Ecuador enshrined Rights for Nature as a part of its new Constitution. In 2010 Bolivia also passed the Law of the Rights of Mother Earth. In contrast, the current UN Sustainable Development Goals and its 2030 Development Agenda failed to mention ecocentrism, the intrinsic value of nature, acknowledge the rights of nature or include Indigenous peoples and their knowledge. Victoria Tauli-Corpuz (2015: np), UN Special Rapporteur on the Rights of Indigenous Peoples from 2014 to 2020, has claimed that 'Indigenous Peoples have been all but erased from the [2030] development agenda'. These erasures raise concerns about the adequacy of these international initiatives to address the urgent environmental challenges facing our planet.

Fostering a supportive ecocentric worldview in ecoSImies of care means bridging Indigenous knowledge systems and scientific knowledge that objectively suits and furthers Indigenous struggles and futures. Symbolically, and by all means also in actuality, 'the Indigenous Scientist plays a leading role in this paradigm shift' (Biemann, 2022: 1). The Indigenous scientist emerges from a shared history of colonial conquest and Western modern natural science, studying the natural world while being part of it. Most importantly, this figure stands for a different kind of economic epistemology that reconnects us to other ways of knowing and understanding the human–nature symbioses and whose rationale has been a major driver in the current ecological crisis.

Uncertainty and dialogue

Economics has long sought to control and mitigate uncertainty through equilibrium formulations aimed at coordinating atomistic agent behaviour. Yet, we inhabit a world marked by the fundamental unknowability of the future. When we refer to 'uncertain times', we imply danger and threat. However, uncertainty is a ubiquitous reality – from physics, a discipline cherished by mainstream economists, to the narratives of our lives. In any condition that lacks absoluteness, human affairs are never exempt from uncertainty. Therefore, ecoSImies of care embrace uncertainty not merely in a defensive or fear-based manner but by acknowledging the possibility of interruption, which is not necessarily construed as failure.

Uncertainty is intrinsic to both the environment and human existence, and consequently, to the economy itself. Environmental systems and humans engage in non-linear relationships and are not necessarily in a state of equilibrium. They are uncertain and can be chaotic and messy. Still, uncertainty should not be viewed solely as a negative attribute that obstructs objectivity. Instead, it is an inherent quality embraced within ecoSImies of care and, for this reason, uncertainty compels us to engage in profound public discussions and critical intercultural dialogues concerning multiple economic estimations, values and perceptions (see Chapter 4).

Not knowing as an ally

Not knowing makes economics nervous. Yet, not knowing is quite the opposite of passive illiteracy. Knowledge is not accumulated against ignorance. All true knowledge involves discovering a relationship between what we know and what we do not know. Currently, when uncertainty seems to be one of the most permanent dimensions of our time, it is even more important and relevant to remember it, so that not knowing does not become a threat or fuel reactive fear. From an extractivist and productivist conception of knowledge, ignorance can only be combated or subdued, annihilated or made profitable. This binary scheme forgets two things: firstly, that what we know is full of other knowledges and other possible ways of life. And secondly, that everything we think we know is full of ignorance (that is prejudices, secrets, hidden interests, and so on). Knowledge and ignorance, thus, must be understood as an alliance.

In that sense, embracing not knowing in ecoSImies of care becomes a counter-hegemonic gesture, an act of disobedience against an ecoNOmic logic that seeks to control and provide self-explanatory answers and 'solutions'. Knowledge is precisely the awareness that what we know has limits. If knowledge has boundaries, it is because there is no object of knowledge that suffices in itself, nor any established science that can explain everything definitively. That is why economic knowledge in ecoSImies of care is an invitation to continue imagining and creating together new notions, perceptions and representations of the world and ourselves of what life we want to live, what economies we want, incorporating plural knowledges, radical solidarities, (anti-)disciplines and imaginations for possible futures. We need, therefore, economies oriented towards providing the conditions so that different knowledge and existences can be incorporated into a common, yet not unique, world.

Sí al Yasuní

The Yasuní region in the Ecuadorian Amazon has a rich history of biodiversity, recognized globally for its unparalleled ecological significance. Designated as a National Park in 1979 and later as a World Biosphere Reserve, Yasuní is celebrated for its astonishing variety of plant and insect species. Home to the Waorani people and other Indigenous groups, Yasuní's conservation has been deeply rooted in ancestral practices passed down through generations.

Despite decades of protection efforts, Yasuní faces threats from extractive projects driven by Ecuador's substantial external debt, notably owed to China. In 2020, Petroamazonas EP awarded a contract to expand oil wells in Yasuní, prompting the YaSunidos collective to call for a national consultation. The question posted to citizens was: *Do you agree with the Ecuadorian government keeping the ITT [Ishpingo-Tambococha-Tiputini], known as Block 43, crude oil indefinitely in the subsoil?* Despite repression tactics, the collective, with support from youth groups, rallied Ecuadorians nationwide, garnering over 757,000 signatures in a remarkable display of public engagement. In August 2023, the Constitutional Court of Ecuador approved the Yasuní Popular Consultation, marking a historic victory for the 'Sí al Yasuní' (Yes to Yasuní) movement – the first instance of a community voting to preserve oil reserves underground without exploitation. Ecuador said 'Yes' to life, to its economic sovereignty, embracing a different economy, envisioning better futures for all. This victory was not only for Ecuador but for the world, fighting against extractivism violence and climate change.

The campaign, led by Indigenous peoples, women and youth, represents a collective effort to prioritize life over economic interests. Amidst ongoing debates about Ecuador's social and economic future, the 'Sí' campaign stands as a beacon of hope for climate change mitigation. Indigenous women, given the disproportionate impact of extractive activities on them, have played a pivotal role in the resistance against oil exploitation in Ecuador, highlighting the importance of their voices in shaping environmental policies and futures. Their daily struggles in the region are crucial to this resistance, as they combat increased health risks and the fragmentation of social fabric caused by oil exploitation.

Zenaida Yasacama, from the Confederation of Indigenous Nationalities of Ecuador, stresses the significance of intersectionality and emphasizes the importance of having created networks with various social organizations and groups in the region, demonstrating the need for radical solidarity between different social struggles to act for climate justice and collective care. She states (Di Paula López et al, 2023: np; translation mine): 'There have been young people, women, academics, and individuals from different sectors, social and different associations, such as women's fronts and others such as students, but the most important thing about this campaign has been that women and youth have been at the forefront of all this.'

As Ecuador faces scrutiny from the Inter-American Court of Human Rights for alleged violations against Indigenous peoples in Yasuní, activists remain committed to defending the referendum's outcome and ensuring its implementation – the cessation of oil extraction from Yasuní National Park. If a low-income country such as Ecuador can do this, how can countries like the United States, United Kingdom, Canada or Australia justify their own plans for new fossil fuel extraction?

Zeneida Yasacama goes beyond the specific problems of Yasuní, taking this as a starting point since 'it is about having a different world, a world that heals our wounds' (Di Paula López et al, 2023: np; translation mine). The Sí al Yasuní movement challenges the extractivist logic of traditional economic models, advocating for a paradigm shift towards radical solidarity and the criteria of ecoSImies of care. By placing the sustainability of life at the centre of their activism, the movement echoes the Colectivo Miradas Críticas del Territorio desde el Feminismo (2014): life at the centre and oil underground.

PART III

7

What Kind of Economies Do We Want?

A little bit of impossible or I will suffocate.

Espai en Blanc, *Pressentiment No. 41* (2015)

Introduction: A little bit of impossible

If contemporary economics wants to regain its civic voice, it must find a way to discuss issues we have forgotten how to raise.[1] When we talk, think or teach about economics, we normally do so about two issues: progress or the distribution of the national product. For instance, in feminist economics, when discussing economic care policies or budgets, we often argue that they will either increase part of the economic pie or distribute part of the pieces of that pie more equitably between men and women. However, this was not always the case. Historical economic debates from different times and places show us that we can ask different questions. In particular, we can ask ourselves how we want to live and what kinds of economies we want, without always having to consider whether the national income is growing or how it is being distributed. We can imagine alternative economic systems. We can imagine just futures.

As we have discussed in earlier chapters, the economy is not some abstract concept removed from our daily lives. It is a very real part of our day-to-day existence. That idea of the economy as an abstract and complicated system far removed from life that many economics courses project, makes us powerless and see economic problems as disproportionate, as if this had nothing to do with us. But it has to do with us. It is, therefore, crucial that we take the economy back into our hands and make it more democratic. We should be able to talk about it, understand it, discern, value and decide together what kinds of economies we want to create to shape just futures. So, what kinds of economies do we want? This is not a naive or utopian question, but an emancipatory one. It reminds us that we urgently need to take the economy back (out of the clouds), making it just, democratic, dignified and sustainable. These are not more perfect or ideal economies, but rather economies that open possibilities of thought, possibilities of other economies.

Questioning what we want is precisely the heart of democratic emancipation. However, when we try to envision the economies we want, many of us, even in discussions around feminist economics, often draw blanks. If we close our eyes, can we imagine an economy that is not based on capitalism? Can we picture a feminist economy that does not rely on growth? Let's be honest. Many times, when we raise these questions, we hear responses like, 'Well, we need growth, but in a fair and feminist way', or 'It is not possible without growth; we will go back to primitive times!'. The underlying idea here, though unintentional, is to make the current, unjust economic system better, even if we say we are changing it or making it more just and sustainable, because, and this is the key: we cannot image an economy otherwise.

In *Pressentiment No. 41* of the Catalan Collective, Espai en Blanc, in the epigraph to this chapter, when they allude to the 'impossible', their intent is not to advocate for some unattainable utopia. Rather, they beckon us to acknowledge that the prison in which we feel ensnared – an unjust, heteropatriarchal, unsustainable economic system bereft of alternatives – is, in fact, an open cell. It is we who cling to the bars, believing ourselves to be condemned to choose from a world devoid of alternatives. While there may be various options inside this prison (more distributive, with a gender perspective and so on) the core belief remains that we are unable to fathom economic alternative possibilities. This chapter is an invitation to think about what economies we want to live and suggests imagination as an urgent and necessary economic faculty that, in an emancipatory way, opens our eyes to see possible just futures.

In the face of paralysis, we can imagine

In times of profound societal upheaval, marked by a multitude of crises, such as health, economic, social and environmental, our capacity for imagination can also waver. The difficulty of envisioning possible better futures, especially when we perceive the future as a scarce commodity (a viewpoint often reinforced in narratives of competition and dispute for the future, as explained in Douglas Rushkoff's book, *Survival of the Richest: Escape Fantasies of the Tech Billionaires* [2022]), can lead us down the path of what Marina Garcés (2017) aptly terms the apocalypse/salvation code – a familiar feature of the prevailing economic discourse. As discussed in the Introduction of this book, the apocalypse future narrative portrays a bleak outlook characterized by ideas like 'this is our end', 'it is what it is' and 'sorry, things work out this way'. Conversely, the salvation (or solutionism) reduces the complexities of the world to techno-economic problems that seemingly demand swift, efficient resolutions, often fixated on the idea that technology will save our economies – yet, for who? This apocalypse–salvation dichotomy stifles our imagination by construing any limit as an ultimate: an end as a catastrophe or an end as a solution or salvation.

This paradigm of thinking fosters opportunism within an economic system of domination, one that is colonialist, capitalist, heteropatriarchal and exercises ecological devastation, where the best response for the citizens is to adapt to these precarious, unjust and unsatisfactory living conditions. Thus, promoting an economy that devalues life and leaves us with no recourse but to conform. This acceptance of an impossible and unsustainable world has become pervasive, and it implies that we are alive but we have embraced the irreversibility of an end, accepting the impossibility of a different economy, a better world.

This apocalyptic context is no longer defined by a singular narrative of progress, as in Western-centric modernity, which has faced substantial critique from postcolonial and decolonial thought. Instead, we are ensnared in a narrative of destruction of life (Mbembe, 2019). The apocalypse–salvation discourse is presented as the exclusive historical perspective, a narrative that imposes itself as an unquestionable dogma (Garcés, 2017). Within this dogma, there are those who suffer as victims and those who benefit. We have, unfortunately, come to see ourselves as destroyers, pinning our hopes on the very technology we have created to save us, often because we have convinced ourselves that we lack the ability to do so. Under this decree, there is no room for an alternative experience of the economy. This fascination with the apocalypse perpetuates a sense of helplessness, combined with an inability to intervene in the economic conditions of our own lives. This leads us back to the question at the beginning of this book: is it not this very surrender that pushes our species to the brink of sustainability?

On closer examination of these adaptive or solutionist economic proposals, we often find behind them investors (banks and investment firms), leading the charge to privatize common resources and creating new opportunities for a select few. This portrayal of an economy as unique, which benefits only a minority, comes at the cost of fear, anxiety and the precariousness of our lives. Ailton Krenak (2019) expressed a relevant perspective in this context: we must summon the courage to be fully alive and not constantly negotiate our survival. Human life does not sustain itself; it requires deliberate effort to be sustained. Hence, human life is not a certainty but a possibility. As we have emphasized throughout this book, the economy must prioritize *intentionally* sustaining life.

How do we steer clear of apocalyptic thinking? Is another kind of economy feasible? How can we escape the collapse engendered by this sense of powerlessness and impotence? In the face of paralysis, we can imagine.

Ecologies of the feminist economic imagination

Imagination breaks the apocalypse/salvation code to open up possible just futures. Imagination, as understood here, far from being an individual treat, operates as a social practice, therefore also economic, creating relationships of meaning (Garcés, 2022). It defies a passive acceptance of the status quo (administration of what is given to us) by propelling us to explore alternative economic thinking. In times of crisis, we must ask new questions again. Can imagination become a tool for economic transformation, fostering trust and resilience in the face of growing crises and isolation?

Imagination is a radically political faculty, inviting us to engage with the world rather than escape from it. Iris Murdoch (1993), an Irish novelist and philosopher, distinguishes between fantasy and imagination. She contends that imaginative thinking allows one's internal image of the world to evolve through encounters with reality. In contrast, fantasy constructs a perspective that wishes the world to be different from what it actually is. Imagination, thus, operates within the boundaries of reality, in the present, as a thought experiment rather than a prophetic vision, as the American feminist science fiction writer Ursula K. Le Guin (2004) would tell us, while fantasy, on the other hand, dwells in the realm of the unreal. Fantasy thrives among those who embrace the allure of a technological panacea (techno-utopia) with excessive optimism, or who are ensnared by the dream of boundless economic growth. Giorgos Kallis (2019) asserts that the prevailing economic model is steeped in the fantasy of invincibility and boundlessness. It perpetuates the idea of a hero, concealing a deep-seated dread of mortality – a characteristic often ingrained in Western thinking. In stark contrast, an imaginative perspective assesses actions and behavioural patterns in relation to their impact on the larger interconnected whole.

Referring to imagination as an 'art', is not to reduce it to mere aesthetics, as the narrow notion of imagination being solely linked to creativity tends to do. Rather, it underscores that imagination is a dynamic activity intertwined with knowledge and meaning, creating new contexts and possibilities (Garcés, 2022). In *The Domain of the Marvelous*, Suzanne Césaire (1941 [2001]: 157) writes:

> No longer is it a matter of the narrow roads … in its clarity and obviousness. … Now it is a question of seizing and admiring … which leaves humankind in its true condition, fragile and dependent, and which nevertheless, in the very spectacle of things ignored or silenced, opens unsuspected possibilities.

Murdoch, as Césaire, asserts that imagination involves reflecting upon people and events, imbuing them with details, infusing colours, and contemplating (unsuspected) possibilities beyond mere facts. Imagination, therefore, is not a spontaneous, isolated force; it is an art of interconnectedness, a practice that navigates the blurry boundaries between what we know and what remains unknown (ignored or silenced), between what we recognize and what lies beyond our recognition, between what exists and what does not. It is an emancipatory practice that can be learned and shared.

Any form of critique today involves thinking about the limits of reality, about what prevents us from thinking about it in any other way or only at the risk of its destruction. To use the imagination in an economic transformative way is, therefore, to situate our concepts, analyses and experiences in what opens (and not in what closes) at these limits. Gayatri C. Spivak (2013) emphasizes the need to train our imagination to shape knowledge and reconfigure desires. This notion of preparation, of getting ready to know and desire, is a compelling one. Is it not precisely what we disrupt when we cease to imagine alternative economies?

Imagination, at its core, is desire – a powerful impulse of attention, intention and yearning for what does not yet exist. To re-signify our economic landscape, we must evoke desire. Longing for another non-fantasy economy opens up the reality of a dispute in a concrete way, how do we want to live? Against the apocalypse and the neoliberal concept of life, can we foster economies rooted in desire? In which ways can economics be reconjugated in new grammars of desire and imagination, as well as responsibility?

In light of this, I define imagination through five interconnected characteristics that can help understand its essential role for economic thought. I also provide concrete examples from post-capitalist movements that envision better futures, exploring post-work futures, post-development futures and post-growth futures, and challenge the very notion of what an economy is.

Imagination is bringing the absent into the present

Imagination involves a dynamic engagement with what is not immediately visible, encompassing both its boundaries and potentials. It serves as a crucible for thought experimentation, connecting elements that thinking often separates: the present and the absent, the sensory and the intellectual, the internal and the external, the possible and the impossible. Imagination is not an isolated, spontaneous or vacuous faculty; rather, it represents a means of constructing our relationship with the constraints of what we observe, comprehend, recall and envision within the world we inhabit.

Whether manifesting in art, science, politics, economics or everyday decision-making, imagination traverses temporal dimensions, disciplines, individuals and diverse aspects of economic, social and cultural life. It is an interconnected endeavour, functioning like an ecosystem – a living system that can be disrupted and impaired or enhanced and nurtured.

For instance, in *After Work*, Helen Hester and Nick Srnicek (2022) imagine a post-capitalist future and propose scenarios for post-work societies. They challenge us to think critically and imagine beyond the current capitalist and welfare-state paradigms centred on paid labour and de-labourify care work, which disproportionately affects women and racialized people.

Their vision includes a post-scarcity world where the necessity of selling one's labour to survive no longer exists. This is not about excess consumer goods but rather about liberating individuals from the compulsion to work. They propose a feminist reimagining of work that is not confined to isolated nuclear families or unrealistic work–life balances. Instead, they advocate for expanding our freedoms by liberating time to do autonomously chosen activities as much as possible and creating institutions that allow us to collectively shape our human development.

The authors draw on the insights of historical anti-housework thinkers and post-autonomist Marxism and, from what is absent, imagine a society where everyone has genuine free time to pursue their passions or simply do nothing at all – while still living well. Achieving this vision, they argue, requires rethinking our living arrangements, societal expectations and urban designs. Contemporary feminist post-work imaginaries offer practical responses to the impending decline of job-centric cultures; imagining possibilities that opened up when we no longer centre our lives and societies around paid labour.

Imagination involves navigating the unfamiliar

Eiman Osman Zein-Elabdin and S. Charusheela (2004: 2–3) state that '[e]conomics can … be soundly characterized as a colonial discourse grounded in exclusion and erasure of the unfamiliar'. Imagination, however, has at its core the power of the unfamiliar (Garcés, 2022). It encourages us to engage with what we do not fully recognize or understand, fostering connections that transcend mere economic considerations.

This means that when we critically use our imagination in economics, we must be willing to become strangers among strangers, existing without needing permission and without facing erasure. The unfamiliar allows us to connect within a common world and time, creating links without closing off possibilities. Our market-driven consumer culture conditions us to see others as interchangeable, with differences that do not truly affect or transform us. Embracing the unfamiliar, however, opens up the possibility for new relationships and economic transformations that leave us changed.

The Kichwa concept of *sumak kawsay* or *buen vivir* ('living well') has become a cornerstone of post-development thought, representing an unfamiliar way of imagining development, including as an alternative to it. It emphasizes the resurgence of Indigenous peoples and the integration of socio-productive models with local territories and cultures. Ontologically, *buen vivir* does not view progress in the familiar linear terms; there is no notion of moving from 'underdevelopment' to 'developed' as in the core of development theory. Instead, it advocates for a way of life that ensures justice for individuals within the context of community and environmental well-being. This includes promoting non-capitalist property relations where individuals act as stewards of the land and resources, using them with community permission rather than owning them, thus breaking away from colonial private property economic frameworks promoted in mainstream development (Acosta, 2013). It is important to note that the complexity of *sumak kawsay* continues to spark theoretical and practical debates and contradictions, importantly feminist ones, making it a dynamic and evolving imaginary rather than a static or exotic one.

Imagination is a condition of suspicion and an activity of comprehension

Imagination serves both as a critical lens for suspicion and as an essential component of understanding. Contemporary mainstream economic thought has been limited by an uncritical reliance on mathematics and the assumption that we are all rational and completely free. It is crucial to challenge these assumptions.

In the context of feminist post-work proposals and the concept of *sumak kawsay*, economic imagination operates as a state of suspicion, questioning rationality and common-sense notions of 'work' and 'development'. However, imagination is not merely a tool for scepticism. As previously discussed, it is also an exercise in vision (post-work; '*buen vivir*') and, therefore, an exercise in comprehension. In fact, imagination is a prerequisite for understanding and a fundamental aspect of all forms of dialogue, including economic discourse.

It is important to clarify that comprehension does not imply blind acceptance. Rather, it means acknowledging and understanding different perspectives without necessarily agreeing with all aspects (essentially, 'I understand because I do not accept everything').

Imagination helps us build bridges to bring closer that which is far away

Imagination is a tool for fostering connections rather than merely producing outcomes. Without imagination, we are confined to 'the narrow roads … in its clarity and obviousness. …' (Césaire, 1941 [2001]: 157) – that is to immediacy, verification and mere administration, lacking the potential for emancipation. Emancipatory imagination serves as the architect of bridges. This economic imagination must be considered alongside its historical contexts, including colonial, heteropatriarchal, postcolonial, extractive and developmentalist histories. It seeks to link rather than unify, allowing for economic diversity and difference instead of forcing everything into a single paradigm. Economic imagination prompts new questions rather than offering definitive answers. It serves as a condition of possibility, charting a course for what can be experienced and realized. Consequently, economic imagination stands as a horizon of significance, deeply entwined with the past, present and future.

In this sense, post-growth or degrowth projects and movements help us to imagine a good life beyond growth, bridging different temporalities and envisioning just futures. Degrowth is a radical project aimed at economic and socio-ecological transformation, advocating for the decolonization of the social imagination from capitalism's relentless pursuit of growth (Kallis, 2019). It is a subversive imaginary that bridges the past into the future and creates the present by making a novel case for limits, acknowledging that scarcity is socially produced, and embracing conflict as a constitutive element. Degrowth does not envisage a return to the past but mobilizes elements of the past to critique the capitalist present, highlighting latent non-capitalist practices such as gift economies, barter markets and urban commons. These practices, degrowthers argue, carry the seeds for a different future (D'Alisa et al, 2014). A future that is not simply the opposite of growth; rather possible futures that, by confronting growth, open up new imaginaries, spaces and key concepts.

To imagine is to create separation from that which is too close and prevents us from thinking

When we have been asked throughout the book what kind of economies we want, we see that in order to question what we want we cannot separate the dimensions of the question itself. Imagination, however, operates differently; it introduces separation, a space of 'in-between' that both connects and detaches us. It fosters relationships among us without advocating for unification (an economic dogma), instead encouraging a multitude of perspectives without being relativist (ecoSImies of care). Imagination, as Hannah Arendt (2006 [1961]) suggests, allows us to establish a certain distance from things, even those that are too close to us. Fina Birulés (2023) highlights the importance of imagination for thinking and explains that only when we can imagine that the situation could be different, can we then categorize it as unjust. Imagination allows us, therefore, to take a position and be critical, to propose new economic scenarios, new narratives. If we always repeat the same patterns, we lose that capacity. And we survive with more of the same. That is, for problems caused by growth-based capitalism we continue to recommend growth in the global North and capitalist solutions everywhere. Is it not absurd to recommend more of what harms us?

Postcolonial and decolonial thought tells us that the world is as diverse as the knowledge it contains. Therefore, the Western view, and specifically the dominant capitalist economic model, represents just one of the many ways we can (dis)organize and (not)sustain our lives materially. There exist, and have existed, alternative approaches, many of which resist the prevailing growth settler colonialist economic model that threatens life. Creating distance from that which suffocates us, as indicated by Espai en Blanc's *Pressentiment*, allows us to think the unthinkable (the end of work, the end of 'development', the end of growth-based economies). It also grants us a broader vision, a necessary condition for representative and critical economic thinking to be just, since it takes into account other possibilities of looking at the economy from other angles and that inserts us into a common world. It opens doors to analytical spaces that uncover economic realities that are 'surprising' due to their novelty or the fact that they have been overlooked, silenced or rendered invisible by the current hegemonic economic model. It allows us, therefore, to identify and value other economies that are not governed by capitalism (or the pursuit of economic growth) and are often relegated to labels like underdeveloped, global South, idealist, utopian or primitive.

There are economies whose conception of a good life or economic prosperity is not, for example, contingent on labour market entry or material accumulation. Instead, these economies are founded on values of reciprocity and sustainability. What do we truly know about them? Are we willing to learn from them? Take them seriously? Or do we simply believe that an economy must be rooted in ecocide, individualism and competition? Economic imagination guides us in dispelling the illusion of a universally applicable economic model and assists us in redefining the economy as ecoSImies of care, the space where we collectively craft potential meanings of a good life together and shared futures. This process allows for the creation of alternative itineraries rooted in dissent.

This separation that the imagination allows us does not imply throwing away everything done in the West, but rather being able to discern, now from a broader panorama of possibilities, which economies we want and which ones harm us. Which imaginaries oppress us and which ones do not. It allows us, as we have said at the beginning of this chapter, to take a position on what we want and what we do not want in our economies. Imagination, therefore, puts distance with reality (not to deny reality, but to gain perspective), allowing us to uphold our commitment to that which is contingent, and that therefore depends on us: the economy can be different.

Living well together

How can we live well without shifting the costs of our way of living onto others, the Earth or future generations? This is perhaps one of the most radical and urgent political questions that can be posed today from an economic perspective. Living well involves having dignified lives, but there is no dignity when it involves treating others unfairly. In this sense, what constitutes a dignified life today? What does it entail to fight for a dignified life and make it possible? There are many national, regional and international legal frameworks that appeal to dignity through the rights of citizens and the safeguarding of human rights, which recognize us as free and equal. However, there are other answers that do not require us to rely solely on the logic of rights.

A dignified life is one that is not characterized by fear. Not specific fears, but the kind of fear that makes us lose control of our lives and fall into impotence and indifference. An undignified life is, therefore, a present without a future. Instead of turning this idea into a self-help proclamation or positive thinking, it is essential to deeply consider how we define, sustain and defend a dignified life when we feel overwhelmed by the lack of a future to extract its implications. In this regard, economic thought must inquire about how to guarantee material life and dignified subsistence without diminishing life.

A dignified life is a life rich in some sense. Can it be called living asked de La Boétie in *The Discourse of Voluntary Servitude* (1577) in the 16th century about the meaning of life? The question arises from astonishment, from the normalization of the misery and suffering of the majority of human lives under the regime of oppression and servitude. The question, directed at each of us, continues to challenge us today and sparks the desire to contemplate if a better life is possible. Because human life, in its self-reflection and self-constitution, contains something that goes beyond mere survival – the coverage of basic vital needs, which is, of course, a necessary condition for everything else but not sufficient. Alongside de La Boétie, we can say that yes, it is possible and indeed the most desirable. Therefore, a dignified life is not about ensuring the survival of the Earth or of human beings – as emphasized today under the hegemonic discourse of sustainability – and thus concealing the violent system itself. A dignified life is a liveable life, a life that does not break us. Life, as Ailton Krenak (2019) reminds us, holds infinite possibilities, and mere survival, death and relationships of domination are just one of them. In my opinion, the least interesting.

A dignified life can be shared in many ways that are not undignified, precarious or servile. This sharing of dignity can span from individual to collective actions. However, it is evident that we are currently experiencing a significant loss of what we have personally and collectively generated and accumulated in recent decades. The question arises: How can we reclaim our richness? It is not about dividing the spoils but understanding that the value of life is at stake here. A value that cannot be appropriated. From land expropriations to housing struggles and the protection of our data: Who assigns value of our lives and with what consequences? Do we ourselves assign value through the specific circumstances and contexts we create, or do we allow our worth to be assessed by abstract entities such as algorithms? In this context, the challenge is not a moral crisis, as often portrayed; rather, it is a conflict between richness and profitability (Garcés, 2017). In 2023, demonstrations against the development of three infrastructures that unlocked the budgets of the Generalitat of Catalonia in Spain were marked by three banners declaring: 'No to the expansion of the airport'; 'No to the Fourth Belt'; and 'Let's not play, let's stop Hard Rock'. The overarching motto was *We defend the land, we build the future.* The manifesto read loud and clear: 'All this does not generate wealth; it only brings benefits to brick-and-mortar entrepreneurs, tourism, casinos, commerce, and real estate speculators' (Marinas, 2023).

Thus, if the economy is to help us affirm our dignity and that of the planet, what economic knowledge and practices are necessary today to develop and share for a sustainable planet and dignified lives for all? To approach this foundational question for critical economic thought today, I present and analyse as follows three movements, both academic and social, which are interconnected to some extent. I further suggest how decolonizing feminist economics can enhance them. These movements hold the radical idea that we can no longer expect a dignified life from capitalism, and therefore, from the imperative of economic growth, only the privilege of a few, and propose possible just futures.

These movements further confront economic and socio-environmental injustices ingrained in patriarchal colonial capitalist dominance and ecological degradation. They do so from situated perspectives that consider the challenges common to the global North and global South, fostering radical solidarity and sustainability. They propose paths of sovereignty, autonomy, liberation and degrowth to organize life in common. In their economic proposals, a dignified life takes on specific forms in various contemporary life contexts and, therefore, in our imaginaries of the future. The following analysis also aims to provide a decolonizing feminist economics reflection for future research and collective action.

The post-extractivist future must be anti-patriarchal

In academic circles, post-extractivism has been associated with the struggles against extractivism in Latin America over the past 20 years and has paved the way for new ethics of life and coexistence. In broad strokes, it has been defined as a critique of the ecological limits of the Earth and offers a critical diagnosis of current extractivist capitalism, not only in terms of economic and cultural crises but also in more global terms, understood as a 'socio-ecological crisis of civilizational scope' (Svampa, 2017: 9; see also Gudynas, 2011; Acosta and Brand, 2017). It points to the deep roots in the process of colonization and the subsequent structuring of criollo elites in the global South. Post-extractivism aims to envision new horizons of change and civilization, different from the economic rationality driving the commodification of life. However, I agree with Ivette Vallejo (in Acosta and Brand, 2017) that current post-extractivist discourse lacks transformative dialogues (not just mentions) with the theoretical contributions, experiences and concrete struggles of feminist/anti-patriarchal Indigenous leaders, activists, thinkers and academics from communitarian feminisms, decolonial feminisms and ecofeminisms in Latin America, and beyond.

Much research, within and beyond Latin America, is nourishing feminist/anti-patriarchal critiques of extractivism and the proposal of post-extractive, anti-patriarchal/feminist futures. For example, in Bolivia, Silvia Rivera Cusicanqui (2017) has detailed the conflict against the construction of the road through the Territory and Isiboro-Sécure National Park as a key aspect of women's territorial defence against the extractivist turn in the government of the Movement for Socialism. In sub-Saharan Africa, WoMin (2020) has analysed the impacts of industrial-scale mining on the land rights and food sovereignty of peasant women and their families in the region. In Chile, several analysis suggest that women resist being treated, in terms of body-territory, as sacrifice zones in the Puchuncaví and Quintero areas (Bolados García and Sánchez Cuevas, 2017). Raul Holz and Paulina Pavez (2022: 29) show the 'distinctive violent impacts', including economic violence, on racialized women in Indonesia and Colombia. In Peru, extractivism as a biopolitical project is presented as rooted in mining activity and entwined with patriarchy and gender discrimination (Silva Santisteban, 2017). Moreover, there is a significant feminist collective production of manifestos and declarations from gatherings that systematize different extractivist situations around the world, update ongoing conflicts and propose alternative imaginaries. An example is the periodic communication from the Organization of Peasant and Indigenous Women (Conamuri) in Paraguay, the African Women Unite Against Destructive Resource Extraction (WoMin), the Escuela Mujer y Minería in Colombia or 'The compost engineers and sus *saberes lentos*: a manifest for regenerative technologies' (Varon and Egaña Rojas, 2024), to just mention a few.

Post-extractive feminist approaches examine extractive violence in its physical, economic, technological and epistemic forms through a *simultaneous* critique of racism, capitalism, colonialism, patriarchy and environmental degradation through struggles that seek the recovery of women's bodies-territories, as the foundation for defending land against various forms of extractivism (mining, oil, forestry, artificial intelligence, among others). These proposals reveal that extractivist capital represents a systemic organization of violence that takes various forms when it impacts racialized women, manifesting in two of the most significant sites of violence in our times: women, particularly racialized women, and nature. Some of these approaches emphasize the analysis of women's experiences specifically due to the separation within extractivism between productive and reproductive labour. In this regard, post-extractive feminisms assert that extractivism was born out of colonialism, which was not just about conquering land; it was also about taking control of women's bodies (WoMin, 2015, 2020).

Communitarian feminists such as Lorena Cabnal (2010: 23) have developed the concept of *cuerpo-territorio* (body-territory) to emphasize 'historical and oppressive violence existing for my first body territory, as well as for my historical territory, the land'. Understanding the body as an extension of the territory-land (meanings within, access to and the power/politics that determine these), as proposed by communitarian feminists, is constitutive of Indigenous women's capacities for self- and community-caring (Zaragocin and Caretta, 2021). It further recognizes their connection and interdependence: humans are not only part of nature, but more-than-human nature is inextricably linked with the social and economic relationships that occur within the territory itself.

A post-extractive feminist approach allows us to question the blurred boundaries between human and more-than-human nature resulting from extractive projects. It enables us to understand that, in advancing extractive capital's control over people and territories, oppression and threats manifest on the bodies, which, in this process, become disputed territories. The predatory occupation of territories expands to 'females and feminized bodies' that inhabit and resist in these territories, to the point that the consequences of plundering only seek 'to leave remains' (Segato, 2011: 3). Thus, the *cuerpo-territorio* is a battleground where economic, heteropatriarchal and colonial power attempts to wage the extractivist and productivist confrontation. However, women, non-normative and feminized bodies are also bodies that resist, rebuild and fight; they are bodies that gestate, give birth and regenerate human life.

The notion of *cuerpo-territorio* is both a post-extractivist feminist methodological and ontological claim as it underscores the imperative that human relationships cannot be examined differently from ecological relationships. Therefore, it allows decolonizing feminist economics to analyse economies beyond Western dualisms. In this sense, Ehuana Yaira Yanomami and Luana Pawë Yanomami (2017), Lorena Cabnal (2010, 2015), Begoña Dorronsoro (2013) and Elizabeth Sweet and Sara Ortiz Escalante (2017: 594) propose to understand physical violence against women from the unity and interconnection of the *cuerpo-territorio*; this 'helps to decenter the public-private divide, which is an important obstacle to eliminating violence against women'. Thus, *cuerpo-territorio* links women's struggles for territorial and embodied defence 'against extractivist resource exploitation with the struggle against intersectional discrimination, racism, and the historic violation of their bodies' (Habersang, 2021: 169). *Cuerpo-territorio* entails, therefore, an expansion of the existing international framework for comprehending violence against women, as put forth by multilateral organizations like the UN Committee on the Elimination of Discrimination Against Women

(CEDAW) (1993), which predominantly addresses physical, psychological and sexual violence (Holz and Pávez, 2022).

Many of the women who are fighting against extractivism, both in the global South and the global North, are confronting significant and powerful economic and political interests, placing at the forefront what is necessary to sustain life. Not only do they often lead these struggles, literally using their own bodies to stop the destruction of their territories, they have also proposed critical views on the patriarchal and racist nature of extractivism. For instance, during the Ugandan sugarcane protests, peasant women used their bodies as a tool of dissent when they exposed their breasts in front of governmental officials to protest of a land grab deal, shouting, 'If you bring sugar here, our breasts will have no milk to feed ourselves' (Martiniello 2015: 662). Another vivid example of the body as a tool for protest is the case of La Puya in Guatemala.

To reach La Puya, situated in the northern region of the Guatemalan central department, one must take the bus route heading east. Along this journey, the bus progresses and the temperature rises. This dusty path, surrounded by trees and vegetation, marks the entrance to the Progreso VII Derivado project – one of the 12 state concessions granted to exploration mining companies as part of the 'El Tambor' extraction megaproject. Initially overseen by the Canadian company Radius Explorations Ltd. and its Guatemalan subsidiary, Exploraciones Mineras de Guatemala, S.A. (Exmingua), the project has since been acquired by the North American company Kappes, Cassiday & Associates.[2] Despite this transition, the local community adjoining the mine asserts that they were never neither informed nor consulted.

The rallying cry of the La Puya Peaceful Resistance movement was the non-violent struggle for water, life and territory. This opposition began in March 2012 when the movement witnessed the passage of heavy machinery through its territory in objection to the 'El Tambor' mining project, which involves the extraction of gold and silver in the municipalities of San José del Golfo and San Pedro Ayampuc. The resistance was initiated by a woman, Estela Reyes, who confronted the machinery, challenging subjugation with her life. On 8 May of the same year, during the early hours of the morning, a convoy of machines arrived at the mine entrance. Spontaneously, *mestizo* and Indigenous Maya-Kaqchikel women lay on the ground, sang and prayed to thwart the entry of bulldozers using their bodies to halt the destruction of the land. In December, women in La Puya faced 25 patrols dispatched to displace the population. Yolanda Oquelí, the movement's leader until 2015 and a member of the Network of Ancestral Healers of Community Feminism (Tzk'at), was attacked in the middle of the night when an unknown assailant shot her from a van in the same year. Although Yolana Oquelí survived, she lives with a bullet lodged near her spine.[3]

In 2012, the Inter-American Commission on Human Rights urged the Guatemalan government to take measures to ensure the safety of Yolanda Oquelí and her family, who faced renewed threats. However, Yolanda Oquelí found herself accused by the prosecutor's office of alleged illegal detention, coercion, minor injuries and threats – a result of complaints filed by former Exmingua workers. Since January 2018, Yolanda Oquelí has been in Catalonia, in Spain, under the Amnesty International protection programme.

Despite a campaign of criminalization and defamation, and an increased military presence in the region, residents established a resistance camp that operates 24 hours a day to effectively oppose the mine. However, complaints surfaced, indicating the company's continued violence and mineral extraction operations through alternative methods even after the Supreme Court of Justice of Guatemala suspended the project. An investigation file was opened for the crime of illegal exploitation. Oquelí has explained on many occasions that the Guatemalan government has launched smear and criminalization campaigns against the members of La Puya, and especially against women.[4]

There is an important thread of radical solidarity and continuity in all these feminist post-extractive forms of defending dignified lives. In South Africa's North West Province, which holds 90 per cent of the world's platinum, particularly in the Platinum Province, the wealth derived from mining fails to benefit the local population. Mineworkers and their families endure impoverished and undignified living conditions. The August 2012 strike by Lonmin PLC's Marikana mine workers in Rustenburg, demanding a wage increase, resulted in the tragic Marikana Massacre, where 34 striking miners were shot and killed by the South African Police.

The women of Marikana play a crucial role, serving as the backbone of their communities. Without the women of Marikana, mining would not be possible. They are the foundation of their communities – they put food on the table, raise children, care for the sick and elderly, and sometimes work as mineworkers themselves (Palesa Madi in Barcia, 2017). Following the massacre, these women faced immense challenges, dealing with grief and the hardships caused by the ongoing strike. Often overlooked in public discourse, they organized protests, fought for representation at the Marikana Commission of Inquiry, and advocated for improved living conditions and post-extractivist just futures.

Establishing the community-based organization Sikhala Sonke – meaning 'we are crying together', but which can also be interpreted as 'we are all in the same pain' – the women sought to address the systemic gendered and racist inequalities and living conditions in the mining industry that led to the strike. Despite their severe impact on the events, the Commission largely ignored their testimonies. The women, persistent in their efforts, reported their living conditions and protest actions in a documentary,[5] using the material as evidence during the Commission's proceedings (Palesa Madi in Barcia, 2017).

In 2015, the women of Marikana filed a complaint with the International Finance Corporation of the World Bank, which had invested in Lonmin. A mediation process began, but in 2016, Sikhala Sonke withdrew, citing Lonmin's bad faith and avoidance of core issues. The International Finance Corporation is now tasked with investigating Lonmin's failure to meet obligations (Palesa Madi in Barcia, 2017).

As a registered non-profit organization, Sikhala Sonke continues the fight for a better Marikana community. Despite challenges from the state and corporations, the women persist in telling their story, engaging in civil society forums and advocating with the government, media, mining companies and the wider community for an improved life free from the violence of extractivism and patriarchy.

Solidarity with those fighting against extractivism in the global South greatly depends on changing consumption habits, economies and perspectives in the global North. Excess consumption in high-income nations is sustained by an ongoing process of net appropriation from the lands and peoples of the global South, on unequal terms. It relies on stopping multimillion-dollar agreements and policies driven by companies and regions, sometimes under 'solidarity' agreements of South–South cooperation or European slogans of 'green and digital transition', which are massacring the lives of people (Carrasco-Miró, 2017). Communitarian feminists suggest communal healing as a rebellion act against patriarchal oppression and extractivism: 'Healing yourself, heals me. And healing me heals you' (Cabnal, 2020). It is the reciprocity and interdependence of healing. Healing, they argue, is a personal and political act 'from the emancipation and rebellion against the patriarchal system' (Cabnal, 2020; translation mine; see also Cabnal, 2018).

Ecofeminism needs to be decolonizing

Ecofeminism stands as a political and intellectual force in resisting extractivism, with diverse strands of thought within this field and with strong connections with post-extractivism. Some emphasize material conditions (for example, see WoMin, 2015, 2020), while others highlight women's personal and spiritual connections to nature (see Allison, 2017). A crucial perspective, ecofeminism envisions and advocates for a post-extractivist, feminist, degrowth and ecologically just economic alternative, countering the dominant, patriarchal, environmentally destructive economic model for the benefit of all people and the planet.

Ecofeminism combines two words: ecology and feminism. The connection between these two words and their potential dialogue revolves around the question 'What sustains life?' When we envision what sustains life, we must recognize that we are fundamentally dependent on the Earth that is not created or controlled at the whim of human beings. This means that there is no economy (nor technology, politics or society) without nature. When we ask what sustains life, we directly encounter the claims and struggles that the feminist movement has historically championed. For a long time, part of feminism, including importantly feminist economics, has sought to redistribute and de-genderize care responsibilities, to make society collectively responsible for the daily and generational reproduction of human life, and to uphold ecological advocacy as a basis for a dignified life.

Can one be an ecofeminist without explicitly naming it as such? Many movements around the world have not explicitly identified as ecofeminist, yet they share a common goal of defending the land, fighting patriarchy and pursuing an emancipatory process to protect and sustain life. In this sense, and while respecting the choices of these movements regarding what they want to be called, a connection and radical solidarity exists among these struggles without the need to unify them under a single banner. Sylvia Tamale (2020: 85) notes in her discussion of Afro-ecofeminism that 'women in the global South may not have self-identified as "ecofeminists," but they have a long history of ecological consciousness and moral obligation towards future generations'.

There are, however, points of conflict within ecofeminism. Sofia Nicolasa Chipana (2018: 161; translation mine) recognizes Lorena Cabnal's (see Cabnal, 2015) communitarian feminist proposal, highlighting the significant 'epistemological, spiritual, and political contribution of the body-territory and the land-territory … cultivated in spaces of indigenous women who self-identify as feminists' and which 'has much in common with ecofeminist proposals'. However, Chipana (2018: 162; translation mine) argues that Indigenous women's starting point differs from ecofeminism, as 'the spirituality linked to the ancestors, from whom [Indigenous women] nourish and accompany their struggles for the land-territories in full connection with their bodies' is absent in ecofeminism. In this sense, as in Afro-ecofeminism, spirituality is an inseparable part of cultural identity for Indigenous women, both emphasizing the need to rescue Indigenous worldviews, worldsenses and their vital principles of life: everything lives, everything has its place and time, and there is a mutual creation of life.

Certain ecofeminist perspectives have been critiqued for homogenizing and essentializing women's experiences. This focus has led to the universalization of women-nature connections across class, culture, and other intersecting factors, particularly positioning women from the global South as the embodiment of nature (Zein-Elabdin, 1996; Kapoor, 2008). Critics argue that ecofeminism is essentialist when it assumes an intrinsic relationship between women and nature. By doing so, it simplifies the responsibility for ecological stewardship to women, thus absolving others from addressing ecological degradation and portraying nature as static and ahistorical. This assumption of a universal parallel between women and nature overlooks the specific institutional contexts in which women and nature interact, lacking the necessary context.

The exploitative nature of capitalism, neoliberal agroeconomy, the current regime of resource colonialism, heteropatriarchy and industrial ecocide does not exclusively impact women. While there are women in certain contexts that are disproportionately affected by ecological degradation and capitalism, it is not due to a different female nature, but rather specific historical and material processes explaining why. Therefore, understanding the connection between heteropatriarchy, capitalism, colonialism and the exploitation of nature results in the exclusion or devaluation of *antithetical practices* such as caregiving or the sustainability of life, whether exhibited by women, men or gender-diverse individuals, and the ideological construction of the groups associated with such practices as natural, 'traditional', irrational, less developed or pre-modern.

The decolonial critique of ecofeminism stems from the recognition that this movement did not originate in the West and acknowledges that Indigenous thought and life have always centred on conceptions of interconnectedness that go beyond human relationships and include nature. Indigenous knowledge systems, often in harmony with nature, can be employed to address environmental injustices through an integrative view of nature and people, transcending the Western-centric modernist dichotomy of nature versus culture.

In today's world, there is an unintentional convergence of three distinct movements: the anti-capitalist movement; the anti-imperialist and anti-colonial movement; and the anti-racist and anti-patriarchal movement. At the intersection of these three movements lies the praxis of challenging and transforming power structures and hierarchies (Tamale, 2020). The same patriarchal, imperialist and colonialist ideologies and institutions that disrupted and displaced Indigenous systems are working to exploit nature. Maina-Okori et al remind us that 'from a colonial perspective, land and the colonized (mostly Indigenous peoples) are considered part of nature and consequently objects and commodities of capitalism' (cited in Tamale, 2020: 83). In this context, ecofeminism and decolonizing feminist economics holds political power, allowing it to strike a balance between the principles of decolonial feminisms, feminist post-extractivism, post-growth politics and Indigenous ontologies in a non-essentialist and non-relativist manner, conducive to a dignified life and antithetical to oppression and exploitation.

We can find ecofeminist struggles everywhere and not just in rural contexts. Western and urban societies also contain elements that can be considered ecofeminist or display ecofeminist traits. For instance, there is a significant alignment with all movements advocating for housing rights. Defending your home in the context of urban society is analogous to defending nearby territory because it encompasses more than just the walls where you cook, sleep or have sex. It also involves preserving a space that connects you to the surrounding territory, maintaining neighbourhood ties, and upholding your belonging to the neighbourhood in which you reside.

Within the *Movimiento por una Vivienda Digna* (Movement for Decent Housing), the Spanish collective *V de Vivienda* circulated posters with a slogan that resonated deeply with a specific and very real fear that still haunts a substantial portion of Western societies: 'No vas a tener casa en la puta vida' (You are never going to have a house in your damn life). This prophetic slogan, which has recently resurfaced, expresses a situation that can no longer be addressed only on an individual level. Not having a house is not merely a private issue. Simultaneously, this slogan stirrers up a sense of anger, directed at the extractive logic of rentiers and debt, and against the prevailing view that justifies the violence imposed on life ideals that extend beyond the need for shelter. This conflict between life and capital remains at the core of struggles related to issues such as air quality, heatwaves and the effects of climate change within the Western urban environment.

The concept of care has always been central in both ecofeminism and feminist economics since their inception. Today 'care' plays a crucial role in shaping future economic solutions, even leading to what is often referred to as a 'care revolution'. But what exactly is meant by 'care'? In feminist economics, care is at the heart of two interconnected debates: whether care, defined narrowly as 'nurturant' or 'direct' care, should be recognized as 'work', and whether paid alternatives for this type of care labour are of equal quality to unpaid care. On the other hand, ecofeminism explores the parallels between the environmental crisis and the care crisis. Both perspectives highlight the devaluation and invisibility of social reproductive work perpetuated by heteropatriarchal social structures and assumed mostly by women, particularly racialized and migrant women.

Nonetheless, many feminist proposals related to care in this 'care revolution' might start to resemble a resignation. While it is crucial to acknowledge the feminist movement for planting the seed of an ethics that places self-care and life at the centre, a pressing question we began to explore in Chapter 2 remains: How can we prevent these efforts from becoming mere 'palliative care' (Garcés, 2017: 26)? Can we think care not just as access to paid labour or social reproduction, but as a form of resistance?

East African women-led anti-colonial movements exemplify resistance in which the reclamation of care mirrored the women's 'relationship to key resources that were central to the colonial capitalist accumulation project – land and labor – and their struggles took on an agrarian form because they affected the overall political and economic structure of the colonial state'

(Ossome, 2021: 48). Through these struggles, women 'articulated an anti imperialist critique of gender (gender labor)' (Ossome, 2021:49), using it as a form of resistance against patriarchy and capitalist accumulation and connecting it to claims over public land and common resources.

In the 21st century, capitalism is no longer legitimized by narratives of progress or promises of a better life for the global population. Instead, it perpetuates itself through quick and substantial benefits to a few, achieved through increasingly intense practices of extractivism, dispossession and the marginalization of large segments of the global population and the planet's territories.In this context, care can become not just a form of resistance, but a revolutionary practice that challenges the oppressive conditions of our time.

In my previous neighbourhood, el Barri de Gràcia, in Barcelona, there is graffiti that reads 'la fragilidad es el alma de la revolución' ('fragility is the soul of the revolution'; see Figure 7.1). I believe it conveys something important and may provide some clues. In the care for a dignified life, we can experience the power of confronting the injustices and inequalities that cause so much suffering. Therefore, it is important to not limit care to a defensive language but to link it to the various ways in which we can simultaneously fight and create collectively, as demonstrated by the East African women led anti-colonial movements, reclaiming life and shared futures. Fighting against economic powers that harm life, both human and more-than-human and creating a habitable world among us. We are not just fragile beings, as

Figure 7.1: Graffiti in the neighbourhood of Gracia, Barcelona, 2021

Source: Photograph by Gisela Carrasco-Miró

emphasized by some branches of feminist economics and ecofeminism today. Is it possible to approach fragility that is not synonymous with impotence, but on the contrary, that is the revelation of our impossibility of being a single individual (Carrasco-Miró, 2020a)? Our fragility, as the graffiti says, is inseparable from a great collective power of creativity, invention and practical resolution of our common challenges (revolution). We must not forget: we are not only nurses to a sick economy, but co-creators of a world in which we want to live with dignity.

Towards a post-growth internationalism that is decolonial and feminist

How do we transition to a different international system – a feminist and decolonizing one, that does not require growth in the first place? Today, post-growth has become one of the key reference points for a future beyond economic growth, industrialism and domination (Jackson, 2021). Post-growth constitutes an additional and radical contribution for a new internationalism that 'seeks to fundamentally alter global relations towards a multi-polar, post-growth internationalism' (Schmelzer et al, 2022: 29). In that sense, post-growth internationalism calls for a range of policy changes and social innovations that prioritize social and ecological well-being for all in a democratic and dignified manner, while respecting planetary boundaries and minimizing major social and economic disruption. This requires a new economics, new value systems and new forms of collaboration.

However, post-growthers and degrowthers do not explicitly address the issue of international relations and the geopolitical ramifications of the transition they envision. Although post-growth may indirectly impact geopolitics by promoting sustainability, environmental justice, and reducing the use of energy and resources, it does not offer a comprehensive answer to the complex challenges facing the global community (Schmelzer et al, 2022). Therefore, it is necessary to articulate a new understanding of internationalism in a post-growth direction that transcends the conventional top-down and grassroots-politics dichotomies and engages with the complex questions of geopolitics and economics.

What would a post-growth internationalism look like? What needs to be done? As a principle, there should not be a post-growth internationalism without decolonization (Hickel, 2021) and feminism/anti-patriarchalism (Feminisms and Degrowth Alliance, nd). Colonialism and patriarchy have been central to capitalism and the exploitation of the global South (Federici, 2004). The exploitation of free labour does not sustain itself without highly devalued labour and non-waged labour provided by racialized bodies (colonialism) and sexualized bodies (heteropatriarchy). However, research on post-growth/degrowth and feminist economics is still very rare. Nascent conversations on post-growth and degrowth with feminist economics remain gender-centred and focused on the social reproductive sphere, without challenging much of its Western-centric modernism. This book proposes a decolonizing feminist critique of growth as a lens to better articulate a post-growth internationalism. Decolonizing feminist economics involves critically examining the assumptions and values that underpin economic theory and international policy making. It seeks to develop, both theoretically and practically, alternative frameworks that move beyond growth-based models in the global North and delink in the global South, promoting ecological sustainability and well-being. Ultimately, decolonizing feminist economics aim to dismantle the interconnected systems of colonialism, heteropatriarchy, growth-driven capitalism and ecological degradation.

In the following, I suggest a series of questions intended to guide further research and practical applications in the realm of post-growth internationalism from a decolonizing feminist economics approach. They hold the potential to offer insights into the geopolitics of today, particularly within the evolving landscape of international economic relations.

Epistemological ruptures are an essential prerequisite for the constitution of a post-growth internationalism. What are the essential features of a post-growth internationalism and what changes can bring it about? How to incorporate, not only through the apology of diversity but also through political, economic, cultural and epistemological conflict, decolonizing feminist knowledges? How does a post-growth internationalism need to be pursued to promote socio-ecological and decolonial feminist justice, without falling into the trap of reproducing colonial and patriarchal continuities? What can be learned from feminist internationalism, communist internationalism, anarchist internationalism, Third-Worldism, the New International Economic Order, human rights and liberal internationalism, and Black internationalism?

Political feasibility and opposition. What would be the potential consequences of transitioning towards a feminist/anti-patriarchal post-growth system in the current world? How can a post-growth internationalism be managed to overcome global inequalities without deepening dependency (delinking), while also addressing centuries of colonial and ecological debt by high-income countries? Can economies that shift away from growth-oriented models still maintain their status as global players despite their current dependence on growth? In a post-growth internationalism, what role would the state and intergovernmental organizations such as the European Union and the United Nations play? Can they be transformed to become independent of growth?

Organization. While it is clear that a post-growth internationalism requires different actors to work together, the decolonizing question here is *how*? How to scale-up counter-hegemonic movements, particularly feminist/anti-patriarchal ones, moving beyond growth economy to the international level? How and what decolonizing feminist economic strategies can advance a post-growth internationalism, which actors to involve, how to connect different political and geographical levels, what currently existing processes and organizations to build on, connect or scale up? What are the multi-level mechanisms and processes of organization (for example, who to involve and how, what is to be decided at what level and by whom, how to resolve conflicts, how to enforce decisions) that will bring about decolonial feminist post-growth transformations?

8

Decolonizing Feminist Economics: A Tentative Map

Introduction: Tentatives

Stepping outside the solutionist logic inherent in projects and their objectives, Marina Garcés (2013) suggests the concept employed by French educator, writer and filmmaker Fernand Deligny: attempts (*tentatives*). Common worlds, tentatively connected. Confronting the efficient logic of projects, Deligny (2009) asserts that an attempt claims ownership of its time, rhythm and value. Its functionality hinges on its capacity to weave a map of alliances with other attempts.

Decolonizing feminist economics questions what kind of economies we want, what shared futures we can imagine. By doing so, it confronts the inequalities that condition the future and ensure possibilities for material life, liberation and dignified subsistence without diminishing life. Situating the proposition of decolonizing feminist economics on a map of attempts is not a romanticized image but rather a space to navigate the confusion and frustration stirred by today's field of economics, both within and beyond academic institutions. It is about producing disruptions into economic thought from its borders – not solely to confront it, but to breach its glass walls and expose it to the contagion of unconventional ideas, transformative practices that dismantle deep-seated injustices and perspectives that envision possibilities of just futures. To avoid becoming a self-indulgent gesture, every act of insubordination requires, therefore, tools for sustaining and sharing its position.

In this chapter, I present eight interconnected approaches to developing a decolonizing feminist economics proposal: *embodying* feminist economics; *recognizing* Indigenous sovereignty and freedom; *interrogating* Orientalism, Eurocentrism and developmentalism; *advocating* for plural economic knowledges; *questioning* the meaning of value; *resisting* capitalist growth economies; *advancing* economic justice – reparations, land return and wealth redistribution; and *embracing* a common world as a political commitment. This map provides both theoretical and practical concepts and tools, building on previously discussed ideas such as *mestiza* methodology, ecoSImies of care and radical solidarity. It aims to transcend existing feminist economics paradigms, offering a decolonizing perspective that breaks free from mainstream economic frameworks and opens up possibilities for just futures. It is important to acknowledge that my proposal for decolonizing feminist economics is inherently limited by the historical conditions of its own production. This limitation, while unavoidable, can be mitigated through constant revision.

The map

Embodying feminist economics

The challenge of decolonizing, once confined to the realm of the mind (Cabral, 1979; Ngũgĩ, 1986), has evolved into a challenge of the body. Yet, how do we incarnate decolonizing? How do feminist economics acquire a body? Often confined to isolated enclaves, decolonial efforts face barriers hindering movement and perpetuating a sense of impotence. The essence lies not in perfecting a decolonial language or citations but in transcending the boundaries of a 'good' feminist and decolonial consciousness, steering clear of facile solutions for academic approval. To embody feminist economics is to explore how we can disrupt our lives to fundamentally reshape the world. It is a battle against inertia, a disruption of the world within and around us. This involves *experiencing* the world collectively – a relearning of our sense of 'we'.

Rosi Braidotti (1994, 2011) argues that the processes of theory development are necessarily embodied and embedded. These positions are unavoidably shaped by active material networks and connections that facilitate theoretical development. These embodied and situated perspectives, however, can be easily overlooked. This happens when feminist economics is practised with the distant gaze of a 'modest witness' (Haraway, 1997: 24), ignoring the partiality, embodiment and embedded position. In such cases, claims of objectivity arise, and, through this 'divine trick', allow the scholar to maintain a privileged 'view from nowhere' (Haraway, 1988: 87; see also Chapter 3).

Embodying feminist economics within one's own body goes beyond understanding the implications of having a specific body (for example, being a woman), but rather as a web of living meanings. On an ontological and epistemological level, Karen Barad (2003) suggests that this recognition has creative implications, affirming multiple, situated and diverse positions for responsible theoretical development that is embodied and embedded. This approach is crucial in the context of feminist materialism, as in the project of decolonizing feminist economics.

According to this perspective, dualism is taken to its extreme, and traditional dualisms are thoroughly reconsidered (Van der Tuin and Dolphijn, 2010, 2011). In this sense, the theorization of feminist economics from embodied and situated perspectives not only subverts the dualisms on which hegemonic economics and *Homo economicus* are based (such as thought versus corporeality, economics versus culture), but also generates ways to engage with and think through difference or differences beyond dualism. This allows feminist economic thought to diverge horizontally and in a pluralistic way.

Drawing from Gloria Anzaldúa's *Borderlands/La Frontera*, and as stated in Chapter 2, decolonizing feminist economics proposes a *mestiza* methodology aiming to dismantle dualistic thinking in economics and embodying feminist economics. It advocates for an 'in-between' space that not only acknowledges but also embraces culture as a vital element in our understanding of economies (Zein-Elabdin, 2016). In this sense, decolonizing feminist economics redefines economic theorization beyond representationalism and dualistic oppositions, shifting focus from 'what' and 'why' to '*how*'. It poses questions that do not assume the object of research as external ('out there') or teleologically explained ('why'), but rather concentrates *on the processes* involved ('the how of becoming'). In this light, the central inquiry of this map is to shift from 'what is feminist economics?' to '*how is feminist economics embodied*?'

This approach ties feminist economics to analyses wherein the existence of elements in the world always establishes a reciprocal relationship with our understanding and articulation of them. In essence, and as emphasized by Barad (2003: 828), 'we are part of [the world] that we are trying to understand'.

Recognizing Indigenous sovereignty and freedom

Naomi Klein (2016) initiated her sold-out talk to a Winnipeg audience in April 2016 by recognizing they were gathered on Treaty 1 Territory. She challenged the audience, stating, '[i]t is not enough for us to simply say that this is Indigenous Land. We need to act like it is Indigenous Land' (25:36–25:46). Indeed, as discussed in Chapter 3, decolonizing requires recognizing Indigenous sovereignty and freedom in its material, psychological, epistemological and spiritual forms (Sium et al, 2012). As Robyn Maynard and Leanne Betasamosake Simpson (2023: 149) emphasize: 'Indigenous freedom means that my sovereignty over my body, mind, spirit, and land is affirmed and respected in all of my relationships.'

Indigenous sovereignty encompasses various dimensions, from asserting rights and countering ongoing colonial experiences to reclaiming ancestral lands, resources, economies, self-governance and preserving cultural knowledge (Barker, 2005). It involves inherent rights derived from spiritual and historical connections to lands and waters, persisting irrespective of the actions or inaction of the nation-state. Fiona Nicoll (2000, 2004) asserts that Indigenous sovereignty is a reality, independent of non-Indigenous responses or failures to acknowledge it. Following Leanne Betasamosake Simpson (2017), only when Indigenous sovereignty is recognized, rather than dismissed, will relationships between Indigenous and non-Indigenous people begin to shift.

It is important, however, to understand sovereignty as a national liberatory project encompassing multiple dimensions, where land but also economic sovereignty are essential. Sovereignty should include water, energy, food and economic sovereignty, allowing Indigenous people to exercise their full power within a global economy. For instance, in Greenland, Indigenous sovereignty movements are achieving victories, but economic vulnerability forces them to consider drilling for oil under melting ice to gain economic freedom. If these issues are not addressed, what does sovereignty mean for Arctic people whose economic survival depends on actions that could lead to their cultural annihilation?

The Red Nation (TRN), a United States-based Indigenous activist organization, advocates a feminist, anti-racist, and anti-capitalist decolonization rooted in Indigenous knowledge. TRN envisions Indigenous sovereignty by dismantling settler-colonial institutions like the police and military. Their call for land repatriation rejects private property, intertwines Indigenous self-determination with Black liberation, and seeks a 'decolonized commons' that promotes emancipation, economic sovereignty and self-determination for Indigenous peoples while rejecting a nationalism that excludes others.

In a similar vein, Indigenous feminists like Andrea Smith strategically challenge the heteropatriarchal, racist and colonial form of the modern nation-state, redefining Indigenous nationality on indigenist, feminist and decolonial grounds (Smith et al, 2006). Indigenous feminisms suggest that 'there are other models of nationhood we can envision … that do not have the heteronormative, patriarchal, nuclear family as their building block. Indigenous sovereignty and nationhood, rather than constituting the antithesis of coalition and alliance building, can serve as a model for how it can be done' (Smith et al, 2006: 271). In this sense, the synergy of national and transnational commitments among Indigenous feminists displaces theories that would oppose national work against transnational work while recognizing economic sovereignty as a crucial site for theorists and activists pursuing decolonizing agendas of radical social and economic change.

Living with an awareness that we are on Indigenous lands, governed by Indigenous protocols, stories and obligations, offers a vital frame for the decolonizing action of feminist economics. This orientation represents the part of settlers not governed by the state, allowing a choice in how they relate to Indigenous peoples, their economies and lands. Engaging deeply with Indigenous sovereignty, including Indigenous economic sovereignty, transforms not only perspectives but also envisions possible just futures for all. This engagement changes relationships, transforms thinking and enables the creation of a different world. In this context, decolonizing feminist economics charts pathways with and for Indigenous peoples, calling for the redistribution of land to them and their economic sovereignty and not just the transformation of market relations.

To achieve decolonizing and economic sovereignty, Ndongo Samba Sylla and Jason Hickel (2024) identified six principles of action that are: 1) reduce material-technical dependency on the global North; 2) regain national control over foreign exchange earnings; 3) make strategic use of foreign exchange for national development; 4) mobilize production around human well-being and national development; 5) establish industrial policy focused on well-being, ecology and sovereignty; 6) cooperate for collective abolition of onerous/odious debts if necessary.

Building on these principles, a decolonizing feminist economic approach would require: a) addressing intersectional gender inequalities in earnings distribution; b) prioritizing marginalized communities over elites through redistributive mechanisms; c) investing in care-centered, sustainable initiatives benefiting marginalized women, trans, and non-binary people; d) supporting sustainable industries with equitable opportunities for marginalized groups; e) promoting community ownership and cooperative models to counter heteropatriarchal and capitalist hierarchies; f) framing debt abolition as a feminist demand due to its disproportionate impact on marginalized women and collective well-being; and g) building regional feminist alliances to resist debt imperialism and advance economic sovereignty.

Interrogating Orientalism, Eurocentrism and developmentalism

Feminist economics seeks to dismantle androcentrism, aligning with postcolonial and decolonial efforts aimed at undoing Orientalism, Eurocentrism and developmentalism. However, feminist economics has not thoroughly explored its engagement with postcolonial, anti-colonial and decolonial ideas (Carrasco-Miró, 2020a; see also Chapter 1 and Chapter 2 in this book).[1] Critical questions raised by postcolonial, anti-colonial and decolonial feminists regarding encounters with 'the Other' – emphasizing non-Western worldviews, worldsenses – remain largely unaddressed. Therefore, interrogating Orientalism, Eurocentrism and developmentalism is essential for any approach that aims to critically unravel colonial and oppressive attitudes and structures towards 'Others'.

Orientalism, Eurocentrism and developmentalism, albeit with differences, share the exposition of a constituted otherness embedded in Western economic scholarship. All can be productively deployed in a feminist critique of economics – orthodox and heterodox – and offer a foundation upon which to construct alternative readings of economy. In economics, Orientalism manifests prominently in the Western-centric modernist concept of 'development', perpetuating a power dynamic entrenched in discourses that label certain people and nations as inherently inferior or backward. This racist classification with imperial designs is often veiled by terms like 'developing', 'third world' or, more recently, 'global South'. Arturo Escobar (1995: 62) points out that 'there is … an orientalism in economics that has to be unveiled – that is, a hegemonic effect achieved through representations that enshrine one view of the economy while suppressing others'. Despite Escobar's observation nearly three decades ago, Orientalism remains entrenched in much of contemporary economic theory.

Edward Said's *Orientalism* is still one of the most influential postcolonial works. It continues to express, and help shape, contemporary thinking about topics such as representation of the 'Orient', European imperialism and how both of these relate to other concepts, including gender and race. A feminist exploration of Orientalism in economics is useful in investigating and dissecting the various ways economic theory have viewed the Orient or the global South. In particular, it serves to unpack colonial attitudes of superiority over '"primitive", "backward" or "traditional" people from the global South with catastrophic gendered and racist effects' (Yeğenoğlu, 1998: 96); it focuses on situated subjects in feminist economics analysis that acknowledges the changing agency of women in non-Western contexts (Charusheela, 2001); as well as the economics methods that shape the study of the non-Western regions (Kongar et al, 2018).

Eiman Osman Zein-Elabdin (2011a: 220) states that '[a]ny faithful application of Said reveals developmentalism as the name of orientalism's 20th century descendant'. In this sense, the Orient is displaced onto the global South. Just as orientalist scholars presented the Orient as exotic and mysterious to the Western imaginary, developmentalists depict the global South as 'underdeveloped' – backward, pre-modern, pre-capitalist, or deviant in some form. However, to attain a materialist understanding of capitalism and imperialism in developmentalism, Orientalism is insufficient. Samir Amin (1988 [2009]) coined Eurocentrism to describe the polarized project reinforcing imperialism and systemic inequalities, highlighting how dominant understandings of capitalism fail to recognize postcolonial experiences of capitalist development (Amin, 1988 [2009]; Kvangraven and Kesar, 2023). With a view of the economics field in particular, and highlighted in Chapter 1, Amin's theory helps us see the ideological foundations of mainstream economics – orthodox and heterodox – and developmentalism, in particular. According to this understanding, developmentalism is presented as a rational and all-pervasive progress (that is, economic growth) that is expected to unfold organically through the world (that is, development).

The driving 'development' forces behind mining, oil, natural gas and agricultural frontiers are becoming increasingly powerful, and anything that stands in their way and blocks their path tends to be destroyed as an obstacle to development (see Chapter 3 and Chapter 5). These highly powerful forces excel in transforming the increasingly disturbing signs of the immense environmental and social debt they create into the inevitable cost of 'progress'/'development'. This model, rooted in an extractivist and productivist mentality (see Chapter 4) perpetuates the global argument for capitalist accumulation.

All social processes that do not align with this developmentalist imagination (that is heteropatriarchal, extractive, growth-based, capitalist), including non-Western views of and forms of economies, identities, rationalities and institutions, are then devalued as in need of 'development' or 'empowerment'. One example of that is the entrepreneurial woman of the global South or the mainstream gender and development discourse advocating for empowering women discussed previously (see Chapter 6). To foster a critical study of economics, we should be able to imagine and invoke relevant and complex economic phenomena from non-Western countries, different from growth and capitalist social relations in order to support our critical study of economics (see Chapter 7).

Decolonizing feminist economics offer the possibility of thinking different from developmentalism and 'the Other' by delinking from the imperatives of globalized capitalism and its oppressive structures and extractivist mentality. This is, therefore, a work of epistemological, material and democratic imagination, pointing to create new and plural notions of economic relations and social emancipation based on freedom and liberation upon the ruins of development. It would also mean creating possibilities to build a shared economic horizon for just futures.

Advocating for plural economic knowledges

In *Decolonizing Methodologies*, Linda Tuhiwai Smith (1999: 39) provides a working definition of decolonization, which 'does not mean and has not meant a total rejection of all theory or research or Western knowledge. Rather it is about centring [Indigenous] concerns and world views and then coming to know and understand theory and research from our own perspectives and purposes'. Central to decolonizing methodologies within decolonizing feminist economics is, therefore, recognizing the coexistence of distinct knowledge systems, where Indigenous knowledges are recognized, strengthened and valued, and how these distinct knowledge systems can work alongside each other. That is, advocating for a feminist economics deeply rooted in plurality – which is not just composed by many voices but voices that express different worldviews.

Yet, to foster contexts that encourage decolonizing feminist economic thinking, what conditions are required? From a perspective that views knowledge wealth as diverse and economics as multifaceted rather than solely growth-oriented, is it possible to consider a shared pool of economic experiences? The premise of decolonizing feminist economics answers 'yes' – it is not only possible but necessary.

Decolonizing feminist economics directly challenges the entrenched norms of Western-centric modernist economics monocultures, disrupting the status quo of linear time, social classifications (including gender), presumed Western superiority and narrow productivity conceptions (see Chapter 2). It cultivates ecoSImies of care and asserts the necessity for alternative perspectives on economic life and socio-economic transformation, paving the way for resistance against heteropatriarchy, colonialism, capitalism and ecological degradation. Consequently, decolonizing feminist economics creates openings for Indigenous and non-Western discursivity and epistemologies, fostering dialogues with prevailing Western-centric modern economic systems of knowledge. Importantly, this pursuit of plurality arises not just from the rights or identities of people marked by specific ethnicities and genders but from the alternative, decolonizing economic epistemologies they offer, that bring to light the antagonisms governing our worlds.

As a guiding principle, decolonizing feminist economics does not reject any form of knowledge outright but encourages public dialogue on economic issues. It challenges the discipline of economics' claim to a monopoly on rigour and asserts that it is not the sole valid form of economic knowledge. This raises three crucial questions: What relevance should be ascribed to the internal pluralism of feminist economics? How do we distinguish decolonizing feminist economic knowledge from other forms of knowledge? And how relevant are non-Western conceptions of economics and economies?

The first question delves into the relevance of the internal pluralism of feminist economics. While aligned with feminist economics' philosophical assumptions of justice and sustainability, alternative decolonizing methodological and theoretical paths may lead to different or even contradictory feminist economic arguments coexisting and being considered valid. This necessitates a rethinking of the relationship of knowledge not only with power but *especially* with emancipation. Reclaiming the vital link between knowledge and emancipation involves understanding the accurate and embodied relationship with various forms of experience and economic knowledge.

However, the capitalist push to commodify knowledge – reducing it to market-driven value – and the prioritization of research aligned with short-term profit goals jeopardize this pluralism. As feminist economists face increasing pressure to align with capitalist objectives, their ability to meaningfully contribute to the fight against systemic oppressions rooted in heteropatriarchy, capitalism, colonialism, and ecological degradation diminishes. This erosion of internal pluralism complicates the transformative and counterhegemonic potential of feminist economics.

Addressing the second question, for feminist economic knowledge to be considered decolonizing, it must engage with non-Western-centric economic ideas, imaginaries and resistances. In that sense, decolonizing feminist economics is marked by:

- Revealing and pushing back against colonialism, (hetero)patriarchy, capitalism and ecological degradation to open spaces for decolonizing critique, imagination, and resistance (outlined particularly in Part I of this book).
- Revaluing and recovering Indigenous knowledges, lands and Indigenous future (outlined particularly in Part II of this book).
- Imagining a world free of these oppressive structures where the sustainability of life is truly at the centre (outlined particularly in Part III of this book).

The third question addresses the significance of alternative, non-Western conceptions of the economy in economics. These perspectives are often dismissed due to dominant consensus on what constitutes 'economics'. However, in certain contexts, non-Western economic frameworks may take precedence. For instance, this is evident in Mayan economies (see Carrasco-Miró, 2020a) or in African economies, as examined by Eiman Zein-Elabdin (2011b). Acknowledging that what qualifies as economics—or feminist economics—varies across specific spatial and temporal contexts challenges conventional and Western-centric understandings of the field.

Resisting capitalist growth economies: sustainability of life

Contemporary economic models, such as 'green growth' and 'sustainable development', heavily rely on perpetual economic growth as a linchpin for their functionality (Carrasco-Miró, 2016, 2017, 2018b). The success of nations and alliances is intricately tied to the idea that firms, industries and nations must increase production every year, regardless of necessity. However, mounting evidence linking growth to ecological breakdown has led institutions and scientists worldwide to reassess their approach (Hickel and Kallis, 2020; see, for example, European Environment Agency, 2021).

Surveys consistently highlight public dissatisfaction with growth-centric economies (capitalism) and growing concerns about ecological, economic and social justice issues (King et al, 2023). People say they want an economy that is organized around well-being and justice rather than growth and capital accumulation. A survey conducted in 34 European countries found that, on average, 61 per cent of people support post-growth (Paulson and Büchs, 2022). However, the study also reveals that support for post-growth is lower among disadvantaged communities, underscoring the importance of emphasizing redistributive policies that can enhance livelihoods and economic security for the working classes (Paulson and Büchs, 2022). In another recent study by Giorgos Kallis, Riccardo Mastini and Christos Zografos (2023), 41 members of the European Parliament were interviewed regarding 'degrowth versus green growth' within the context of climate policy and the Green New Deal. The study reveals that, at least in the European Parliament, green growth is seen primarily a liberal and right-wing concept, challenging the notion of it being a solid foundation for political economic consensus. The authors question why this diversity of opinions is not reflected in 'real policies'. One possible answer, they assert: the balance of power.

Reconciling the sustainability of the planet with economic growth as proclaimed by 'green growth' narratives is based on a structural and unsolvable conflict between capital and life (see Chapter 6). The dilemma is stark: either we ensure the relentless accumulation of capital, or we prioritize the sustainability of life. Feminist economics advocates for the latter, positioning the preservation of life as the central goal for our economic systems (Pérez Orozco, 2014; Carrasco-Miró, 2017, 2018b; Federici, 2018). Yet, how can we transition to an alternative economic system – one that does not necessitate growth in high-income countries? How can we create and sustain post-growth economies and post-extractivist economies where the means are subjected to the sustainability of life, and that respond to the cultural and spiritual needs and possibilities, as well as material ones? What needs to be done? These are central questions for decolonizing feminist economics.

What is now at issue is the very premise of limitless growth as a condition for economic activity. In the 18th century, the connection between growth and political economy made sense due to colonial expansion, wealth increase, industrialization and demographic growth. However, the current perception is the opposite. Why should a principle be maintained that contradicts the real experience we are having today about our living conditions? This is when a principle, asserted by itself and against all evidence, becomes dogma. A dogma that once again relies on the idea of sustainability. Take, for example, the Agenda 2030 for sustainable development: 'What, exactly, is to be sustained in sustainable development?' (Carrasco-Miró, 2017: 89). The preached sustainability is not only for natural resources but for the economic system as a whole. The new slogan is: make the (unjust) system sustainable.

Decolonizing feminist economics stands in opposition to unlimited growth and capitalism, aiming to dismantle hierarchies and dispel myths guiding exploitative global economic activities. It fights for societies and economies centred on the sustainability of life, generating plural economic knowledge and action beyond growth for well-being and economic justice. Collaboration with anti-colonial movements, anti-capitalist movements, Indigenous movements, feminist/anti-patriarchal movements, ecological justice movements, post-extractivist struggles, degrowth movements and progressive governments in the global South is crucial in this decolonizing path.

Hence, putting the sustainability of life at the centre of the economy ensures that the economy serves people and the Earth, rather than the other way around. It opens up a radical way of imagining the economy and economics as ecoSImies of care: that is, as multiple, polyvocal and decolonizing, and as bringing together social, political and economic insights in a situated and contextual manner for sustainable just futures.

Questioning the meaning of value

To transform our current unjust and violent economic system into one that is sustainable and works for all, we must urgently question the very meaning of wealth: What is wealth, and where does value come from? A critical examination reveals that much of what is hailed as value creation is, in reality, a concealed form of value extraction (Mazzucato, 2017). Decolonizing feminist economics explores the meaning of wealth beyond mere economic growth and personal accumulation, seeking to understand how value – what enables material sustenance and general well-being – manifests in contemporary economic landscapes. In that sense, decolonizing feminist economics confronts value, power and justice as a mutually constitutive problem.

By examining what constitutes value and how it is determined, this discourse influences our approach to measuring growth, directing economies towards certain activities, compensating certain endeavours more than others, and shaping our understanding of work, nature and impoverished countries' contribution to life in high-income parts of the world. Mainstream economics often reduces value to a single metric: price (assuming that if a good is traded in the market, it inherently possesses value). As Mariana Mazzucato (2017) contends, our prevailing economic theory establishes a framework where price and exchange uncover value, rather than the reverse. In essence, our societies rely on the price system to reveal value, creating the illusion that monetary measurements accurately indicate value derived from other dimensions.

However, economic estimation is just one of several ways of valuing. Measuring simplifies diverse values to technical instrumentalization, as explored in Chapter 3, and precludes public discourse about these valuations. Furthermore, equating value with price underestimates the contribution of low-income economies to high-income ones. As many have noted, these terms merely reinforce global inequalities that originated under colonial rule. Instead, what if the value of 'raw materials' were more closely tied to the value of the final products they help create (Zein-Elabdin, 2024)? For instance, consider the cobalt case in the Democratic Republic of Congo discussed in Chapter 4. What if the level of income in the Democratic Republic of Congo were determined by how much its people and materials support affluent life in other regions of the world (Zein-Elabdin, 2024)? A contemporary theory of value must be critically aware of its implications for past, present and future inequities, systems of domination, and current global power dynamics.

In economics, value has shifted from being a core economic theory category, tied to production dynamics (division of labour, changing production costs), to a subjective category tied to the 'preferences' of economic agents. Many issues, such as stagnant real wages, are interpreted in terms of the 'choices' that agents make; for example, unemployment is seen as related to workers' choice between work and leisure. Entrepreneurship – the praised motor of capitalism – is viewed as a result of individualized choices rather than the productive system surrounding entrepreneurs, essentially the fruit of collective effort. By understanding value solely as price, there is a tendency to assume that the money someone earns reflects their contribution to the common good, but this is a mistake. Michael Sandel (2013, 2020) argues that, if we assume that, we avoid reasoning and deliberating about what counts as a valuable contribution to the common good. What is truly valuable? What are the purposes and ends of our societies?

Sandel's (2020) work on the tyranny of meritocracy is particularly pertinent in this discussion. He contends that meritocracy, a system allocating income, wealth, power and honour based on perceived deservingness, fosters a dangerous mindset. Winners attribute their success solely to their efforts, while losers feel looked down upon by those at the top. This transforms meritocracy into a tyranny, as success becomes synonymous with deservingness, justifying growing inequalities.

As income and wealth disparities have expanded, meritocratic attitudes towards success have tightened, leading winners to believe in the absolute merit of their accomplishments. Unfortunately, as meritocracy solidifies its hold on public life, it has shifted from being a potential remedy for inequality to a justification for it. This mindset encourages the successful to overlook the role of luck and good fortune in their achievements, eroding social cohesion and diminishing our shared sense of fate.

Sandel explains that the economists behind neoliberal globalization, deregulation and the financial crisis were credentialed under meritocratic principles, unlike their predecessors. In the United States, for instance, this led to four decades of stagnant wages, income inequality reminiscent of the 1920s, the Iraq War, a protracted failed effort in Afghanistan, financial deregulation and the 2008 financial crisis. Governing elites in the age of meritocracy have overseen a decaying infrastructure, the highest incarceration rate globally, and a compromised democratic system through campaign finance and gerrymandered congressional districts.

The COVID-19 pandemic has further exposed the shortcomings of meritocracy in shaping our societies, particularly in the West. Who sustained our lives and the lives of the people we care about, and how are they treated in our economies? As the economic focus shifted to managing money, rewarding hedge fund managers and Wall Street bankers, traditional work lost prestige. However, the pandemic prompted a re-evaluation of roles, emphasizing the importance of those providing essential services linked to traditional work (garbage collectors, supermarket cashiers and stockers, nursing assistants, guards, home caregivers, truck drivers, and so on). Moving forward, it is crucial not only to express gratitude to essential workers but also to restructure economies to recognize and compensate their contributions adequately.

The exploitation of cobalt producers in the Democratic Republic of Congo is not as distant from the plight of exploited workers in the United States as colonial development discourse suggests. Both groups share an institutionalized conception of value that reflects a vast disparity between their pay and the social value of their work, as well as between cobalt producers' income and the price of high-end products like iPhones or Teslas (Zein-Elabdin, 2024).

The debate on the meaning of value has tangible implications, extending beyond the abstract to influence societal, political and economic realms as well as suggesting imaginaries such as contemporary feminist post-work proposals. Conversations about value shape the behaviour of all economic actors, from corporations to consumers, influencing and being influenced by performance measurements. Without a clear definition of value, we risk being unable to generate or distribute it equitably. Therefore, the notion of wealth generation as a collective effort, rather than an individual triumph, and the need to move beyond the monetary value of life are crucial considerations in the pursuit of more just economic systems. Decolonizing feminist economics seeks spaces governed not by market values but by what benefits the entire community and the planet, fostering a new economic culture and imagination rooted in radical solidarity, dignity and the collective management of common wealth.

Advancing economic justice: reparations, land return and wealth redistribution

The process of decolonization involves healing and moving away from anger, loss and grief towards a place where Indigenous peoples can thrive. Key elements of this process include reparations, land return and wealth redistribution, which are crucial for advancing economic justice. However, these efforts require that Indigenous people tell their stories and that these stories are heard. This necessitates a shared understanding of our common past and a shared vision of the future centred on Indigenous lives and futures. It also requires the global North to acknowledge its role, take accountability and stop exploiting resources from the global South. This demands concrete actions.

In that sense, reparations and land return are one part of the process of restoring economic justice for the land theft, genocide, feminicide and enslavement committed in the spirit of capitalism, because the generational privilege is still real and the harm to Indigenous communities and peoples persists. In this regard, Eve Tuck and Wayne Yang (2012) caution that discussions of decolonization that overlook Indigenous sovereignty and rights, neglecting the unsettling and de-occupation of the land, sidestep engagement with settler colonialism.

Despite its significance, the call for reparations and land restitution in the global South often finds itself marginalized or entirely absent from key feminist economics literature on international economics and development (see, for example, Zein-Elabdin and Charusheela, 2004; Berik and Kongar, 2021; Ambler et al, 2022). For feminist economics to align with global justice objectives, it must prioritize reshaping the international economic system – an urgent demand articulated prominently by movements in the global South and decolonizing initiatives, yet still pending in post-growth/degrowth narratives (see Chapter 7). Failure to adopt this global justice outlook may risk rendering feminist economics an insular, localized endeavour within the Europe and global North academic landscape. Going one step further, neglecting to integrate a decolonizing approach into feminist economics could lead to its misuse, potentially perpetuating old colonial patterns when imposed on the global South.

Today, according to the UN Global Crisis Response Group (2023), 3.3 billion people – four out of every ten – reside in states where the expenditure on debt interest surpasses allocations for health or education. As highlighted in the latest Debt Service Watch Report (2023), low-income countries are compelled to allocate 57.7 per cent of their funds to repayments and interest. In 2021, the burden of an external debt totalling nine trillion dollars affected both low- and middle-income countries, as reported by the World Bank (2022). Understanding the proportion of this proves challenging in countries like Spain given that the Ministry of Economy refrains from disclosing such information, citing its non-public status. This lack of transparency regarding the extent and nature of debt stands as a primary challenge faced by analysts. Íñigo Macías, Oxfam Intermón's research coordinator, underscores this issue, stating '[t]hat is one of the main problems that those of us who analyse the debt situation from the point of view of creditors and debtors encounter – the lack of transparency regarding the level of debt and its characteristics' (Otero, 2023; translation mine).

Reparations, land return and wealth redistribution encompass policies and measures implemented by states or corporations to rectify historical and ongoing systematic injustices. These measures aim to rebuild the global economy in ways that ensure justice and well-being for all. Examples of reparations and wealth redistribution range from debt cancellation and unconditional cash transfers to funding climate adaptation, technology transfer and the return of land ownership to local communities. In 1953, Germany's debt was cancelled in London, in the United Kingdom, to facilitate its post-war prosperity, underscoring the acknowledgement that such measures are essential for economic recovery. However, demands for debt cancellation for the global South have been consistently denied, perpetuating a colonial power dynamic that has allowed ongoing exploitation and inequalities.

Reparations compel us to recognize that the global North owes much more to the global South than any financial debt incurred by the latter. For some, reparations involve financial compensation, addressing the trillions that the global North has extracted through the large-scale appropriation of labour, land, energy and materials from the global South, embodied in traded goods (US$152 trillion since 1960, as per Hickel et al [2021]). This amount, as noted by Jason Hickel et al (2021), would be enough to end extreme poverty in the global South 70 times over. This extraction drains the global South of resources necessary for development, perpetuates mass deprivation, and imposes the social and ecological costs of Northern growth overwhelmingly on the global South. Others view reparations holistically, extending beyond the material realm to encompass internal self-emancipation through psychological, cultural and relationship repairs. Many also consider debt justice integral to reparations, entailing the cancellation or repudiation (when a country refuses to pay) of debt and rectifying inequalities embedded in the debt system. As articulated by David Graeber (2014: 390): 'Debt cancellation would not only relieve human suffering, but it would also remind us that money is not ineffable; these are human arrangements. If democracy is going to mean anything, it is the ability for all to agree to arrange things in a different way.'

Decolonizing feminist economics must grapple with issues of reparation and land return addressing and subverting pre-existing unequal and discriminatory structures, as well as devise mechanisms for the redistribution of wealth. In that sense, reparative principles articulated by Black and Indigenous peoples should be central. For Indigenous communities globally, land must be returned, allowing reparations to fall under Indigenous governance and challenging the perpetuation of colonialism, capitalism, heteropatriarchy and ecological degradation.

There exists a profound intersection between decolonizing feminist economics and arguments for reparations, as both fight for economic justice and raise critical questions about Indigenous economic sovereignty, visibility, representation, reparation women's rights and land rights. Insights from global reparations movements offer valuable perspectives on achieving a more anti-racist, anti-patriarchal and economically just transition, particularly in settler-colonial contexts like the United States and Canada. These insights direct attention to fundamental dynamics within the extractivist economic global system that must be reconfigured to ensure lasting, just and shared futures – moving away not only from fossil fuels but also from patriarchy and white supremacy in all its manifestations (Ferdinand, 2022; see also Chapter 5 and Chapter 6).

Efforts towards land return can be integrated into multifaceted feminist economic policies that promote Indigenous economic sovereignty, support decolonization, identify the root causes of economic injustice (including intersectional gender injustice), encourage sustainable resource use, preserve cultural sites, develop community assets, and improve economic outcomes for Indigenous people. Strategies for land reparations may differ depending on distinct Indigenous histories, particular needs, desires and local opportunities for land restitution. These efforts may involve reforming laws and bureaucracies that hinder Indigenous peoples from achieving economic and political independence and justice.

In the United States, the Land Back movement, which calls for the return of the nation's land – especially federal public lands – to Native ownership, shares similarities with broader examples of land reparations. The movement gained significant attention, particularly after the Dakota Access Pipeline protests at Standing Rock, and has witnessed noteworthy achievements. Partnerships with state bodies and conservation organizations have facilitated the acquisition of ancestral land for Indigenous tribes (Johnson, 2023). For instance, the Tübatulabal Tribe secured 1,240 acres bordering the Sequoia National Forest through collaboration with the state Wildlife Conservation Board and the Sierra Nevada Conservancy (Walker, 2023). In Minnesota, land ownership was transferred from the Upper Sioux Agency State Park to the Upper Sioux Community as part of land back and reparations efforts linked to the United States Dakota War of 1862 – the largest mass hanging in United States history (*The Guardian*, 2023).

Individuals can also play a role in supporting land return and tribal restitution. A notable example is Art Tanderup, a Nebraska farmer, who returned a 1.6-acre parcel of ancestral tribal land to the Ponca Tribe in 2018. This land, forcibly taken by the United States government 137 years prior, is now used for growing and restoring the Ponca Tribe's sacred corn (EcoWatch, 2018).

It is crucial to emphasize that merely halting the accumulation of wealth and centralization of power is insufficient to correct global economic inequalities.

Similarly, relying solely on resource transfers through reparations would not be adequate. A decolonizing feminist economics approach is indispensable to opposing the processes of capital accumulation and extractivism, radically transforming heteropatriarchal socio-economic dynamics, and reshaping the imaginary of how we organize to live well, together (see Chapter 7).

Embracing a common world as a political commitment

In academic circles, commitment is often understood in two ways: as a voluntary and unilateral decision or as a contractual agreement between parties. The voluntarist model involves scholars who choose to align themselves with ideas or movements, such as decolonization, without direct involvement. The contractual model, on the other hand, encompasses agreements such as employment, scholarships or grants. However, both models tend to distance us from the true commitments we are already engaged in, creating a sense of immunity – what Tuck and Yang (2012: 1) describe in the context of decolonizing as 'settler moves to innocence' – and the possibility of withdrawal. This makes it easy to avoid honouring commitments, leading to a pervasive 'lack of commitment' in academic projects.

To overcome this detachment, we must step back and truly experience our involvement in the world we share. In this sense, commitments cannot be decided or calculated in the usual way. Making a commitment means allowing oneself to be committed, relinquishing the barriers of immunity and the superficial freedom that comes with it. Every commitment inherently brings change, without guaranteed outcomes. Our personal and collective freedom, therefore, depends on our ability to navigate the obligatory interdependence of our past, present and future lives.

We are not all Indigenous, but this does not mean we are not already committed to Indigenous peoples. Whether we like it or not, we are all implicated in a world we share, and the positions we occupy in this common world depend on how we accept and shape this fundamental commitment. Thus, commitment to others and the realities we share is not only a demand but also the starting point of any idea, decision, project or endeavour (Garcés, 2013).

The question of a common world invites decolonizing feminist economics to ponder what binds us without simplifying it into a unity – whether of a discipline, a topic, an essence, system or identity. Decolonizing feminist economics strives to dismantle oppressive structures, envision an Indigenous future and cultivate connections from a position immersed in the diversity of common problems, where the feminist subject gains relevance by creating new meanings and decentring the viewpoint without disconnecting from shared issues.

Amidst the ongoing privatization of our lives within a capitalist, heteropatriarchal, settler-colonialist framework, and the perceived 'connected isolation' of our globalized world (Sloterdijk, 2016: 294), the modern individual finds themselves distanced from a gift economy. However, when viewed through the lens of the common world, decolonizing feminist economics embraces a political commitment: accepting life as it unfolds, rather than yearning for what was never meant to be. This involves understanding economics as a body (not in anatomic sense but as a web of living meanings) engaged in the world, not merely as an observer.

This shift in economics requires, firstly, stepping away from academic detachment and embodying feminist economics. Secondly, a common world is not merely the world we recognize as ours, but the world that extends beyond us and inscribes us into the concrete and the totality of the unfinished (Garcés, 2013). Thus, the idea of decoloniz*ing* feminist economics does not solely aim to break away from the existing world; it addresses the problem of duration – the ongoing effort to reclaim our capacities and possibilities for a sustainable life, and thus, to envision just futures.

The sustainability of life is a common problem. Yet, decolonizing feminist economics does not view this problem as specific to its framework but rather embraces it as a political commitment to a reality in which we are always already involved. Commitment, understood in this radical sense, exposes decolonizing feminist economics and binds us to others, breaking down the detachment of the Western-centric modern individual and opening a possible way to imagine connections with others and to articulate shared futures.

Decolonizing feminist economics begins with the conviction that a common world is not the world we see as our own, but rather the world that does not end with us – a continuum of human and more-than-human beings, for which we are responsible but of which we are not the sole part. In this way, we can think about how we relate to everything that is yet to be done, desired and lived.

Glossary for Confabulating Futures

From 12 to 25 August 2024, I participated in the artistic residency *The Word for World is Forest: Resilience at the Edge of Collapse* at Konvent in Berga, Catalonia, Spain. The following glossary emerged from a series of confabulative dialogues between the manuscript *Decolonizing Feminist Economics: Possibilities for Just Futures* and each of the eight artistic projects of the residency. I compiled this glossary using words that resonated throughout these dialogues, aiming to capture not just the dialogue but the conspiracy for possible futures that was being woven.

The *Glossary for Confabulating Futures* was presented on Saturday, 25 August, during the Open Studio at Konvent, where the general public was invited to participate in the confabulations.

Special thanks to the artists with whom I engaged in confabulative dialogue to create the glossary: Abgott project (Gianluca Patrizi and Marco Garofalo), Anna Cornudella and Eliza Lu Doyle, Laura del Vecchio, Luka Lenzin, Luzia G. Pardo, Mona Mohagheghi, Nour Kara and Sabina M. Entrocassi. Additional thanks to Laia Llobera and Gil Roca Culí for their organization, curation and care throughout the residency. A heartfelt thank you to everyone at Konvent.

Glossary for confabulating futures

Confabulate has its origins in conversation and *fable*, thus opening the possibility of collectively reviewing and conspiring possible futures. In the face of apocalyptic discourses, we wanted to come together to breathe better, to confabulate better, to reappropriate the past, present and future.

From complicity and dialogue, we have distanced ourselves from urgency to take a moment to think, question and imagine, together, new ways of being and connecting. Rather than *reflecting on* our artistic and creative practices, we have created gatherings to *engage from within*, activating future imaginaries in the present.

This glossary was created from a series of confabulative dialogues between the manuscript *Decolonizing Feminist Economics: Possibilities for Just Futures* and each of the eight artistic projects of the residency *The Word For World is Forest: Resilience at the Edge of Collapse* at Konvent during August 2024. From these confabulations, the following ideas-action for other possible futures have emerged.

***

Humans are insignificant and precarious, but we have an extraordinary power.

Rehearsing

Examining, recognizing, testing, and experiencing, with others, different ways of living to avoid dwelling in impotence and indifference. *Synonym*: Betting on the future together.

Cultivating

Giving to the earth, being gardeners. Providing for things to happen. Meeting at welcoming tables that do not start from a closed group, but rather open and invite the possible senses of communal life. Welcoming the stranger is learning to estrange ourselves.

Glimmer

A deep and momentary surge of desire that arises from within, as a yearning for something that does not yet exist. Glimmers dwell underground, they appear rather than being sought. Attentive listening is needed.

Fragile ideas

Concepts of great collective power for creativity, invention and practical resolution of our common problems. They make us uncomfortable, put us on alert. They must be accompanied because they can break. Fragility is the soul of the revolution.

(Im)possibles

Their intention is not to advocate for an unattainable utopia. Rather, they invite us to recognize that the prison in which we feel trapped – an unjust, colonial, heteropatriarchal, unsustainable economic system – is, in fact, an open cell. It is we who cling to the bars. How do we want to live? What kind of economies do we want?

Traces

Phantasmagoric voices of lives beyond our own, the humans. They narrate times that indicate that a trace, like time, has no original. It is a crossed-out origin that always refers to another trace. Traces are political, measured by the realities they draw. What to do with those who impose their traces? *Synonyms*: Clues, scars, imaginaries, trails.

Bridges

Foster connections without focusing solely on results. Link without unifying, allowing for diversity and difference without forcing everything into a single paradigm.

Familiar voices

What separates us is what unites us. Simone Weil tells us about two prisoners confined in a prison. Between them is a thick stone wall, but over the years, they learn to communicate by tapping on the stone. The wall is what separates them, but it is also the only means they have to communicate. Every separation is always a bond.

Notes

Preface

1 I am most grateful to Albert Lladó for his helpful comments and suggestions on the Preface of this book. For all errors of commission or omission that remain, I am to be held responsible.

Introduction

1 I recognize the problematic nature of homogenizing dichotomies such as West(ern) and the global South. Drawing on Kapoor (2008), I use these terms to refer to an unequal structure of knowledge and material production rooted in colonial hierarchies.

2 The term heterodox, while somewhat ambiguous and in contention, serves to distinguish a diverse group of economic philosophies – most notably Marxian, institutionalist, post-Keynesian and feminist – from the neoclassical approach (orthodox).

3 It is interesting to note that while mainstream economics often presents a disembodied narrative, it also embodies cis-heteronormative logic. As a system that organizes the world, cis-heteronormativity imposes a universal subject – whether male or female – with supposedly universal problems, a body that shares the same challenges, difficulties and, above all, potentials.

4 Oyěwùmí (1997: 3) explains the inadequacy of the term 'worldview' as a synonym for cosmology in Yoruba contexts and suggests '"world sense" as a more inclusive way of describing the conception of the world by different cultural groups'.

5 Coloniality maintains the matrix of power established during active colonization through contemporary institutional, financial and genopolitical world orders. And also through knowledge systems (Quijano, 2000).

6 Land, water, air, oceans and the subterranean earth (hereinafter collectively referred to as 'land').

7 Although scholars such as Tim Jackson (2021) distinguish degrowth and postgrowth quite strongly, I use degrowth and postgrowth interchangeably in this book, as both are grounded in the post-capitalist hypothesis that societies can live better with less, alongside an acknowledgement of the necessity for a social-ecological transformation of the economy and of economics, including a fundamental critique of the hegemony of growth. For the purposes of this book, I consider their differences as not particularly relevant, viewing post-growth as encompassing degrowth, and degrowth as a step toward achieving a post-growth world (Kallis, 2018; Hickel, 2020; Schmelzer et al, 2022; Kallis et al, 2023).

8 Neoclassical economics presents the model of *Homo economicus* as an isolated, self-sufficient, rational and selfish individual who makes decisions through a personal and rational process of utility maximization. This model suggests that the individual's character is composed of calculable components such as self-interest, short-term perspective and immediate expediency, with a tendency towards materialism. This individual is conceptualized as

without a body (Pérez Orozco, 2014) but yet embodies a cis-heteronormative logic (see endnote 3).

Chapter 1

1 The neoclassical variant refers to the choice game-theoretical model, which is based on the premise that aggregate social behaviour results from the behaviour of individual actors, each of whom is making their individual decisions. According to this model, rational decisions culminate in the supremacy of the market as a medium for resource allocation.

2 See, for example, the open letter from economic students to professors and others responsible for the teaching of this discipline (2000). Available at: http://www.paecon.net/PAEtexts/a-e-petition.htm

3 An international student call for pluralism in economics, open letter (2014). Available at: http://www.isipe.net/open-letter

4 An open letter to Greg Mankiw (2011). Available at: https://harvardpolitics.com/an-open-letter-to-greg-mankiw/

5 I developed these questions within the framework of a collaboration with the Program for Gender Analysis in Economics at the Department of Economics, American University (Washington, DC), and the University Programme of Studies on Asia and Africa at the National Autonomous University of Mexico, as part of an effort towards decolonizing the feminist economics curriculum. Special thanks to Professor Mieke Meurs and Professor Alicia Girón.

Chapter 2

1 International Association for Feminist Economics (IAFFE) Official Web Page: https://www.iaffe.org/pages/about-iaffe/miss/

2 Examples of postcolonial feminist economists are S. Charusheela (2001, 2003, 2009), Cynthia Wood (2003), Suzanne Bergeron (2004), Eiman Osman Zein-Elabdin and S. Charusheela (2004), J.K. Gibson-Graham (2006) and Eiman Osman Zein-Elabdin (2009, 2016, 2024).

3 One of the few works in feminist economics works that incorporates queer theory is Colin Danby's (2007) critique of heteronormativity in feminist economics.

4 For a different understanding of developmentalism as internationalism, see Christy Thornton (2023).

5 See here the Sustainable Development Index: https://www.sustainabledevelopmentindex.org

6 'Gender equality is a human right', is recognized as such in Article 23 of the Charter of Fundamental Rights of the European Union (2007/C 303/01). Available at: https://www.europarl.europa.eu/charter/pdf/text_en.pdf

7 I presented some of these reflections during the seminar 'Touch but Not Wounded by the Institution', which I delivered to postgraduate students in the Research Lab II: Designing Gender Research at Utrecht University on 24 January 2023. The seminar was coordinated by Dr Adriano José Habed. I am grateful to the students and Dr Habed for their engaging discussions on the topic.

Chapter 3

1 Orientalism is frequently linked with Edward Said's seminal work *Orientalism* (1978). Said contended that cultural hegemony played a pivotal role in colonial relationships and continues to be a means by which the West sustains its hegemonic power over the non-Western world. Though criticisms of European ethnocentrism existed prior to Said, his book marked the beginning of a comprehensive examination of how European

thought an imagined non-Western (Oriental) Other. This construct, according to Said, was instrumental in shaping Europe's modernist imagination.

2 Tactics have included the cancellation of events and lectures, the termination of critical visiting scholars, threats to de-matriculate pro-Palestinian students, censorship of frameworks like Apartheid and settler colonialism, and draconian measures against student protesters. Governments have also pressured universities to suppress students' rights to free speech and assembly.

Chapter 4

1 Cobalt is necessary for the batteries used in our electronic devices. Before this material, there were other raw materials in the Democratic Republic of the Congo: graphite, palm oil, diamonds, wood, copper and, above all, people (Kara, 2023).

2 https://www.rtve.es/noticias/20241108/aumentan-223-muertos-dana-valencia-castilla-mancha-andalucia/16322569.shtml

Chapter 5

1 It included Cleo Reece (Fort McMurray First Nation), Eriel Tchekwie Deranger (Athabasca Chipewyan First Nation) and Melina Laboucan-Massimo (Little Buffalo First Nation). The last walk took place in 2014, as the organizers felt their goals of spreading awareness were achieved (Leahy, 2014).

Chapter 6

1 For further insights into commercial lithium production, readers may refer to 'An Overview of Commercial Lithium Production', available at: https://www.thoughtco.com/lithium-production-2340123

2 For example, for a more-than-human mode of relationality as an experimentation of an inter-species dialogue see the artistic work of Paula Bruna (nd).

Chapter 7

1 This chapter incorporates material from the master class I delivered at the National Autonomous University of Mexico (UNAM) titled '*Qué economía(s) queremos? Ecologías de la imaginación económica*', part of the *Epistemologías Feministas, Economía y Cultura: Diálogos con Asia y África* graduate programme at the University Program of Asian and African Studies (PUEAA). The class was held virtually and open to the public on 9 August 2022. My heartfelt thanks to Professor Alicia Girón.

2 Global Atlas of Environmental Justice, EjAtlas, available at: https://ejatlas.org/print/proyecto-minero-el-tambor

3 Global Atlas of Environmental Justice, EjAtlas, available at: https://ejatlas.org/print/proyecto-minero-el-tambor

4 Yolanda Oquelí, Ajuntament de Barbará, available at: https://www.bdv.cat/es/yolanda-oqueli-guatemala-0

5 The documentary is available at: https://www.youtube.com/watch?v=mbfdyBX4J8I

Chapter 8

1 Some efforts have been made by scholars such as Ulla Grapard (1995), Drucilla Barker and Edith Kuiper (2003), Eiman Osman Zein-Elabdin and S. Charusheela (2004), Jennifer Olmsted (2004), Natalia Quiroga Diaz and Daniela Gómez Correal (2013), Ebru Kongar, Jennifer Olmsted and Elora Shehabuddin (2018) and Gisela Carrasco-Miró (2020a).

References

Achiume, T. (2019) *Report of the Special Rapporteur on Contemporary Forms of Racial Discrimination, Xenophobia and Related Intolerance: Global Extractivism and Racial Inequality*. UN Doc A/HRC/41/54, 14 May.

Acosta, A. (2013) *El Buen Vivir: Sumak Kawsay, una oportunidad para imaginar otros mundos*. Ecuador: Antrazyt.

Acosta, A. and Brand, U. (2017) *Salidas del laberinto capitalista: Decrecimiento y postextractivismo*. Barcelona: Editorial Icaria.

Adefarakan, E.T. (2011) (Re)conceptualizing 'indigenous' from anti-colonial and Black feminist theoretical perspectives: Living and imagining indigeneity differently. In G.J. Sefa Dei (ed), *Indigenous Philosophies and Critical Education: A Reader* (vol 379, pp 34–52). Berkeley: Counterpoints.

Ahmad, S. (2020) The lithium triangle: Where Chile, Argentina, and Bolivia meet. *Harvard International Review*, 15 January. Available at: https://hir.harvard.edu/lithium-triangle/

Ahmed, A.K. (2017) #RhodesMustFall: Decolonization, praxis and disruption. *Journal of Comparative and International Higher Education*, 9(2), 5–9. Available at: https://www.lse.ac.uk/sociology/assets/documents/events/UCT-Rhodes-Must-Fall-Statement.pdf

Ake, C. (1979) *Social Science as Imperialism: A Theory of Political Development*. Ibadan: Ibadan University Press.

Albán Achinte, A. (2013) Pedagogías de la re-existencia: Artistas indígenas y afrocolombianos. In C. Walsh (ed), *Pedagogías decoloniales: Prácticas insurgentes de resistir, (re)existir y (re)viver* (vol 1, pp 443–468). Quito: Ediciones Abya Yala.

Alexander, N. (2022) Walking the Tar Sands: Poetry and the fossil economy. *Green Letters*, 26(3), 231–240. https://doi.org/10.1080/14688417.2022.2102526

Allison, J.E. (2017) Ecofeminism and global environmental politics. *Oxford Research Encyclopaedia of International Studies*. https://doi.org/10.1093/acrefore/9780190846626.013.158. Available at: https://oxfordre.com/internationalstudies/view/10.1093/acrefore/9780190846626.001.0001/acrefore-9780190846626-e-158?print=pdf

Altamirano-Jiménez, I. (2021) Indigenous women refusing the violence of resource extraction in Oaxaca. *AlterNative*, 17, 215–223.

Amadiume, I. (1997) *Reinventing Africa: Matriarchy, Religion and Culture*. London: Zed.

Ambler, L., Earle, J. and Scott, N. (2022) *Reclaiming Economics for Future Generations*. Manchester: Manchester University Press.

Amin, S. (1976) *Unequal Development: An Essay on the Social Formations of Peripheral Capitalism*. New York: Monthly Review Press.

Amin, S. (1988 [2009]) *Eurocentrism*. New York: Monthly Review Press.

Anchorage Declaration (2009) Available at: http://unfccc.int/resource/docs/2009/smsn/ngo/168.pdf

Anderson, K. and Real, M.J. (2023) *Women on the Frontlines of Extractivism: How Funders Can Support Women Environmental Defenders*. Global Alliance for Green and Gender Action (GAGGA), Global Greengrants Fund, and SAGE Fund. Available at: https://gaggaalliance.org/women-on-the-frontlines-of-extractivism-how-funders-can-support-women-environmental-defenders/

Anzaldúa, G. (1999 [1987]) *Borderlands/La frontera: The New Mestiza*. San Francisco: Aunt Lute Books.

Arendt, H. (2006 [1961]) *Between Past and Future*. New York: Penguin Books.

Bakare-Yusuf, B. (2003) 'Yorubas don't do gender': A critical review of Oyèrónkẹ́ Oyěwùmí's *The invention of women: Making an African sense of Western gender discourses*. *African Identities*, 1(1), 119–140.

Bal, M. (2002) *Travelling Concepts in the Humanities: A Rough Guide*. Toronto: University of Toronto Press.

Banks, N. (2021) Intersectional identities and analysis. In G. Berik and E. Kongar (eds), *The Routledge Handbook of Feminist Economics* (pp 118–126). London: Routledge.

Barad, K. (2003) Posthumanist performativity: Toward an understanding of how matter comes to matter. *Signs: Journal of Women in Culture and Society*, 28(3), 801–831.

Baran, P. (1957) *The Political Economy of Growth*. New York: Monthly Review Press.

Barcia, I. (2017) *Weaving Resistance Through Action: Strategies of Women Human Rights Defenders Confronting Extractive Industries*. Available at: https://www.awid.org/sites/default/files/atoms/files/eng_weaving_resistance_through_action-web.pdf

Barker, D. (2000) Dualisms, discourse, and development. In U. Narayan and S. Harding (eds), *Decentering the Center: Philosophy for a Multicultural, Postcolonial, and Feminist World* (pp 177–188). Bloomington: Indiana University Press.

Barker, D. (2005) Beyond women and economics: Rereading 'women's work'. *Signs*, 30(4), 2189–2209.

Barker, D. (2006) A seat at the table: Feminist economists negotiate development. In E. Kuiper and D. Barker (eds), *Feminist Economics and the World Bank: History, Theory and Policy* (pp 209–217). London: Routledge.

Barker, D. and Kuiper, E. (eds) (2003) *Toward a Feminist Philosophy of Economics*. London: Routledge.

Barker, J. (2005) *Sovereignty Matters: Locations of Contestation and Possibility in Indigenous Struggles for Self-determination*. Lincoln: University of Nebraska Press.

Basic Income Earth Network (nd) Available at: https://basicincome.org

Battiste, M. (2002) *Indigenous Knowledge and Pedagogy in First Nations Education: A Literature Review with Recommendations*. Prepared for the National Working Group on Education and the Minister of Indian Affairs, Indian and Northern Affairs Canada (INAC). Ottawa: Ontario.

Benería, L. (1981) Conceptualizing the labor force: The underestimation of women's economic activities. *The Journal of Development Studies*, 17(3), 10–28.

Bergeron, S. (2004) *Fragments of Development: Nation, Gender, and the Space of Modernity*. Ann Arbor: University of Michigan Press.

Berik, G. and Kongar, E. (eds) (2021) *The Routledge Handbook of Feminist Economics*. London and New York: Routledge.

Bermúdez Rico, R., Rodríguez Maldonado, T. and Roa Avendaño, T. (2011) Mujer y minería: Ámbitos de análisis e impactos de la minería en la vida de las mujeres. Enfoque de derechos y perspectiva de género. Cordaid y al Programa Mujeres y Violencias de la Fundación Synergia. Available at: http://www.indepaz.org.co/wp-content/uploads/2013/04/Mujer_y_Mineria.pdf

Bhambra, G.K. (2014) Postcolonial and decolonial dialogues. *Postcolonial Studies*, 17(2), 115–129.

Biemann, U. (2013) *Deep Weather* [Video]. 9 minutes.

Biemann, U. (2015) Deep weather. *Intervalla*, 3.

Biemann, U. (2020) Ursula Biemann interview by Hélène Guenin: Indigenous knowledge and cosmological fictions. *Environment Ecology*, 10 December. Available at: https://www.switchonpaper.com/en/environment/ecology/indigenous-knowledge-cosmological-fictions/

Biemann, U. (2022) *Geobodies*. Available at: https://geobodies.org

Birulés, F. (2023) *Hannah Arendt: El món en joc*. Barcelona: Arcadia.

Blaser, M. and de la Cadena, M. (eds) (2018) *A World of Many Worlds*. Durham, NC: Duke University Press.

Bolados García, C. and Sánchez Cuevas, P. (2017) Una ecología política feminista en construcción: El caso de las 'Mujeres de zonas de sacrificio en resistencia', Región de Valparaíso, Chile. *Psicoperspectivas*, 16(2), 33–42. https://doi.org/10.5027/psicoperspectivas-vol16-issue2-fulltext-977

Braidotti, R. (1994) *Nomadic Subjects: Embodiment and Sexual Difference in Contemporary Feminist Theory*. New York: Columbia University Press.

Braidotti, R. (2011) *Nomadic Theory: The Portable Rosi Braidotti*. New York: Columbia University Press.

Brum, E. (2024) *La Amazonia viaje al centro del mundo*. Barcelona: Ediciones Salamandra.

Bruna, N. (2022) Going beyond efficiency-driven extractivism: A climate-smart world and the rise of green extractivism. *Journal of Peasant Studies*, 49(4), 1–26.

Bruna, P. (nd) *Embolismo por soleá*. Available at: https://paulabruna.com/embolismo-por-solea/

Business & Human Rights Resource Centre (2024) Kenya government compensates 4,102 fishermen harmed by Lamu Port-South Sudan-Ethiopia Transport (LAPSSET) project, 14 June. Available at: https://www.business-humanrights.org/en/latest-news/kenya-government-compensates-4102-fishermen-harmed-by-lamu-port-south-sudan-ethiopia-transport-lapsset-project/

Butler, J. (1997) Merely cultural. *Social Text*, 52/53, 265–277. https://doi.org/10.2307/466744

Butler, J. (2000) Competing universalities. In J. Butler, E. Laclau and Ž. Slavoj (eds), *Contingency, Hegemony, Universality: Contemporary Dialogues on the Left* (pp 136–181). London and New York: Verso Books.

Butler, J. (2006 [1990]) *Gender Trouble: Feminism and the Subversion of Identity*. New York: Routledge.

Byrne, D. (2020) Decolonial African feminism for white allies. *Journal of International Women's Studies*, 21(7), 37–46. Available at: https://vc.bridgew.edu/jiws/vol21/iss7/4

Cabnal, L. (2010) Acercamiento a la construcción de la propuesta de pensamiento epistémico de las mujeres indígenas feministas comunitarias de Abya Yala. In *Feminismos diversos: El feminismo comunitario* (pp 11–25). Madrid: ACSUR Las Segovias.

Cabnal, L. (2015) De las opresiones a las emancipaciones: Mujeres indígenas en defensa del territorio cuerpo-tierra. *Pueblos: Revista de Información y Debate*. Available at: http://www.revistapueblos.org/blog/2015/02/06/de-las-opresiones-a-las-emancipaciones-mujeres-indigenas-en-defensa-del-territorio-cuerpo-tierra/

Cabnal, L. (2018) Lorena Cabnal: Sanar y defender el territorio-cuerpo-tierra. *Avispa Media*. Available at: https://avispa.org/lorena-cabnal-sanar-y-defender-el-territorio-cuerpo-tierra/

Cabnal, L. (2020) *Lorena Cabnal: La sanación, un acto feminista emancipatorio*. Available at: https://decolonial.hypotheses.org/2147

Cabral, A. (1966) The weapon of theory. Address delivered to the first Tricontinental Conference of the Peoples of Asia, Africa and Latin America, Havana, January. Available at: https://www.historyisaweapon.com/defcon1/cabralwepthe.html

Cabral, A. (1979) *Unity and Struggle: Speeches and Writings of Amilcar Cabral*. New York: Monthly Review Press.

Cameron, P.D. and Stanley, M.C. (2017) *Oil, Gas, and Mining: A Sourcebook for Understanding the Extractive Industries*. Washington, DC: World Bank Group. Available at: http://documents.worldbank.org/curated/en/222451496911224999/Oil-gas-and-mining-a-sourcebook-for-understanding-the-extractive-industries

Carastathis, A. (2016) *Intersectionality: Origins, Contestations, Horizons*. Lincoln and London: University of Nebraska Press.

Carrasco-Miró, G. (2016) A critical look at the gender responsive budgeting approach in the development discourse: A feminist contribution to postcolonial politics of development. *Tijdschrift voor Genderstudies*, 19(1), 57–75. https://doi.org/10.05117/TVGN2016.1.CARR

Carrasco-Miró, G. (2017) EcoSImies of care: A proposal for decolonizing 'sustainable development'. *Insurgencies from the South and Human Rights. A Transdisciplinary Journal of Postcolonial Humanities*, 2, 89–108.

Carrasco-Miró, G. (2018a) *Epistemologies at a Crossroads: Decolonising Knowledges on Politics of Development, Economics, and Feminism* (PhD thesis). Available at: https://dspace.library.uu.nl/handle/1874/371558

Carrasco-Miró, G. (2018b) South-South cooperation and trilateral development cooperation: New donors, same colonial practices? Towards decolonizing solidarity. *CIDOB Journal on International Relations*, 120. https://doi.org/10.24241/rcai.2018.120.3.147

Carrasco-Miró, G. (2020a) Decolonizing feminist economics: Interrogating the women's economic empowerment and gender equality development framework. *Social Politics: International Studies in Gender, State and Society*. https://doi.org/10.1093/sp/jxaa033

Carrasco-Miró, G. (2020b) Encountering the colonial: Religion in feminism and the coloniality of secularism. *Feminist Theory*, 21(1), 91–109.

Carrasco-Miró, G. (2021) Decolonising development: Putting life at the centre. *E-International Relations*. Available at: https://www.e-ir.info/2021/04/14/decolonising-development-putting-life-at-the-centre/

Carrasco-Miró, G. (2025a) Recognizing intersectionality and epistemological plurality in feminist economics. In *Feminist Economics: Women, Work and the Home*. London: Routledge (forthcoming).

Carrasco-Miró, G. (2025b) Interrupting whatever seems inevitable: Decolonising knowledge to make another experience of 'we'. *Third World Quarterly* (forthcoming).

Carvajal, L. (2016) *Extractivismo en América Latina: Impacto en la vida de las mujeres y propuesta de defensa del territorio.* FAU – AL Fondo Acción Urgente – América Latina 2016. Available at: https://movimientom4.org/wp-content/docs/Extractivismo-en-Am%C3%A9rica-Latina.-Impacto-en-la-vida-de-las-mujeres-y-propuestas-de-defensa-del-territorio.pdf

Castoriadis, C. (1997) *The Imaginary Institution of Society.* Cambridge, MA: MIT Press.

Cerwonka, A. (2008) Traveling feminist thought: Difference and transculturation in Central and Eastern European feminism. *Signs*, 33(4), 809–832. https://doi.org/10.1086/528852

Césaire, A. (1972 [1950]) *Discourse on Colonialism.* New York: Monthly Review Press.

Césaire, S. (1941 [2001]) The domain of the marvelous. In M.A. Caws (ed), *Surrealist Painters and Poets: An Anthology* (pp 1–20). Achorn Graphic Services, Inc.

Chagnon, C.W., Durante, F., Gills, B.K., Hagolani-Albov, S.E., Hokkanen, S., Kangasluoma, S.M.J., et al (2022) From extractivism to global extractivism: The evolution of an organizing concept. *The Journal of Peasant Studies*, 49(4), 760–792. https://doi.org/10.1080/03066150.2022.2069015

Chant, S. and Sweetman, C. (2012) Fixing women or fixing the world? 'Smart economics,' efficiency approaches, and gender equality in development. *Gender & Development*, 20(3), 517–529. https://doi.org/10.1080/13552074.2012.731812

Charusheela, S. (2001) Women's choices and the ethnocentrism/relativism dilemma in postmodernism, economics, and knowledge. In J. Amariglio, S.E. Cullenberg and D.F. Ruccio (eds), *Postmodernism, Economics, and Knowledge* (pp 159–174). London: Routledge.

Charusheela, S. (2003) Empowering work? Bargaining models reconsidered. In D. Barker and E. Kuiper (eds), *Toward a Feminist Philosophy of Economics* (pp 287–301). London: Routledge.

Charusheela, S. (2009) Social analysis and the capabilities approach: A limit to Martha Nussbaum's universalist ethics. *Cambridge Journal of Economics*, 33(6), 1135–1152.

Charusheela, S. and Zein-Elabdin, E.O. (2003) Feminism, postcolonial thought, and economics. In M. Ferber and J. Nelson (eds), *Feminist Economics Today: Beyond Economic Man* (pp 175–192). Chicago: University of Chicago Press.

Chipana, S. (2018) De la sanación a la liberación. In D. Rufín and L. Marrero (eds), *Reencantos y reencuentros: Caminos y desafíos actuales de las teologías de la liberación* (pp 157–166). Buenos Aires: JUAN UNO.

Christoffersen, A. and Emejulu, A. (2023) 'Diversity within': The problems with 'intersectional' white feminism in practice. *Social Politics: International Studies in Gender, State & Society*, 30(2), 630–653. https://doi.org/10.1093/sp/jxac044

Clifford, J. (1997) *Routes: Travel and Translation in the Late Twentieth Century*. Cambridge, MA: Harvard University Press.

Colectivo Miradas críticas del territorio desde el feminismo (2014) *La vida en el centro y el crudo bajo tierra: El Yasuní en clave feminista*. Available at: https://miradascriticasdelterritoriodesdeelfeminismo.files.wordpress.com/2014/05/yasunienclavefeminista.pdf

Collins, P.H. (1990) *Black Feminist Thought: Knowledge, Consciousness and the Politics of Empowerment*. New York: Routledge.

Collins, P.H. (2000) Gender, Black feminism, and Black political economy. *The Annals of the American Academy of Political and Social Science*, 568, 41–53. http://www.jstor.org/stable/1049471

Colpani, G., Mascat, J.M.H. and Smiet, K. (2022) Postcolonial responses to decolonial interventions. *Postcolonial Studies*, 25(1), 1–16. https://doi.org/10.1080/13688790.2022.2041695

Combahee River Collective (1977) A Black feminist statement. In B. Smith (ed), *Homegirls: A Black Feminist Anthology* (pp 272–292). New York: Women of Color Press.

Costa, C.L. and Alvarez, S.E. (2014) Dislocating the sign: Toward a translocal feminist politics of translation. *Signs: Journal of Women in Culture and Society*, 39(3), 557–563.

Crenshaw, K. (1989) Demarginalizing the intersection of race and sex: A Black feminist critique of antidiscrimination doctrine, feminist theory and antiracist politics. *University of Chicago Legal Forum*, 1, Article 8. Available at: http://chicagounbound.uchicago.edu/uclf/vol1989/iss1/8

Cumes, A. and Iñigo, M. (2017) Conversación sobre epistemología Maya, teoría poscolonial y procesos de lucha identitaria con Aura Cumes. *Re-visiones*, 7(5).

Curiel, O. (2007) Crítica poscolonial desde las prácticas del feminismo antirracista. *Nómadas*, 26, 92–101.

D'Alisa, G., Demaria, F. and Kallis, G. (eds) (2014) *Degrowth: A Vocabulary for a New Era*. New York and London: Routledge.

Danby, C. (2007) Political economy and the closet: Heteronormativity in feminist economics. *Feminist Economics*, 13(2), 29–53. https://doi.org/10.1080/13545700601184898

Dar, S., Martinez Dy, A. and Rodriguez, J.K. (2018) Is decolonizing the new black? *Sisters of Resistance* [blog]. Available at: https://sistersofresistance.wordpress.com/2018/07/12/is-decolonizing-the-new-black/

Davis, A. (1983) *Women, Race and Class*. New York: Vintage.

Davis, K. (2008) Intersectionality as buzzword: A sociology of science perspective on what makes a feminist theory successful. *Feminist Theory*, 9(1), 67–85. https://doi.org/10.1177/1464700108086364

Debt Service Watch Report (2023) *The Worst Ever Global Debt Crisis: New Data from Debt Service Watch.* Available at: https://assets.nationbuilder.com/eurodad/pages/3195/attachments/original/1696947958/Debt_Service_Watch_Briefing_Final_Word_EN_0910.pdf?1696947958

D-Econ (Diversifying and Decolonising Economics) (nd) Available at: https://d-econ.org/mission/

De Capitani, L. and Bassi, S. (eds) (2023) Exploring New Routes in the Postcolonial Environmental Humanities. *From the European South*, 13, 4–9. https://www.fesjournal.eu

de Henau, J. and Himmelweit, S. (2021) A care-led recovery from COVID-19: Investing in high-quality care to stimulate and rebalance the economy. *Feminist Economics*, 27(1–2), 453–469. https://doi.org/10.1080/13545701.2020.1845390

de Jong, S. (2022) Writing rights: Suturing Spivak's postcolonial and de Sousa Santos' decolonial thought. *Postcolonial Studies*, 25(1), 89–107. https://doi.org/10.1080/13688790.2022.2030596

de La Boétie, É. (2008 [1578]) *The Politics of Obedience: The Discourse of Voluntary Servitude* (H. Kurz, trans). Auburn: Ludwig von Mises Institute.

de la Cadena, M., Lien, M.E., Blaser, M., Bruun Jensen, C., Lea, T., Morita, A., et al (2015) Anthropology and STS: Generative interfaces, multiple locations. *HAU: Journal of Ethnographic Theory*, 5(1), 437–475. https://doi.org/10.14318/hau5.1.020

Deligny, F. (2009) *Permitir, trazar, ver.* Museu d'Art Contemporani de Barcelona.

Dell'Angelo, J., Navas, G., Witteman, M., D'Alisa, G., Scheidel, A. and Temper, L. (2021) Commons grabbing and agribusiness: Violence, resistance, and social mobilization. *Ecological Economics*, 184, Article 107004.

Del Mármol, C. and Vaccaro, I. (2020) New extractivism in European rural areas: How twentieth-first century mining returned to disturb the rural transition. *Geoforum*, 116, 42–49.

Demos, T.J. (2020) *Beyond the World's End: Arts of Living at the Crossing.* Durham, NC: Duke University Press.

Deonandan, K., Tatham, R. and Field, B. (2017) Indigenous women's anti-mining activism: A gendered analysis of the El Estor struggle in Guatemala. *Gender & Development*, 25, 405–419.

Despentes, V. (2018) Pour les manants de demain. In J. Lindgaard (ed), *Éloge des mauvaises herbes: Ce que nous devons à la ZAD.* Paris: Les Liens Qui Libèrent.

Dhamoon, R.K. (2015) A feminist approach to decolonizing anti-racism: Rethinking transnationalism, intersectionality, and settler colonialism. *Feral Feminisms*, 4, 20–36.

Di Paula López, M., Fernández Álvarez, S., Kelly Fernández, E., Delgado, M. and Juventud por el Clima (2023) SI Al Yasuní. *Pikara Magazine*, 8 November. Available at: https://www.pikaramagazine.com/2023/11/si-al-yasuni/

Djerbi, D. (2024) The social reproductive roots of agrarian contention: Gendered labor amid peasant struggles in Tunisia. *Antipode*. https://doi.org/10.1111/anti.13081

Dorronsoro, B. (2013) El territorio cuerpo-tierra como espacio-tempo de resistencias y luchas en las mujeres indígenas y originarias. In *Cabo dos Trabalhos. IV Colóquio Internacional de Doutorandos/as do CES, 6–7 dezembro 2013*. Available at: https://cabodostrabalhos.ces.uc.pt/n10/documentos/11.3.1_Begona_Dorronsoro.pdf

EcoWatch (2018) *Nebraska Farmers and Keystone XL*. Available at: https://www.ecowatch.com/nebraska-farmers-keystone-xl-2578444895.html

EIP (European Innovation Partnership on Raw Materials) (2018) *Raw Materials Scoreboard*. European Commission, Joint Research Centre. Available at: https://publications.europa.eu/en/publication-detail/-/publication/117c8d9b-e3d3-11e8-b690-01aa75ed71a1

Ellman, H. (2013) 'Stop the destruction, start the healing': Tar Sands healing walk. *Cultural Survival*, 22 July. Available at: https://www.culturalsurvival.org/news/stop-destruction-start-healing-tar-sands-healing-walk

Escobar, A. (1995) *Encountering Development: The Making and Unmaking of the Third World*. Princeton: Princeton University Press.

Escobar, A. (2016) Thinking-feeling with the Earth: Territorial struggles and the ontological dimension of the epistemologies of the South. *Revista de Antropología Iberoamericana*, 11(1), 11–32.

Espai en Blanc (2015) *Pressentiment No. 41*. Available at: http://elpressentiment.net/no-41?lang=en

Espinosa, Y., Gómez, D. and Ochoa, K. (eds) (2014) *Tejiendo de otro modo: Feminismo, epistemología y apuestas descoloniales*. Popayán: Editorial Universidad del Cauca.

Esquivel, V. (2017) The rights-based approach to care policies: Latin American experience. *International Social Security Review*, 70, 87–103.

Estes, N. (2019) *Standing with Standing Rock: Voices from the #NoDAPL Movement*. Minneapolis: University of Minnesota Press.

European Environment Agency (2021) *Reflecting on Green Growth: Creating a Resilient Economy within Environmental Limits*. Available at: https://www.eea.europa.eu/publications/reflecting-on-green-growth

Fanon, F. (1963) *The Wretched of the Earth* (C. Farrington, trans). New York: Grove Press.

Federici, S. (2004) *Caliban and the Witch: Women, the Body and Primitive Accumulation*. New York: Autonomidia.

Federici, S. (2012) *Revolution at Point Zero: Housework, Reproduction, and Feminist Struggle*. Oakland: Common Notions/PM Press.

Federici, S. (2018) *El patriarcado del salario: Críticas feministas al marxismo*. Madrid: Traficantes de Sueños.

Feminisms and Degrowth Alliance (nd) Available at: https://degrowth.info/blog/feminisms-and-degrowth-alliance-fada-newly-launched

Ferber, M. and Nelson, J.A. (eds) (1993) *Beyond Economic Man*. Chicago: University of Chicago Press.

Ferdinand, M. (2022) *Decolonial Ecology: Thinking from the Caribbean World*. Cambridge: Polity Press.

Fernández-Llamazares, Á., Garteizgogeascoa, M., Basu, N., Brondizio, E.S., Cabeza, M., Martínez-Alier, J., et al (2020) A state-of-the-art review of indigenous peoples and environmental pollution. *Integrated Environmental Assessment and Management*, 16, 324–341.

Fernández-Llamazares, Á., Lepofsky, D., Lertzman, K., Armstrong, C.G., Brondizio, E.S., Gavin, M.C., et al (2021) Scientists' warning to humanity on threats to indigenous and local knowledge systems. *Journal of Ethnobiology*, 41, 144–169.

Fisher, M. (2009) *Capitalist Realism: Is There No Alternative?* London: Zero Books.

Franquesa, J. (2018) *Power Struggles: Dignity, Value, and the Renewable Energy Frontier in Spain*. Bloomington: Indiana University Press.

Fraser, N. (2008) *Scales of Justice: Reimagining Political Space in a Globalizing World*. Milton: Polity Press.

Fraser, N. (2021) Climates of capital. *New Left Review*, 127, January–February.

Fruean, B. (2021) Nos enfrentamos al colonialismo climático: Compañías ricas y contaminantes se lucran de nuestra destrucción. *El País*, 2 November. Available at: https://elpais.com/clima-y-medio-ambiente/2021-11-02/nos-enfrentamos-al-colonialismo-climatico-companias-ricas-y-contaminantes-se-lucran-de-nuestra-destruccion.html

Gago, V. and Mezzadra, S.A. (2017) A critique of the extractive operations of capital: Toward an expanded concept of extractivism. *Rethinking Marxism*, 29(4), 574–591.

Galindo, M. (2013a) *A Despatriarcar! Feminismo urgente*. Lavaca.

Galindo, M. (2013b) *No se puede descolonizar sin despatriarcalizar: Teoría y propuesta de la despatriarcalización*. La Paz: Mujeres Creando.

Galindo, M. (2021) *Feminismo bastardo*. La Paz: Mujeres Creando.

Galindo, M. (2023) María Galindo: 'El feminismo deja de incomodar cuando se vuelve un patrimonio elegante de pequeñas élites'. Interviewed by B.B. Morales. *Palabra Pública Universidad de Chile*, 9 January. Available at: https://palabrapublica.uchile.cl/maria-galindo-el-feminismo-deja-de-incomodar/

Garcés, M. (2002) *En las prisiones de lo posible*. Barcelona: Edicions Bellatera.

Garcés, M. (2013) *Un mundo común*. Barcelona: Edicions Bellatera.

Garcés, M. (2017) *Nova il.lustració radical*. Barcelona: COLECCIÓN, Nuevos cuadernos Anagrama.

Garcés, M. (2022) Imaginación crítica. In M. Garcés (ed), *Ecología de la imaginación*. Artnodes, no. 29. Barcelona: UOC.

Garcés, M. (2023) *El temps de la promesa*. Barcelona: COLECCIÓN, Nuevos cuadernos Anagrama.

Gargallo, F. (2007) Feminismo latinoamericano. *Revista Venezolana de Estudios de la Mujer*, 12(28), 17–34.

Gay, A. (2018) La crise d'une utopie blanche? In J. Lindgaard (ed), *Éloge des mauvaises herbes: Ce que nous devons à la ZAD* (pp 157–165). Paris: L'Arche.

Gaztambide-Fernández, R., Tuck, E. and Yang, W.K. (2015) *Critical Ethnic Studies* blog post. Available at: http://www.criticalethnicstudiesjournal.org/citation-practices

Gibson-Graham, J.K. (2006) *The End of Capitalism (As We Knew It)*. Minneapolis: University of Minnesota Press.

Global Witness (2022) *Decade of Defiance: Ten Years of Reporting Land and Environmental Activism Worldwide*. Available at: https://www.globalwitness.org/en/campaigns/environmental-activists/decade-defiance/#foreword-dr-vandana-shiva

Global Witness (2023) *Annual Report 2022: Rising to the Challenge of a World in Crisis*. Available at: https://www.globalwitness.org/en/about-us/annual-report-2022-rising-challenge-world-crisis/

González-Hidalgo, M. (2021) The ambivalent political work of emotions in the defence of territory, life and the commons. *Environment and Planning E: Nature and Space*, 4(4), 1291–1312. https://doi.org/10.1177/25148486211029231

Government of Canada (2017) *Canada's Feminist International Assistance Policy*. Available at: https://www.international.gc.ca/world-monde/issues_development-enjeux_developpement/priorities-priorites/policy-politique.aspx?lang=eng

Graeber, D. (2014) *Debt: The First 5,000 Years* (updated and expanded edn). New York: Melville House Publishing.

Graeber, D. (2019) Against economics. *The Anarchist Library*. Available at: https://davidgraeber.org/articles/against-economics/

Grapard, U. (1995) Robinson Crusoe: The quintessential economic man? *Feminist Economics*, 1(1), 33–52.

Greenpeace (2018) Hambach Forest in Germany [photographs]. Available at: https://media.greenpeace.org/archive/Hambach-Forest-in-Germany-27MZIFJWNA7P0.html

Gregory, D. (2000) Culture of travel and spatial formations of knowledge. *ERDKUNDE*, 54, 297–319. https://doi.org/10.3112/erdkunde.2000.04.02

Gregory, D. (2011) Travelling theory. In D. Gregory, R. Johnston, G. Pratt, M. Watts and S. Whatmore (eds), *The Dictionary of Human Geography* (5th edn, p 775). West Sussex: Wiley.

Grosfoguel, R. (2016) Del 'Extractivismo Económico' al 'Extractivismo Epistémico' y 'Extractivismo Ontológico': Una forma destructiva de conocer, ser y estar en el mundo. *Tabula Rasa*, 24, 123–143. https://doi.org/10.25058/20112742.60

The Guardian (2023) Native tribe Upper Sioux agency US Dakota War. Available at: https://www.theguardian.com/us-news/2023/sep/03/native-tribe-upper-sioux-agency-us-dakota-war

Gudynas, E. (2004) *Ecología, economía y ética del desarrollo sostenible*. Montevideo: Ediciones Coscoroba.

Gudynas, E. (2011) Alcances y contenidos de las transiciones al Post-Extractivismo. In *Ecuador Debate. Problemas y perspectivas del extractivismo* (No. 82, abril 2011, pp 61–80). Quito: Centro Andino de Acción Popular CAAP.

Gudynas, E. (2018) Extractivisms: Tendencies and consequences. In R. Munck and R. Delgado Wise (eds), *Reframing Latin American Development* (pp 61–76). Oxon: Routledge.

Habersang, A. (2021) Resisting body-territories: Indigenous women negotiating racism as a pandemic. *Interface: A Journal for and about Social Movements*, 13(2), 168–198.

Hamouchene, H. (2019) *Extractivism and Resistance in North Africa*. Amsterdam: Transnational Institute. Available at: https://www.tni.org/en/publication/extractivism-and-resistance-in-north-africa

Haraway, D. (1988) Situated knowledges: The science question in feminism and the privilege of partial perspective. *Feminist Studies*, 14(3), 575–599.

Haraway, D. (1997) *Modest_Witness@Second_Millennium.FemaleMan_Meets_OncoMouse: Feminism and Technoscience*. New York and Oxon: Routledge.

Haraway, D. (2016) *Staying with the Trouble: Making Kin in the Chthulucene*. Durham, NC: Duke University Press.

Harding, S. (1995) Can feminist thought make economics more objective? *Feminist Economics*, 1(1), 7–32.

Hargreaves, S. (2019) Neo-extractivism. In A. Kothari, A. Salleh, A. Escobar, F. Demaria and A. Acosta (eds), *Pluriverse: A Post-Development Dictionary* (pp 62–64). Chennai: Tulika Books.

Harvey, D. (2014) *Seventeen Contradictions and the End of Capitalism*. London: Profile Books.

He, M., Ditto, J.C., Gardner, L., Machesky, J., Hass-Mitchell, T.N., Chen, C., et al (2024) Total organic carbon measurements reveal major gaps in petrochemical emissions reporting. *Science*, 383, 426–432. https://doi.org/10.1126/science.adj6233

Henseleit, M., Venghaus, S. and Kuckshinrichs, W. (2022) The Hambach Forest in the German debate on climate protection: Is there a symbolic value beyond the environmental value? In O. Özçatalbaş (ed), *Sustainable Rural Development Perspective and Global Challenges* (pp 1–21). London: Intech Open.

Hester, H. and Srnicek, N. (2023) *After Work: A History of the Home and the Fight for Free Time*. New York: Verso.

Hickel, J. (2020) *Less is More: How Degrowth Will Save the World*. London: Penguin Random House.

Hickel, J. (2021) The anti-colonial politics of degrowth. *Political Geography* 88, Article 102404. https://doi.org/10.1016/j.polgeo.2021.102404

Hickel, J. (2022) *Reimagining the Human-Environment Relationship: A New Political Economy for a Healthy Planet.* UNU Centre for Policy Research and UNEP.

Hickel, J., Dorninger, C., Wieland, H. and Suwandi, I. (2022) Imperialist appropriation in the world economy: Drain from the global South through unequal exchange, 1990–2015. *Global Environmental Change*, 73.

Hickel, J. and Kallis, G. (2020) Is green growth possible? *New Political Economy*, *25*(4), 469–486.

Hickel, J., Sullivan, D. and Zoomkawala, H. (2021) Plunder in the post-colonial era: Quantifying drain from the Global South through unequal exchange, 1960–2018. *New Political Economy*, 26(6), 1030–1047. https://doi.org/10.1080/13563467.2021.1899153

Holz, R. and Pavez, P.J. (2022) The feminization of extractive violence: A comparative study from Colombia and Indonesia. In C. Olivieri and J. Serrano-Muñoz (eds), *East Asia, Latin America, and the Decolonization of Transpacific Studies: Historical and Cultural Interconnections between Latin America and Asia.* Cham: Palgrave Macmillan. https://doi.org/10.1007/978-3-030-74528-8_6

hooks, b. (1981) *Ain't I a Woman: Black Women and Feminism.* Boston: South End.

Human Rights Watch (2019) 'When we lost the forest, we lost everything': Oil palm plantations and rights violations in Indonesia. Available at: https://www.hrw.org/sites/default/files/report_pdf/indonesia0919_web.pdf

ICTA-UAB (2023) The voices of indigenous peoples and local communities as an important part of the climate fight. Universitat Autònoma de Barcelona. Available at: https://www.uab.cat/web/newsroom/news-detail/the-voices-of-indigenous-peoples-and-local-communities-as-an-important-part-of-the-climate-fight-1345830290613.html?detid=1345895220389

Ingham, G. (2013) *Capitalism.* Chichester: Wiley.

IPCC (Intergovernmental Panel on Climate Change) (2023) *Climate Change 2023: Synthesis Report: Contribution of Working Groups I, II and III to the Sixth Assessment Report of the Intergovernmental Panel on Climate Change.* IPCC. https://doi.org/10.59327/IPCC/AR6-9789291691647.001

Jackson, T. (2021) *Post Growth: Life after Capitalism.* Queensland: Polity Press.

Johnson, C.A. (2023) 'Land back' achievement: Land that was for centuries an Indigenous village is now a permanent home for the Native American Youth and Family Center in Portland, Oregon. *Indian Country Today*, 5 September.

Jordan, J. (2018) Revenge against the commons: Why France's biggest police operation since May '68 is prepared to kill for Macron's neoliberal nightmare [blog post], 2 May. Available at: https://www.versobooks.com/blogs/3776-revenge-against-the-commons

Kabeer, N. (2018) Locked out and left behind? Gender, intersecting inequalities and the SDGs. *Facebook*. Available at: https://www.facebook.com/Tropeninstituut/videos/1756423001083309

Kallis, G. (2018) *Degrowth*. Newcastle upon Tyne: Agenda Publishing.

Kallis, G. (2019) *Limits: Why Malthus was Wrong and Why Environmentalists Should Care*. Redwood City: Stanford Briefs.

Kallis, G., Mastini, R. and Zografos, C. (2023) Perceptions of degrowth in the European Parliament. *Nature Sustainability*, 6, 1316–1320. https://doi.org/10.1038/s41893-023-01246-x

Kapoor, I. (2008) *The Postcolonial Politics of Development*. Abingdon: Routledge.

Kara, S. (2023) *Cobalt Red: How the Blood of the Congo Powers Our Lives*. Macmillan.

Kayatekin, S. (2009) Between political economy and postcolonial theory: First encounters. *Cambridge Journal of Economics*, 33(6), 1113–1118. https://doi.org/10.1093/cje/bep067

Khumalo, T. (2015) South Africa's ill miners take gold mines to court. *DW News*, 12 October. Available at: https://www.dw.com/en/south-africas-sick-miners-take-gold-mines-to-court/a-18777363

King, L.C., Savin, I. and Drews, S. (2023) Shades of green growth scepticism among climate policy researchers. *Nature Sustainability*, 6, 1316–1320. https://doi.org/10.1038/s41893-023-01198-2

Kirui, D. (2021) How Kenyans are resisting one of the largest development projects in East Africa. *Waging Nonviolence*, 19 June. Available at: https://wagingnonviolence.org/2021/06/kenyans-lapsset-save-lamu/

Klein, J.T. (1990) *Interdisciplinarity: History, Theory and Practice*. Detroit: Wayne State University Press.

Klein, N. (2014) *This Changes Everything: Capitalism vs. the Climate*. New York: Simon & Schuster.

Klein, N. (2016) An evening with Naomi Klein: This changes everything [Video file]. Available at: https://www.youtube.com/watch?v=TyVymaIe9EI

Kongar, E., Olmsted, J.C. and Shehabuddin, E. (2018) *Gender and Economics in Muslim Communities: Critical Feminist and Postcolonial Analyses*. London: Routledge.

Krause, S.R. (2020) Environmental domination. *Political Theory*, 48(8), 443–468. https://doi.org/10.1177/0090591719890833

Krenak, A. (2019) *Ideias para adiar o fim do mundo*. São Paulo: Companhia das Letras.

Krenak, A. (2023) *O futuro ancestral*. São Paulo: Companhia das Letras.

Kröger, M. (2021) *Extractivisms, Existences and Extinctions: Monoculture Plantations and Amazon Deforestation*. Oxon and New York: Routledge.

Kuiper, E. (2022) *A Herstory of Economics*. Chichester: John Wiley and Sons Ltd.

Kumar, A. (2005) *Perilous Passage: Mankind and the Global Ascendancy of Capital*. Lanham: Rowman & Littlefield.

Kvangraven, I.H. (2022) Colonial legacies and racial hierarchies in the global economy: A review article. *Race & Class*, 63(3), 103–108. https://doi.org/10.1177/03063968211060325

Kvangraven, I. and Kesar, S. (2023) Standing in the way of rigor? Economics' meeting with the decolonization agenda. *Review of International Political Economy*, 30(5), 1723–1748. https://doi.org/10.1080/09692290.2022.2131597

Lakhani, N. (2020) Who killed Berta Cáceres? Behind the brutal murder of an environment crusader. *The Guardian*, 2 June. Available at: https://www.theguardian.com/world/2020/jun/02/berta-caceres-honduras-dam-murder-investigation

LaRocque, E. (2010) *When the Other Is Me: Native Resistance Discourse, 1850–1990*. Winnipeg: University of Manitoba Press.

Leahy, D. (2014) June 28th: Final 'Tar Sands Healing Walk' simply a new beginning, say organizers. *The Narwhal*, 20 May. Available at: https://www.thenarwhal.ca

Le Grange, L. (2016) Decolonising the university curriculum. *South African Journal of Higher Education*, 30(2), 1–12.

Le Guin, U.K. (2004) *The Wave in the Mind: Talks and Essays on the Writer, the Reader and the Imagination*. Boulder: Shambhala Publications.

Lindgaard, J. (ed) (2018) *Éloge des mauvaises herbes: Ce que nous devons à la ZAD*. Paris: Les Liens Qui Libèrent (LLL). Available at: https://reporterre.net/Les-mauvaises-herbes-de-la-Zad-creent-d-autres-mondes

Loomba, A. (2002) *Colonialism/Postcolonialism*. London and New York: Routledge.

Luescher, T.M. (2016) Student representation in a context of democratization and massification in Africa: Analytical approaches, theoretical perspectives and #RhodesMustFall. In T.M. Luescher, M. Klemenčič and J.O. Jowi (eds), *Student Politics in Africa: Representation and Activism* (pp 27–60). Cape Town: African Minds.

Lugones, M. (2008) The coloniality of gender. *Worlds & Knowledges Otherwise*, 2(Spring), 1–17.

Lugones, M. (2010) Toward a decolonial feminism. *Hypatia*, 25(4), 742–759.

Malthus, T.R. (1798) *An Essay on the Principle of Population*. London: J. Johnson.

Mama, A. (1997) Sheroes and villains: Conceptualizing colonial and contemporary violence against women in Africa. In A. Jacqui and C.T. Mohanty (eds), *Feminist Genealogies, Colonial Legacies, Democratic Futures* (pp 46–62). New York: Routledge.

Managua Declaration (2018) Available at: https://viacampesina.org/en/managua-declaration-the-meeting-of-the-broadened-international-collective-on-environmental-and-climate-justice/

Mankiw, N.G. (2021 [1998]) *Principles of Economics* (9th edn). Nashville: South-Western College Publishing.
Mansel, T. (2019) The coal mine that ate Hambacher forest. *BBC*, 16 July. Available at: https://www.bbc.com/news/stories-48931062
Marinas, R. (2023) Protesta contra la ampliación de El Prat, Hard Rock y el Cuarto Cinturón: 'El PSC y Esquerra han vendido la tierra'. *El País*, 4 March. Available at: https://elpais.com/espana/catalunya/2023-03-04/protesta-contra-la-ampliacion-de-el-prat-hard-rock-y-el-cuarto-cinturon-el-psc-y-esquerra-han-vendido-la-tierra.html
Martiniello, G. (2015) Social struggles in Uganda's Acholiland: Understanding responses and resistance to Amuru sugar works. *Journal of Peasant Studies*, 42(3/4), 653–669. https://doi.org/10.1080/03066150.2015.1056705
Marx, K. (1976) *Capital: A Critique of Political Economy, Volume 1*. London: Penguin Classics.
Mauvaise Troupe (2018) *The Zad and NoTAV: Territorial Struggles and the Making of a New Political Intelligence*. London and New York: Verso.
Maynard, R. and Simpson, L.B. (2023) *Rehearsals for Living*. Toronto: Penguin Random House Canada.
Mazzucato, M. (2017) *The Value of Everything: Making and Taking in the Global Economy*. London: Penguin Random House.
Mbembe, A. (2019) *Necropolitics*. Durham, NC: Duke University Press.
McFadden, P. (2018) Contemporarity: Sufficiency in a radical African feminist life. *Meridians*, 17(2), 415–431.
McKittrick, K. (2021) *Dear Science and Other Stories*. Durham, NC: Duke University Press.
Mendoza, B. (2016) Coloniality of gender and power: From postcoloniality to decoloniality. In L. Disch and M. Hawkesworth (eds), *The Oxford Handbook of Feminist Theory* (pp 100–121). Oxford: Oxford University Press.
Mezzadra, S. and Neilson, B. (2017) On the multiple frontiers of extraction: Excavating contemporary capitalism. *Cultural Studies*, 31(2–3), 185–204. https://doi.org/10.1080/09502386.2017.1303425
Mitchell, T. (2011) *Carbon Democracy: Political Power in the Age of Oil*. London: Verso.
Mohanty, C.T. (1991) Under western eyes: Feminist scholarship and colonial discourse. In C. Mohanty, A. Russo and L. Torres (eds), *Third World Women and the Politics of Feminism* (pp 51–80). Bloomington: Indiana University Press.
Mohanty, C.T. (1995) Feminist encounters: Locating the politics of experience. In L. Nicholson and S. Seidman (eds), *Social Postmodernism: Beyond Identity Politics* (pp 68–86). Cambridge: Cambridge University Press.
Moore, J.W. (2016) Anthropocene or capitalocene? Nature, history, and the crisis of capitalism. *Sociology Faculty Scholarship*, 1. Available at: https://orb.binghamton.edu/sociology_fac/1

Moosavi, L. (2020) The decolonial bandwagon and the dangers of intellectual decolonisation. *International Review of Sociology*, 30(2), 332–354. https://doi.org/10.1080/03906701.2020.1776919

Mott, C. and Cockayne, D. (2017) Citation matters: Mobilizing the politics of citation toward a practice of 'conscientious engagement'. *Gender, Place & Culture: A Journal of Feminist Geography*, 24(7), 954–973.

Murdoch, I. (1993) *Metaphysics as a Guide to Morals*. New York: Penguin.

Murikira, J. (2023) *Coal is not the answer, declares Lamu people in a win for the environment*. One Earth. Available at: https://www.oneearth.org/coal-is-not-the-answer-declares-lamu-people-in-a-win-for-the-environment/

Murrey, A. and Mollett, S. (2023) Extraction is not a metaphor: Decolonial and Black Geographies against the gendered and embodied violence of extractive logics. *Transactions of the Institute of British Geographers*, 1–20. https://doi.org/10.1111/tran.12610

Nasong'o, S. and Ikpe, E. (2022) *Beyond Disciplines: African Perspectives on Theory and Method*. Dakar: CODESRIA.

National Geographic (2018) Ancient forest home of squatter communities is doomed by coal. *National Geographic*, 13 April. Available at: https://www.nationalgeographic.com/science/article/hambach-forest-germany-logging-coal-conservation-science

Ngũgĩ wa Thiong'o, N. (1986) *Decolonising the Mind: The Politics of Language in African Literature*. Suffolk: Boydell and Brewer.

Nicoll, F. (2000) Indigenous sovereignty and the violence of perspective: A white woman's coming out story. *Australian Feminist Studies*, 15(33), 369–386. https://doi.org/10.1080/08164640020009802

Nicoll, F. (2004) Reconciliation in and out of perspective: White knowing, seeing, curating and being at home in and against Indigenous sovereignty. In A. Moreton-Robinson (ed), *Whitening Race: Essays in Social and Cultural Criticism* (pp 17–31). Canberra: Aboriginal Studies Press.

Nikiforuk, A. (2010) *Tar Sands: Dirty Oil and the Future of a Continent*. Vancouver: Greystone Books.

Nixon, R. (2011) *Slow Violence and the Environmentalism of the Poor*. Cambridge, MA: Harvard University Press.

Nkrumah, K. (1965) *Neo-colonialism: The Last Stage of Imperialism*. Nashville: Thomas Nelson and Sons Ltd. Available at: http://www.marxists.org/subject/africa/nkrumah/neo-colonialism/introduction.htm

Nuccitelli, D. (2018) Switching to electric cars is key to fixing America's 'critically insufficient' climate policies. *The Guardian*, 22 January. Available at: https://www.theguardian.com/environment/climate-consensus-97-per-cent/2018/jan/22/switching-to-electric-cars-is-key-to-fixing-americas-critically-insufficient-climate-policies?ref=hir.harvard.edu

Nuñez, S., Herrera, F. and Flores, M. (2018) *Extractivismo y resistencia comunitaria en Honduras*. Amsterdam: Transnational Institute.

OHCHR (Office of the United Nations High Commissioner for Human Rights) (2016) Berta Cáceres' murder: UN experts renew call to Honduras to end impunity, 16 April. Available at: https://www.ohchr.org/EN/NewsEvents/Pages/DisplayNews.aspx?NewsID=19805&LangID=E

Olmsted, J. (2004) Orientalism and economic methods: (Re)reading feminist economic discussions of Islam. In E. Zein-Elabdin and S. Charusheela (eds), *Postcolonialism Meets Economics* (pp 165–182). London and New York: Routledge.

Ossome, L. (2021) Pedagogies of feminist resistance: Agrarian movements in Africa. *Agrarian South*, 10(1), 41–58. https://doi.org/10.1177/09730051211005774

Otero, N. (2023) Deuda por oportunidades: Cómo gestiona España el dinero que le deben los países en vías de desarrollo. *El País*, 9 January. Available at: https://elpais.com/planeta-futuro/2024-01-09/deuda-por-oportunidades-como-gestiona-espana-el-dinero-que-le-deben-los-paises-en-vias-de-desarrollo.html

Oxfam International (2017) *Position Paper on Gender Justice and the Extractive Industries* [Report]. March. Available at: https://www.oxfamamerica.org/static/media/files/EI_and_GJ_position_paper_v.15_FINAL_03202017_green_Kenny.pdf

Oyěwùmí, O. (1997) *The Invention of Women: Making an African Sense of Western Gender Discourses*. Minneapolis: University of Minnesota Press.

Oyěwùmí, O. (2002) Conceptualizing gender: The Eurocentric foundations of feminist concepts and the challenge of African epistemologies. *Jenda: A Journal of Culture and African Women Studies*, 2.

Paul, H.K. (2021) Towards reparative climate justice: From crises to liberations. *Common Wealth*, 12 April. Available at: https://www.common-wealth.co.uk/reports/towards-reparative-climate-justice-from-crises-to-liberations

Paulson, L. and Büchs, M. (2022) Public acceptance of post-growth: Factors and implications for post-growth strategy. *Futures*, 143, Article 103020. https://doi.org/10.1016/j.futures.2022.103020

Peck, J. and Theodore, N. (2010) Mobilizing policy: Models, methods, and mutations. *Geoforum*, 41(2), 169–174. https://doi.org/10.1016/j.geoforum.2010.01.002

People's Agreement of Cochabamba (2010) Available at: https://pwccc.wordpress.com/2010/04/24/peoples-agreement/

Pérez Orozco, A. (2014) *Subversión feminista de la economía*. Madrid: Traficantes de Sueños.

Peter, F. (2003) Foregrounding practices: Feminist philosophy of economics beyond rhetoric and realism. In D.K. Barker and E. Kuiper (eds), *Toward a Feminist Philosophy of Economics* (pp 105–121). London: Routledge.

Plumwood, V. (1993) The politics of reason: Towards a feminist logic. *Australasian Journal of Philosophy*, 71(4), 436–462. https://doi.org/10.1080/00048409312345432

Polanyi, K. (1957) The economy as instituted process. In G. Dalton (ed), *Primitive, Archaic and Modern Economies: Essays of Karl Polanyi* (pp 139–174). New York: Doubleday Anchor.

Pollard, J., McEwan, C. and Hughes, A. (2011) *Postcolonial Economies*. London: Zed Books.

Prasse-Freeman, E. (2022) Necroeconomics: Dispossession, extraction, and indispensable/expendable laborers in contemporary Myanmar. *The Journal of Peasant Studies*, 49(7), 1466–1496. https://doi.org/10.1080/03066150.2021.1943366

Preciado, P. (2021) *Can the Monster Speak? Report to an Academy of Psychoanalysts*. London: Fitzcarraldo Editions.

Prügl, E. (2021) Smart economics. In G. Berik and E. Kongar (eds), *The Routledge Handbook of Feminist Economics* (pp 468–476). London and New York: Routledge.

Quijano, A. (2000) Coloniality of power, Eurocentrism, and Latin America. *Nepantla: Views from South*, 1, 533–580.

Quijano Valencia, O. (2008) *Posibles y plurales: Analíticas para no perder el acontecimiento*. Bogotá: Editorial Universidad del Cauca Serie Estudios Sociales. Available at: http://www.unicauca.edu.co/porik_an/imagenes_5tienda/Posibles_y_Plurales.pdf

Quijano Valencia, O. (2016) *Ecosimias: Visiones y prácticas de diferencia económico/cultural en contextos de multiplicidad* (2nd edn). Bogotá: Editorial Universidad del Cauca Serie Estudios Sociales.

Quiroga Diaz, N. and Gómez Correal, D. (2013) ¿Qué tiene que aportar una economía feminista decolonial a las otras economías? *América Latina en Movimiento*, 8 February. Available at: https://www.alainet.org/es/articulo/164499

Ra, D. (2022) *Challenging Extractivism in Kachin State: From Land of Jade to Land for the People*. Amsterdam: Transnational Institute (TNI). Available at: https://www.tni.org/en/article/challenging-extractivism-in-kachin-state-from-land-of-jade-to-land-for-the-people

Ramamurthy, P. and Tambe, A. (2017) Preface. *Feminist Studies*, 43(3), 503–511. https://doi.org/10.15767/feministstudies.43.3.0503

Red Nation, The (2021) *The Red Deal: Indigenous Action to Save Our Earth*. Philadelphia: Common Notions.

Rege, S. (1998) Dalit women talk differently: A critique of 'difference' and towards a Dalit feminist standpoint position. *Economic and Political Weekly*, 33(44), WS39–WS46. http://www.jstor.org/stable/4407323

Reisenberg, K. (2022) Struggles at the 'peripheries': Situated knowledge production and feminist visions for post-extractive environments. *Cidades*. Available at: http://journals.openedition.org/cidades/6197

Reyes-García, V., García-del-Amo, D., Álvarez-Fernández, S., Benyei, P., Calvet-Mir, L., Junqueira, A.B., et al (2024) Indigenous peoples and local communities report ongoing and widespread climate change impacts on local social-ecological systems. *Communications Earth & Environment*, 5, Article 29. https://doi.org/10.1038/s43247-023-01164-y

Rich, A. (1987) *Blood, Bread and Poetry*. London: Virago.

Rivera Cusicanqui, S. (1987) El potencial epistemológico y teórico de la historia oral: De la lógica instrumental a la descolonización de la historia. *Temas Sociales*, 11, 49–64.

Rivera Cusicanqui, S. (2012) Ch'ixinakax utxiwa: A reflection on the practices and discourses of decolonization. *South Atlantic Quarterly*, 111(1), 95–109.

Rivera Cusicanqui, S. (2017) La larga marcha por nuestra dignidad. *Cuestión Agraria*, 4, 7–38.

Rivera Cusicanqui, S. (2018) *Un mundo ch'ixi es posible: Ensayos desde un presente en crisis*. Buenos Aires: Tinta Limón.

Robins, J. (2020) The case for calling climate change 'genocide'. *The New Republic*, 23 September.

Rodney, W. (1972) *How Europe Underdeveloped Africa*. London: Bogle-l'Ouverture Publications Ltd.

Roi, L. (2022) Challenging extractivism in Kachin State: From land of jade to land for the people. *Transnational Institute (TNI)*, 7 July. Available at: https://www.tni.org/en/article/challenging-extractivism-in-kachin-state-from-land-of-jade-to-land-for-the-people

Romanello, M., Walawender, M., Hsu, S.C., Moskeland, A., Palmeiro-Silva, Y. and Scamman, D., et al (2024) The 2024 report of the Lancet Countdown on health and climate change: Facing record-breaking threats from delayed action. *The Lancet*, 404(10465), 1847–1896. https://doi.org/10.1016S0140-6736(24)01822-1

Romero Epiayú, J. and Barón Romero, D. (2013) *Impacto de la explotación minera en las mujeres rurales: afectaciones al derecho a la tierra y el territorio en el sur de La Guajira, Colombia*. Bogotá: Sütsüin Jieyuu Wayúu – Fuerza de Mujeres Wayúu. Equipo de Tierras y Derecho al Territorio del Centro de Investigación y Educación Popular CINEP/PPP. Available at: http://www.oidhaco.org/uploaded/content/article/2091974838.pdf

Rushkoff, D. (2022) *Survival of the Richest: Escape Fantasies of the Tech Billionaires*. Melbourne: Scribe Publications.

Said, E. (1978) *Orientalism*. New York: Pantheon Books.

Said, E. (1983) *The World, the Text, and the Critic*. Cambridge, MA: Harvard University Press.

Said, E. (2000) *Reflections on Exile and Other Essays*. Cambridge, MA: Harvard University Press.

Sandel, M. (2013) *What Money Can't Buy: The Moral Limits of the Market*. London: Penguin Random House.

Sandel, M. (2020) *The Tyranny of Merit: What's Become of the Common Good?* London: Penguin Random House.

Santos, B.d.S. (2008) *Another Knowledge Is Possible: Beyond Northern Epistemologies*. London: Verso.

Santos, B.d.S. (2014) *Epistemologies of the South: Justice Against Epistemicide*. London: Paradigm Publishers.

Santos, B.d.S. (2015) *If God were a Human Rights Activist*. Stanford: Stanford University Press.

Santos, B.d.S. (2018) *The End of the Cognitive Empire*. Durham, NC: Duke University Press.

Santos, B.d.S. (2021) Postcolonialism, decoloniality, and epistemologies of the South. *Oxford Research Encyclopedia of Literature*, 29 November. Available at: https://oxfordre.com/literature/view/10.1093/acrefore/9780190201098.001.0001/acrefore-9780190201098-e-1262

Scheidel, A., Fernández-Llamazares, A., Bara, A.H., Del Bene, D., David-Chavez, D.M., Fanari, E., et al (2023) Global impacts of extractive and industrial development projects on Indigenous peoples' lifeways, lands, and rights. *Science Advances*, 9, eade9557. https://doi.org/10.1126/sciadv.ade9557

Schlissel, D. (2019) *The proposed Lamu coal plant: The wrong choice for Kenya*. Institute for Energy Economics and Financial Analysis. Available at: https://ieefa.org/wp-content/uploads/2019/05/The-Proposed-Lamu-Coal-Project_June-2019.pdf

Schmelzer, M., Vansintjan, A. and Vetter, A. (2022) *The Future Is Degrowth: A Guide to a World Beyond Capitalism*. London and New York: Verso.

Schrecker, T., Birn, A.-E. and Aguilera, M. (2018) How extractive industries affect health: Political economy underpinnings and pathways. *Health and Place*, 52, 141–148.

Segato, R. (2011) Género y Colonialidad: En Busca de Claves de Lectura y de un Vocabulario Estratégico Descolonial. In K.A. Bidaseca and V. Vazquez Laba (eds), *Feminismos y Poscolonialidad – Descolonizando El Feminismo Desde y en América Latina* (2nd edn, pp 17–48). Buenos Aires: Ediciones Godot. Available at: https://nucleodegenerounr.files.wordpress.com/2013/03/bidaseca-karina-y-vazquez-laba-vanesa-comps-feminismos-y-poscolonialidad-descolonizando-el-feminismo-desde-y-en-amc3a9rica-latina.pdf

Segato, R. (2016) *La guerra contra las mujeres*. Madrid: Traficantes de Sueños.

Segato, R. (2018) *Contrapedagogías de la crueldad*. Prometeo: Buenos Aires.

Sen, A.K. (1977) Rational fools: A critique of the behavioral foundations of economic theory. *Philosophy & Public Affairs*, 6(4), 317–344. http://www.jstor.org/stable/2264946.

Sharma, G. (nd) Hambach: An ancient forest at the centre of Germany's struggle with coal. *TRT World Magazine*. Available at: https://www.trtworld.com/magazine/hambach-an-ancient-forest-at-the-centre-of-germany-s-struggle-with-coal-25150

Silva Santisteban, R. (2017) Mujeres y conflictos ecoterritoriales: Impactos, estrategias, resistencias. *ENTREPUEBLOS*. Available at: https://www.entrepueblos.org/wp-content/uploads/2018/03/Mujeresyconflictos_Convenio_-2017.pdf

Simpson, L.B. (2001) Aboriginal peoples and knowledge: Decolonising our processes. *The Canadian Journal of Native Studies*, 21(1), 137–148.

Simpson, L.B. (2013) Restoring nationhood: Addressing land dispossession in the Canadian reconciliation discourse [video file], 13 November. Available at: http://www.sfu.ca/tlcvan/clients/sfu_woodwards/2013-11-13_Woodwards_VOCE_Restoring_Nationhood_12308/

Simpson, L.B. (2017) *As We Have Always Done: Indigenous Freedom Through Radical Resistance*. Chicago: University of Minnesota Press.

Simpson, L.B. and Klein, N. (2013) Dancing the world into being: An interview with Idle No More's Leanne Betasamosake Simpson. Interview by L. Simpson. *Yes! Magazine*, 5 March. Available at: http://www.yesmagazine.org/peace-justice/dancing-the-world-into-being-a-conversation-with-idle-no-more-leanne-simpson

Sium, A., Desai, C. and Ritskes, E. (2012) Towards the 'tangible unknown': Decolonization and the indigenous future. *Decolonization: Indigeneity, Education & Society*, 1(1), i–xiii.

Slameršak, A., Kallis, G., O'Neill, D.W. and Hickel, J. (2024) Post-growth: A viable path to limiting global warming to 1.5°C. *One Earth*, 7(1), 44–58. https://doi.org/10.1016/j.oneear.2023.11.004

Sloterdijk, P. (2016) *Foams: Spheres III*. Cambridge, MA: MIT Press.

Smiet, K.B. (2021) *Sojourner Truth and Intersectionality: Traveling Truths in Feminist Scholarship*. Abingdon and New York: Routledge. https://doi.org/10.4324/9780429424120

Smith, A., Pesantubbee, M., Stewart, D.M., Gonzalez, M.A., Johnson, S. and Tinker, T. (2006) Roundtable discussion: Native/First Nation theology [with response]. *Journal of Feminist Studies in Religion*, 22(2), 85–121.

Smith, L.T. (1999) *Decolonising Methodologies: Research and Indigenous Peoples*. London: Zed Books.

Solnit, R. (2002) *Wanderlust: A History of Walking*. London: Verso.

Spivak, G.C. (1996) Post-structuralism, marginality, post-coloniality, and value. In P. Mongia (ed), *Contemporary Postcolonial Theory: A Reader* (pp 198–222). London: Arnold.

Spivak, G.C. (1999) *A Critique of Postcolonial Reason: Toward a History of the Vanishing*. Cambridge, MA: Harvard University Press.

Spivak, G.C. (2005) Use and abuse of human rights. *boundary 2*, 32(1), 131–189.

Spivak, G.C. (2013) *An Aesthetic Education in the Era of Globalization*. Cambridge, MA: Harvard University Press.

Spivak, G.C. (2016) Development. *Political Concepts*. Available at: http://www.politicalconcepts.org

Srnicek, N. and Williams, A. (2015) *Inventing the Future: Postcapitalism and a World Without Work*. London: Verso Books.

Standing, G. (2023) *The Politics of Time: Gaining Control in the Age of Uncertainty*. London: Penguin.

Sullivan, D. and Hickel, J. (2023) Capitalism and extreme poverty: A global analysis of real wages, human height, and mortality since the long 16th century. *World Development*, 161, 1–15.

Sultana, F. (2023) Decolonizing climate coloniality. In R. Solnit and T.Y. Lutunatabua (eds), *Not Too Late: Changing the Climate Story from Despair to Possibility* (pp 58–65). Chicago: Haymarket Books.

Sultana, F. (ed) (2024) *Confronting Climate Coloniality: Decolonizing Pathways for Climate Justice*. London: Routledge.

Susam-Sarajeva, Ş. (2006) *Theories on the Move: Translation's Role in the Travels of Literary Theories*. Amsterdam: Editions Rodopi BV.

Svampa, M. (2017) Prólogo. La Difícil Tarea de Pensar Alternativas al Capitalismo. In A. Acosta and U. Brand (eds), *Salidas del Laberinto Capitalista: Decrecimiento y Postextractivismo* (pp xiii–xxii). Barcelona: Editorial Icaria.

Svampa, M. (2019) *Las Fronteras del Neoextractivismo en América Latina: Conflictos Socioambientales, Giro Ecoterritorial y Nuevas Dependencias*. Guadalajara: CALAS.

Sweet, E.L. and Ortiz Escalante, S. (2017) Engaging Territorio Cuerpo-Tierra through body and community mapping: A methodology for making communities safer. *Gender, Place & Culture: A Journal of Feminist Geography*, 24(4), 594–606. https://doi.org/10.1080/0966369X.2016.12193

Sylla, N. and Hickel, J. (2024) Proposals for unilateral decolonization and economic sovereignty. *Progressive International*. Available at: https://progressive.international/blueprint/e994437c-ce94-4980-99c1-470464cfbc15-proposals-for-unilateral-decolonization-and-economic-sovereignty/en

Tamale, S. (2020) *Decolonization and Afro-feminism*. Ottawa: Daraja Press.

Tauli-Corpuz, V. (2015) Don't leave indigenous peoples behind in SDGs. *News and Views from the Global South*, 11 May. Available at: https://rightsandresources.org/blog/inter-press-service-opinion-dont-leave-indigenous-peoples-behind-in-sdgs/

Taylor, K.-Y. (2020) Until Black women are free, none of us will be free. *The New Yorker*. Available at: https://www.newyorker.com/news/our-columnists/until-black-women-are-free-none-of-us-will-be-free

Thornton, C. (2023) *Developmentalism as Internationalism: Toward a Global Historical Sociology of the Origins of Development*. Berkeley: University of California Press.

Tilley, L. (2020) A strange industrial order: Indonesia's racialized plantation ecologies and anticolonial estate worker rebellions. *History of the Present*, 10(1), 67–83.

Timm Hidalgo, A. (2018) Feminicidio Extractivista: Reflexiones Sobre La Violencia Hacia Las Mujeres Defensoras Del Agua y Los Territorios. In *Mujeres En Defensa de Territorios: Reflexiones Feministas Frente al Extractivismo* (1st edn, pp 91–99). Santiago de Chile: Fundación Heinrich Böll, Oficina Regional Cono Sur. Available at: https://cl.boell.org/sites/default/files/mujeres_defensa_territorios_web.pdf

Tuck, E. and Yang, K.W. (2012) Decolonization is not a metaphor. *Decolonization: Indigeneity, Education & Society*, 1(1), 1–40.

UCT Rhodes Must Fall Mission Statement (2015) Available at: https://www.lse.ac.uk/sociology/assets/documents/events/UCT-Rhodes-Must-Fall-Statement.pdf

UN (2021) *Transforming Extractive Industries for Sustainable Development*, May. Available at: https://www.un.org/sites/un2.un.org/files/sg_policy_brief_extractives.pdf

UN Committee on the Elimination of Discrimination Against Women (CEDAW) (1993) *General Recommendation No. 19: Violence against Women*. Available at: https://www.refworld.org/docid/52d920c54.html

UN General Assembly (2023) *Promoting the Social and Solidarity Economy for Sustainable Development* (A/77/L.60). Seventy-seventh session General Assembly, 27 March. Available at: https://unsse.org/wp-content/uploads/2023/04/A-77-L60.pdf

UN Global Crisis Response Group (2023) *A World of Debt: A Growing Burden to Global Prosperity*, July. Available at: https://unctad.org/system/files/official-document/osgmisc_2023d4_en.pdf

Van der Tuin, I. and Dolphijn, R. (2010) The transversality of new materialism. *Women: A Cultural Review*, 21(2), 153–171.

Van der Tuin, I. and Dolphijn, R. (2011) Pushing dualism to an extreme: On the philosophical impetus of a new materialism. *Continental Philosophy Review*, 44(4), 383–400.

Varon, J. and Egaña Rojas, L. (2024) Compost engineers and sus *saberes lentos*: A manifest for regenerative technologies. Available at: https://codingrights.org/docs/compost_engineers.pdf

Velez, E. (2019) Decolonial feminism at the intersection: A critical reflection on the relationship between intersectionality and decolonial feminism. *The Journal of Speculative Philosophy*, 33(3), 390–406.

Vergés, F. (2021) *A Decolonial Feminism*. London: Pluto Press.

Vicenzotti, V. and Qviström, M. (2018) Zwischenstadt as a travelling concept: Towards a critical discussion of mobile ideas in transnational planning discourses on urban sprawl. *European Planning Studies*, 26(1), 115–132.

Visvanathan, S. (1997) *A Carnival for Science: Essays on Science, Technology and Development*. Delhi: Oxford University Press.

Visvanathan, S. (2009) *The Search for Cognitive Justice*. Available at: https://www.india-seminar.com/2009/597/597_shiv_visvanathan.htm

Vogel, J. and Hickel, J. (2023) Is green growth happening? An empirical analysis of achieved versus Paris-compliant CO2–GDP decoupling in high-income countries. *Lancet Planet Health*, 7, e759–e769.

Walker, R.A. (2023) Tübatulabal Tribe acquires 1,240 acres of ancestral land: Chairman says site will be 'the nucleus of everything we do from now on'. *Indian Country Today*, 2 October.

Walsh, C. (2023) *Rising Up, Living On: Re-existences, Sowings, and Decolonial Cracks (on Decoloniality)*. Durham, NC: Duke University Press.

Waring, M. (1988) *If Women Counted: A New Feminist Economics*. San Francisco: Harper.

Warlenius, R., Pierce, G. and Ramasar, V. (2015) Reversing the arrow of arrears: The concept of 'ecological debt' and its value for environmental justice. *Global Environmental Change*, 30, 21–30.

WEDO (2021) *A Feminist Agenda for People and Planet: Principles and Recommendations for a Global Feminist Economic Justice Agenda*. Available at: https://wedo.org/wp-content/uploads/2021/06/Blueprint_A-Feminist-Agenda-for-People-and-Planet.pdf

Westman Clinton, N. and Joly, T. (2019) Oil sands extraction in Alberta, Canada: A review of impacts and processes concerning indigenous peoples. *Human Ecology*, 47(2), 233–243.

Whyte, K.P. (2017) Is it colonial Déjà Vu? Indigenous peoples and climate injustice. In J. Adamson and M. Davis (eds), *Humanities for the Environment: Integrating Knowledges, Forging New Constellations of Practice* (pp 88–105). London and New York: Routledge.

Willow, A.J. (2018) *Understanding ExtrACTIVISM: Culture and Power in Natural Resource Disputes*. New York: Routledge.

Women's Budget Group (2020) *Spirals of Inequality: How Unpaid Care is at the Heart of Gender Inequalities*. Available at: https://wbg.org.uk/wp-content/uploads/2020/04/Accompanying-paper-FINAL.pdf

WoMin (2015) *Country Studies: The Impacts of Extraction on Women in Africa*. Available at: https://womin.africa/archive/country-studies/

WoMin (2020) *Women, Gender and Extractivism in Africa: A Collection of Papers.* Available at: https://womin.africa/download/full-collection-women-gender-and-extractivism-in-africa/

Wong, F. and Tomasky, M. (Hosts) (2023) How feminist economics brought us the care agenda (with Nancy Folbre). *Roosevelt Institute Podcast*, 25 May. Available at: https://rooseveltinstitute.org/2023/05/25/how-feminist-economics-brought-us-the-care-agenda-with-nancy-folbre/

Wong, R. (2015) *undercurrent.* Gibsons, BC: Nightwood Editions.

Wood, C. (1997) The first world/third party criterion: A feminist critique of production boundaries in economics. *Feminist Economics*, 3(3), 47–68.

Wood, C. (2003) Economic marginalia: Postcolonial readings of unpaid domestic labor and developments. In D. Barker and E. Kuiper (eds), *Toward a Feminist Philosophy of Economics* (pp 304–320). London: Routledge.

World Bank (2022) *International Debt Report 2022: Updated International Debt Statistics.* Available at: https://openknowledge.worldbank.org/server/api/core/bitstreams/49da23a2-bcc9-5593-bc96-470cae6b3665/content

Wynter, S. (2003) Unsettling the coloniality of being/power/truth/freedom: Towards the human, after man, its overrepresentation – an argument. *CR: The New Centennial Review*, 3(3), 257–337.

Yaira, Y.Y. and Pawë, L.Y. (2017) Yẽpɨmuwi Thëã Oni: Palavras escritas sobre menstruação. *Fino Traço.* Available at: https://acervo.socioambiental.org/sites/default/files/publications/yal00038_0.pdf

Ye, J., Van der Ploeg, J., Schneider, S. and Shanin, T. (2019) The incursions of extractivism: Moving from dispersed places to global capitalism. *Journal of Peasant Studies*, 47(1), 155–183.

Yeğenoğlu, M. (1998) *Colonial Fantasies: Towards a Feminist Reading of Orientalism.* Cambridge: Cambridge University Press.

Yusoff, K. (2018) *A Billion Black Anthropocenes or None.* Minneapolis: University of Minnesota Press.

Zaragocin, S. and Caretta, M.A. (2021) Cuerpo-Territorio: A decolonial feminist geographical method for the study of embodiment. *Annals of the American Association of Geographers*, 111(5), 1503–1518. DOI: 10.1080/24694452.2020.1812370

Zein-Elabdin, E.O. (1996) Development, gender, and the environment: Theoretical or contextual link? Toward an institutional analysis of gender. *Journal of Economic Issues*, 30(4), 929–947. https://doi.org/10.1080/00213624.1996.11505859

Zein-Elabdin, E.O. (2003) The difficulty of a feminist economics. In D. Barker and E. Kuiper (eds), *Toward a Feminist Philosophy of Economics* (pp 321–333). London: Routledge.

Zein-Elabdin, E.O. (2004) Articulating the postcolonial (with economics in mind). In E.O. Zein-Elabdin and S. Charusheela (eds), *Postcolonialism Meets Economics* (pp 21–39). London and New York: Routledge.

Zein-Elabdin, E.O. (2009) Economics, postcolonial theory, and the problem of culture: Institutional analysis and hybridity. *Cambridge Journal of Economics*, 33(6), 1153–1167. http://www.jstor.org/stable/23601939

Zein-Elabdin, E.O. (2011a) Postcolonial theory and economics. In J. Pollard, C. McEwan and A. Hughes (eds), *Postcolonial Economies* (pp 37–62). London: Zed Books.

Zein-Elabdin, E.O. (2011b) Postcoloniality and development: Development as a colonial discourse. In L. Keita (ed), *Philosophy and African Development: Theory and Practice* (pp 215–230). Dakar: Council for the Development of Social Science Research in Africa (CODESRIA).

Zein-Elabdin, E.O. (2016) *Economics, Culture and Development*. New York: Routledge.

Zein-Elabdin, E.O. (2024) Is it possible to 'decolonize' economics? *Developing Economics: A Critical Perspective on Development Economics*, 15 July. Available at: https://developingeconomics.org/author/eimanzeinelabdin/

Zein-Elabdin, E. and Charusheela, S. (2004) Introduction: Economics and postcolonial thought. In E. Zein-Elabdin and S. Charusheela (eds), *Postcolonialism Meets Economics* (pp 1–18). London and New York: Routledge.

Index

References to figures appear in *italic* type. References to endnotes show both the page number and the note number (171n1), and, where required for clarity, the chapter number (171ch4n1).

E

F

Printed and bound by CPI Group (UK) Ltd, Croydon, CR0 4YY

15/09/2026

14962385-0007